The Gaddi Beyond Pastoralism

The Gaddi Beyond Pastoralism
Making Place in the Indian Himalayas

Anja Wagner

berghahn
NEW YORK • OXFORD
www.berghahnbooks.com

Published in 2013 by

Berghahn Books

www.berghahnbooks.com

© 2013 Anja Wagner

All rights reserved. Except for the quotation of short passages for the purposes of criticism and review, no part of this book may be reproduced in any form or by any means, electronic or mechanical, including photocopying, recording, or any information storage and retrieval system now known or to be invented, without written permission of the publisher.

Library of Congress Cataloging-in-Publication Data

Wagner, Anja, 1979-
 The Gaddi beyond pastoralism : making place in the Indian Himalayas / Anja Wagner.
     pages cm
  Includes bibliographical references.
  ISBN 978-0-85745-929-9 (hardback) —
  ISBN 978-0-85745-930-5 (institutional ebook)
  1. Gaddis (Indic people)—India, North. 2. Human ecology—India, North. 3. India, North—Environmental conditions. 4. Himalaya Mountains Region—Environmental conditions. I. Title.
  DS432.G275W34 2013
  305.8914′96—dc23

2012037872

British Library Cataloguing in Publication Data

A catalogue record for this book is available from the British Library

Printed in the United States on acid-free paper

ISBN 978-0-85745-929-9 (hardback)
ISBN 978-0-85745-930-5 (institutional ebook)

Contents

List of Illustrations	vii
Acknowledgments	ix
Note on Transliteration and Spelling	xi
Abbreviations	xii
Introduction	1
Chapter 1. The Study of Environment Reconsidered	10
Rethinking Nature and Society:	
Toward an Anthropology of Environment 10	
Between Adaptation and Ideology:	
Himalayan Pastoralism in the Literature 19	
Chapter 2. The Gaddi in Images	25
Popular Imagery 28	
Ethnographic Representations 31	
Evaluation of Popular Representations 33	
Chapter 3. A Sheep for Shiva	39
Living Like Śiv-ji: Shiva and Gaddi Identity 39	
A Sheep for Shiva: The *Nuālā* Ritual 46	
Identity and Performative Creation of Community 59	
Chapter 4. Doing Kinship, Doing Place	65
Seasonal Migration and Ancestral Villages 65	
Belonging to Multiple Places 73	
Ancestral Villages and Family Deities 77	
Kinship and the Inside Space 79	
How Children Do Kinship and Place 83	
Kinship, Place, and Habitus 85	
Extending Networks, Accessing New Places 87	
The Landscape of the Dhauladhar: From Metaphor to Practice 89	

Chapter 5. Walking   93

Chapter 6. Visiting the Deities, Enacting the Mountains   100
    Gaddi Deities   101
    To Go With a Goat: *Jāgrā* and *Jātar*   108
    Gūne Mātā and Bannī Mātā   112
    Enacting Environment through Movements   120
    High-Altitude Lakes, *Nāg* Deities, and the Practice of *Nhaun*   121
    Power of Place: Performing Altitude   129

Chapter 7. Environment and the Body: Understanding Water Change   137
    The Phenomenon of Water Change   137
    On the Connection between Person and Place in India   139
    Ethnographic Findings: The Concept of *Ādat*   143
    Getting Attuned to Place   146
    Water as a Vehicle   148

Chapter 8. Cool Water, Short Green Grass, and Fir Trees: The Aesthetics of Environment   152
    The Aesthetics of Environment   153
    Good Places: The Mountains Revisited   155
    Environmental Aesthetics in Photographic Motifs   160
    What Is in a Picture? Photography as Socially Defined Practice   161
    Gaddi Photography Collections   162
    On the Meaning of Short Green Grass and Fir Trees   166

Conclusion: Doing Place   173

Appendix: Songs and Translations   178

Glossary   182

References   189

Index   199

Illustrations

Figures

2.1. Framed poster with a pastoral motif next to an image of the god Krishna on a living room wall. Photo by A. Wagner (2008). 35

2.2. In-married women of the groom's family dancing in *nuāncarī* at the groom's house on the morning of the day they will welcome the young bride into her new home. Photo by A. Wagner (2007). 36

3.1. A groom on his way to "beg." Photo by A. Wagner (2007). 44

3.2. *Nuālā* mandala. Note that here the priest drew thirty-three instead of thirty-two houses. Photo by A. Wagner (2007). 50

3.3. *Nuālā* ritual space after a sacrifice, here with a fashionable light-adorned garland. Photo by A. Wagner (2007). 53

6.1. Markings drawn along the path of a *jātar*. Photo by A. Wagner (2007). 110

6.2. At Gūne Mātā with the temple on the right and the view over the Dhauladhar in the background. Photo by A. Wagner (2007). 113

6.3. View of Bannī village—the cluster of houses on the ridge in the center. Photo by A. Wagner (2008). 115

6.4. Bannī Mātā statue(s) decorated with cloths donated by devotees in the temple at Bannī. Ribbons tied on the wooden frame at the time devotees made a wish can be seen. Photo by A. Wagner (2008). 117

6.5. Water sources inside Bhagsu Nag temple. Photo by A. Wagner (2008). 126

8.1. Gathering the flocks at Laka below the Indrahar Pass. Photo by A. Wagner (2007). 158

8.2. "Short green grass." Photo by A. Wagner (2008). 165

8.3. The author with a *tos*. Photo by A. Wagner (2008). 165

Maps

0.1. Map of Himachal Pradesh. Cartography by N. Harm, Department of Geography, South Asia Institute, University of Heidelberg. Used with permission of the Department of Geography. 3

6.1 Map of important places on the southern slope of the Dhauladhar around Dharamshala. Map is not to scale. (Based on a public domain map, University of Texas Libraries, scale of original 1:250,000.) 123

Acknowledgments

This book is based on fifteen months of anthropological fieldwork carried out in the districts of Kangra and Chamba in the North Indian State of Himachal Pradesh between March 2006 and October 2008. It owes a great debt to many persons in India who let me into their lives and extended their help to make my research possible. They are too numerous to be named in exchange for the many interviews and conversations, cups of tea, and servings of rājmā and kicharī I received during my fieldwork.

I would like to extend a special word of thanks, in chronological order of my movements in India, to Dharam Singh Dogra and his wife Kamla in Chandigarh and their children, who not only introduced me to life in India, but also activated their contacts, especially their relatives in Mand, to get me settled in Himachal Pradesh. Kusum Lata acted as my assistant during my first month in the field. In Kangra I especially thank Sohan Lal and Lajjia Devi of Maitti who adopted me into their family as well as Subhkaran Lal and his wife Kaya Devi with all their family and relatives. I am equally grateful to Subedar Prem Singh and Lakshmi Devi of Bandi who accepted me into their home as a member of their family and to their relatives and neighbors who welcomed me into their village. Anil Kumar and Biti Devi always looked after me and my equipment in Bhagsu. I would further like to express my gratitude to Nand Lal for his support of my work. In Chamba, Kamal Prashad Sharma extended his help to me; I warmly thank Prakash Chand Sharma and his wife in Khani for their hospitality and assistance. Special thanks go to the District Library in Chamba and the Public Library at Dharamshala for making their books available to me.

I am indebted to Jyoti Sambyal for transcribing the songs reproduced in this book and translating them into Hindi for me. The translations into English are mine. Arup K. Datta proofread the translations of song texts and interview transcriptions from Hindi. David Whybra took on the task of straightening out my English. I claim all remaining mistakes for myself.

This book is based on my doctoral dissertation, defended at the University of Heidelberg, Germany, Faculty of Behavioural and Cultural Studies, on November 10, 2010. William Sax has been my doctoral supervisor and this work has profited greatly from his insights and ideas. I am also grateful to my second supervisor Annette Hornbacher for her stimulating comments and discussions on my topic.

I thank Krishan Sharma, Department of Anthropology, Panjab University Chandigarh, for acting as a local supervisor of my work in India. Sherry Sabbarwal, on a less official note, has greatly helped my research with her advice throughout my stays in India. Peter Phillimore and Vasant Saberwal have given me valuable recommendations during fieldwork preparation and choosing of a fieldwork site. Special thanks go to Eva Ambos, Christoph Bergmann, Deepra Dandekar, Lokesh Ohri, Karin Polit, Johannes Quack, Ferdinand Okwaro, and Constanze Weigl for their comments and support during my research and writing process. I would also like to thank Georg Pfeffer, who encouraged me to continue with postgraduate studies.

On a more personal note, I thank Daniel Norek for his support of my project in the field and at home.

Last, but not least, I thank my parents.

My postgraduate studies were supported by a doctoral fellowship of the Studienstiftung des deutschen Volkes (German National Academic Foundation), who also funded my fieldwork trips.

Note on Transliteration and Spelling

The transliteration of the Devanagari script follows the conventions for Hindi of the Department of Modern South Asian Languages, South Asia Institute, University of Heidelberg. Long vowels are indicated by a macron (Harder and Liu 2008). Concerning diacritics of Devanagari letters, I follow local pronunciation and omit them if not pronounced, for example, in *khuś*. Not pronounced inherent vowels as well as the *halant* are not transliterated. I further transliterate the nasals, including the *anusvār*, respectively as *ṅ, ñ, ṇ, n, m*. The candrabindu sign, in accordance with Harder and Liu, is indicated by *m̐*.

The spelling of place names follows the common English spelling, if their English usage is widespread. In case of alternative spellings, the variation closest to the Hindi pronunciation is used (Bharmaur, Dharamshala). Other local names are transliterated.

Abbreviations

Following Barnard and Good (1984) the following abbreviations of relationship terms and their compounds are used:

M	mother	W	wife
F	father	H	husband
S	son	B	brother
D	daughter	Z	sister
C	child	P	parent
e	elder	y	younger

Example of compounds:

MBD   mother's brother's daughter   FeZ   father's elder sister

Introduction

One day during my fieldwork, I was walking back from a day of work in the fields with a woman of the family I was staying with. It was a bright sunny day. As we walked up the road to the house, we faced the Dhauladhar Mountains, which stood out clearly against the November sky. Looking at the mountains, I asked if then, as previously in May and June, people would be going up to temples in the mountains on small pilgrimages. No, she replied, at least not many. It would be cold up there. Remember, she asked me, when we went last time, how many people we met? If people are up there, she said, it is fun to go—*kitnī muzū ātā hai*. But in winter, there is no one in the mountains—*sardī mem paharom mem koī nahīm hai*. She was right, during the warm season the mountains had been full of people. We had gone up to a small temple with her husband and their small son and stayed up there two nights with his flock of sheep and goats. On the way back and forth, we had met shepherds on the way to their flock, women from a lower village taking their cows up to graze, people going to a temple. If in winter there is no one in the mountains, in summer one runs into people everywhere. There are also tourists, European trekkers and Indians from Delhi or Punjab on their way to the snow line, and only rarely other people from the villages in the valley. But on the more remote mountain paths, the majority of people are Gaddi. And it is not only the shepherds that one meets in the mountains in summer, but also the school teacher, the office clerk, and the college student.

In this book I describe engagements with the environment among the Gaddi in the North Indian state of Himachal Pradesh. The Gaddi people are known as agropastoralists. They are famous for their large flocks of sheep and goats. During the course of the year, Gaddi shepherds move between the high Himalayan summer pastures in Lahul in the district Lahul and Spiti, and the winter grazing grounds in the Shivalik foothills of the Himalaya on the Himachal Pradesh–Punjab border. According to

Richard Tucker, this transhumant movement is "the largest-scale transhumant sheep and goat herding in the entire Himalayan region" (Tucker 1986: 18). However, it is not the only cyclical movement associated with the Gaddi: Gaddi families practice or used to practice a seasonal migration between summer and winter villages on the northern and southern side of the Dhauladhar range, respectively.

The Dhauladhar (the white mountains) are the first range of the Lesser Himalayas in Himachal Pradesh. In the western part of the state, the Dhauladhar runs roughly from west to east rising between the Beas River, which runs through the Kangra Valley, and the Ravi River in district Chamba. With an elevation of over 4,500 meters around Dharamshala, it acts as a barrier for the monsoon, making Dharamshala the place with the highest annual rainfall in the state. Parallel to the Dhauladhar range in Chamba runs the second Himalayan range, the Pir Panjal, which separates the Bharmaur subdistrict from the district Lahul and Spiti.

When I first decided to write on environment, I had the physical environment I saw in the landscape of the Dhauladhar in mind. I was impressed by the steep mountains, rising seemingly rectangularly from the river beds in Bharmaur, where I started my fieldwork, and which appear like a huge wall to the northern edge of the Kangra Valley, where I shifted after the first month. My questioning of the inhabitants of the Bharmaur village about seasonal migration, transhumance, and their relation with the Kangra Valley, initially led my respondents to talk a lot about distinctions between Bharmaur and Kangra rather than their immediate village surroundings. That they referred to Bharmaur and Kangra as *ūpar* and *nīce* (up and down, respectively), supported my impression that vertical directions must be very important for local people indeed. It is also the vertical movements of the Gaddi that have apparently seemed most intriguing to foreign observers (e.g., Kaushal 2001b).

Publications dealing with the topic of environment among pastoralist societies largely either describe the pastoralists' adaptation to their physical environment or treat environment from a purely symbolic perspective (see chapter 1). In the context of the Himalayas, a focus on resource use and environmental degradation in the study of environment has thus led to a view on environment that is "already defined by the researcher in bio-physical terms" (Guneratne 2010: 2; see also Smadja 2009a). Writing against the outside and technocratic view on environment of, for example, development planners, Arjun Guneratne argues for the study of the *cognized environment* (2010), or the study of how human beings who live in the Himalayas conceptualize their surroundings.

Eric Hirsch has pointed out that the landscape we initially see when starting fieldwork is not necessarily the same as what local people see

Introduction • 3

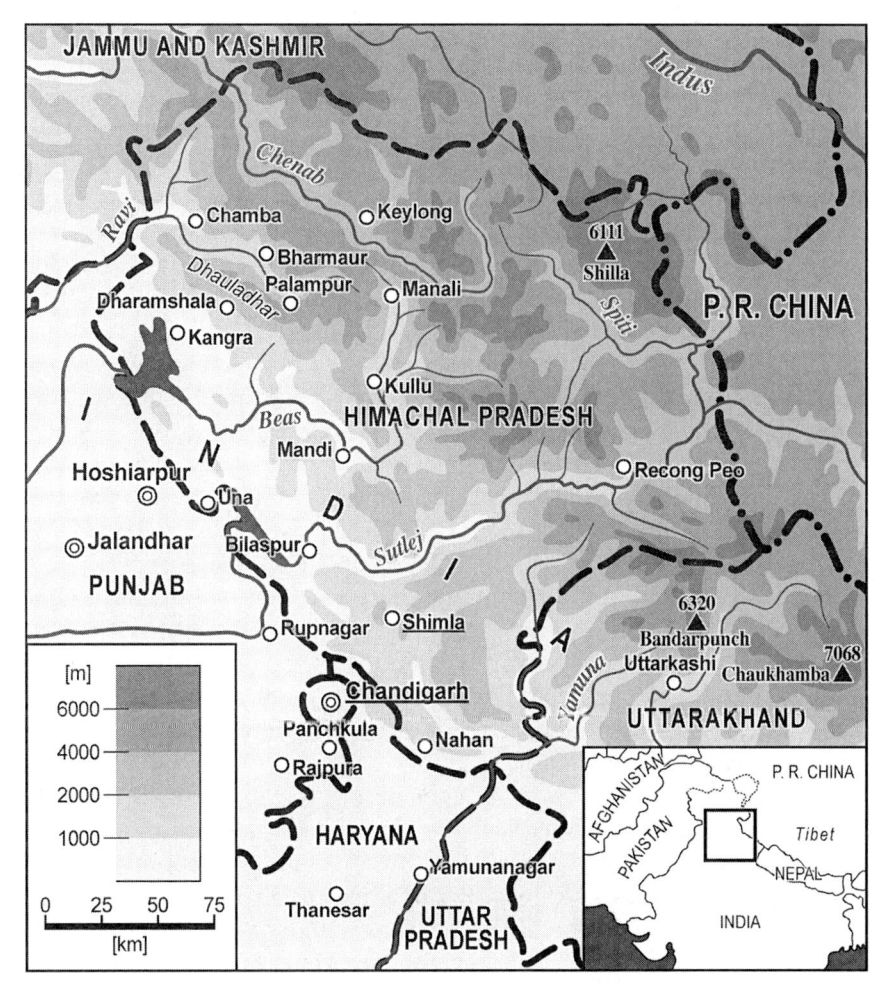

Map 0.1 Map of Himachal Pradesh. Cartography by N. Harm, Department of Geography, South Asia Institute, University of Heidelberg. Used with permission of the Department of Geography.

in their environment (Hirsch 1995).[1] The more I listened to how people talked about places, the more I realized that notwithstanding general ideas about the mountains and the plains—up and down—it is the places in between that are much more emphasized in local discourse than the extremes. It is also the places in between that are interesting in terms of the activities that take place there. A first case in point is the system of transhumance. Here the extreme points—Lahul and Punjab—become the reference points when talking about the Gaddi's pattern of transhumance, while the shepherds spend much more time in the places in between. My own data confirm the respective analysis of the shepherding cycle by Vasant Saberwal and Richard Axelby (Axelby 2005, 2007; Saberwal 1999).

Similar to Guneratne's approach, I aim at developing an explanatory framework for understanding human-environment relations that gives priority to local conceptions rather than preconceived understandings of environment. However, I am not merely interested in the local meanings of environment and more specifically the mountains in the Himalayas. My objective is to contribute to an anthropological perspective for understanding human-environment relations in terms of what Latour calls a *symmetric* anthropology (1993).

The concern with a symmetric or monistic approach (Descola 2005) to human-environment relations as well as the foregrounding of local concepts has stimulated debates on the anthropological study of environment in the emerging field of environmental anthropology. Central to environmental anthropology is the critical discussion of a dualistic understanding of nature and culture (see Descola 2005; Descola and Pálsson 1996; Escobar 1999; Hornborg 2009; Ingold 2000; Latour 1993, 2004). At stake here is not only a particular understanding of nature as opposed to culture that has been characteristic of a historically specific line of thought in the West, but also the influence this conceptualization has had on social science (see Descola; Ingold; Latour). In the context of the present work, the latter calls for a critical assessment of the approaches to environment among pastoralists prevalent in the literature.

My explanatory framework further builds on the idea that environment, and in this case particularly the landscape of the mountains, is not to be understood as a readily laid-out entity. As the philosopher Edward Casey argues, a landscape, no matter how vast, is always "a composition of places" and never an abstract space (Casey 2001: 689). Place rather than space, according to Casey, is the general and primary category for human perception. The phenomenological argument put forward by Casey is that perception is the primary form of experience. The philosophy of perception puts direct experience (place) before abstract reason (space). The idea that "time and space are operative *in places*" (Casey 1996: 44; emphasis in original) amounts to a view of the environment similar to what Casey calls a *place-world*. Casey defines place-world first as a world "bedecked in places" (ibid.: 43), and second, as "a world that is not only perceived or conceived but also actively *lived* and receptively *experienced*" (Casey 2001: 687; emphasis in original). With William Sax, Casey's approach that understands place as an event rather than as a thing "seems a fruitful approach for ethnographers, and because it starts with human activity rather than with ostensibly universal categories, it offers the opportunity of grasping indigenous conceptions 'from the inside'" (Sax 2009: 52).

Understanding place as an event means to study ways in which people do or make place. The study of place-making is interesting precisely because places and their meanings are not already existing somewhere out there independent of human beings (Basso 1996; Rodman 1992). From an anthropological perspective, place-making is a *"cultural* activity," and thus "can be grasped only in relation to the ideas and practices with which it is accomplished" (Basso 1996: 7; emphasis in original). In taking place-making as my approach to an understanding of the environment among the Gaddi, I propose to join ideas from environmental anthropology and the anthropology of place with new approaches in the theory of practice.

The study of practice has recently received a renewed interest within the social sciences: to focus on what people do—that is to study "the enactment of reality in practice" (Mol 2002: ix), has been strongly argued for by Science and Technology Studies as well as Philosophy and of late increasingly found entrance into anthropological discussions on environment (Casey 1996; Ingold and Vergunst 2008; Latour 1993, 2004, 2005; Mol 2002; Pickering 1995). Following Mol, who forwards an approach for which *"ontology* is not given in the order of things, but that instead *ontologies* are brought into being, sustained, or allowed to wither away in common day-to-day socio-material practices" (Mol 2002: 6; emphasis in original), I attempt to foreground events and practices in the study of environment. This approach takes into account ongoing engagements that make the mountains meaningful for the Gaddi, thus including the perspective of shepherds as well as that of teachers and college students.

If places come into being through practices, this also implies being in place, which in turn involves a sensory bodily presence and a perceptual engagement with the place (Feld 1996: 94; see also Casey 1996, 2001). Steven Feld has drawn attention to the role of an anthropology of the senses for understanding place-making. In relation to his ethnography of the Kaluli (Papua New Guinea), where the sense of hearing dominates perceptions of the tropical rain forest, he emphasizes that anthropologists should pay attention to the different senses involved in place-making. Feld criticizes that "ethnographic and cultural-geographic work on senses of place has been dominated by the visualism deeply rooted in the European concept of landscape," while the "overwhelmingly multisensory character of perceptual experience should lead to some expectation for a multisensory conceptualization of place" (Feld 1996: 94).

The inquiry into how places are bodily sensed among the Gaddi involves paying attention to expressions of the relation between body and ecology—that is, between person and place—as well as to notions of aesthetics. A central topic of the present work are moreover religious practices. The study is located in the Indian Himalayas. The Himalayas are considered the abode of the gods in larger (Hindu) Indian narratives, on a regional scale, as well as in local meanings. Gaddi people in turn have their own way of relating to the mountains and making place through religious practices that I will explore in this book.

A further aspect of place-making that is not fully separable from religious practices are social relations. Kinship relations are important for how people engage with places on a conceptual as well as on a practical level and place-making along kinship lines physically guides people through the landscape of the Dhauladhar. However, contemporary meanings of the mountains are not only to be found in physical visits, but also in visual images such as family photographs and in the production and reception of a "virtual" Gaddi identity (Adams 1996) created, for instance, through Himachali music video CDs (VCDs). I have therefore included the analysis of visual media in my approach.

Do Gaddi themselves engage in a discourse about environment or nature? This question has to be answered with "No." At least, *prakṛti* (nature) or *paryāvaraṇ* (environment) as such is not a common topic. I am not writing on environment because it was presented as a discourse by the people among whom I conducted my research. Rather, I am writing about environment because it provides a framework for uniting topics that proved to be relevant during my fieldwork. Topics people talked about and commented on were, for example, the mountains, plains, seasons, deities, or water. And my counterparts referred repeatedly and in different contexts to specific places and things associated with them. Environment and place-making as the overall framework for presenting an understanding of these ideas and connected activities is my proposition.

Before I begin chapter 1 by elaborating on the approach to the study of environment I follow in this book, a few preliminary remarks on the Gaddi as a community and my fieldwork setting are necessary.

The name Gaddi (*gaddī*) is a foreign as well as a self-designation. Gaddi literally means seat in Hindi. This meaning is explained in reference to the perceived ancestral land of the Gaddi, the Bharmaur subdistrict of Chamba. The reference to the seat is either made concerning Mount Kailash in Bharmaur, the seat of the Hindu god Shiva, or to Bharmaur town as the old capital of the kingdom of Chamba. So the meaning of Gaddi is explained either as the Gaddi—themselves Hindu—being the people from the seat of the god Shiva, or from the seat of the Chamba king. The derivation of the name Gaddi highlights a regional affiliation of the Gaddi. Notwithstanding this derivation of the name, there are several migration stories that recount stories of the Gaddi migrating to Bharmaur from the North Indian plains (see *Gazetteer of the Chamba State 1904* 1996: 60; *Gazetteer of the Kangra District 1883–1884* 1884: 91–93; Handa 2005: 32).

Gaddi is also a Hindi dialect. The definition as a language group is maybe the widest definition of the Gaddi community. Gaddi is classed as a Western Pahari dialect. It is also referred to as Bharmauri and is closely related to Chambiali, a dialect spoken in and around Chamba town, but shows common features with Kashmiri as well as Kullu dialects (cf. Grierson 1986). In Kangra, the vernacular dialect is called Pahari or Kangriali. Pahari speakers often claim not to understand the Gaddi dialect in spite of living in the same villages as Gaddi speakers—I involuntarily tested this during the beginning of my fieldwork by mistakenly trying the Gaddi vocabulary I had learned on Pahari speakers who were puzzled even by my few expressions. However, those Pahari speakers who have close relations with Gaddi families do understand Gaddi. Gaddi speakers, on the contrary, generally master at least three dialects, and in my experience even primary school children switch languages without problem: Gaddi is spoken at home, while Pahari is spoken with the non-Gaddi neighbors. Furthermore, with the exception of a few elderly people, Hindi is spoken as a lingua franca, for example, in schools.

The Gaddi are differentiated into three large *jātī* (caste groups): Brahmans, usually called Gaddi Brahmans, the Gaddi who align themselves with the Kshatriya varna (i.e., twice-born castes), and the lower castes or so called Gaddi small castes, namely Sipi and Hali.[2] In Bharmaur, people use the expressions *Gaddi Brahman* and *Gaddi Rajput* for the higher castes, acknowledging that anybody in Bharmaur can call him- or herself a Gaddi. In Kangra, people refute the designation Gaddi Rajput, identifying the name Rajput with non-Gaddi castes. They use Gaddi itself as their *jātī* (caste) name, concretizing it as *Gaddi Gaddi* if necessary, or simply naming clans as *jātī*.[3] Gaddi Brahman men who do not work as priests do not differ in their occupation from men of Gaddi Kshatriya castes, whether as schoolteachers or as shepherds. Neither did I discover any difference regarding forms of regional identifications. In ritual practices, there are however slight differences, and here my data refer to the practices of Gaddi, not Gaddi Brahmans. I have not collected substantial data on Gaddi speaking lower castes where further differences might emerge, although these differences are hard to predict since reference to lower castes apart from their role as *celā* (oracles/healers) is scant in the literature.

I started my fieldwork in a village close to Bharmaur town in Chamba. My main research focus, however, has been on Kangra, where I shifted after the first month. From then on I alternately lived in two villages about ten kilometers west of Dharamshala. Most villages in the Kangra Valley are not nuclear villages centered around a temple and village square (as often in Bharmaur), but rather a spread-out settlement of several *mahal* (house clusters or neighborhoods) that form around the houses of patrilineal descent groups and are situated alongside the fields (see also Baker 2005: 54–55). In one village, I stayed with a family of flock owners who had settled in Kangra several generations ago. The village of about five hundred inhabitants has about ten Gaddi households belonging to one descent group.[4] I spent most of the time with one (extended) family and their closest neighbors and was regularly invited by all their relatives, including the (out-married) sisters and sisters' daughters and the wives' natal relatives. This way I not only got to know their relations, but also got to visit several other villages and places. In the second village, which has more than a thousand inhabitants and on its borders directly joins other settlements—adding to its practical size—there are three Gaddi descent groups. I mainly stayed with one family and the house cluster of their relatives, but also visited houses of the other Gaddi descent groups. The family I lived with, which is not involved in pastoralism, owns two homes, one in Kangra and one in Bharmaur, as do their neighbors. I have traveled back to Bharmaur with both of my Kangra families to visit their old village and second village, respectively. Furthermore, I have spent time with the shepherds and their flocks, mainly on the southern slopes of the Dhauladhar.

Although the largest amount of my fieldwork time was spent in villages, my focus on environment did lead me to not take the village itself as a unit of study. Rather, I took an approach unbounded by locality in concentrating on forms of mobility carried out from the village and in following people in their activities of making place. In this my ethnographic approach differs from previous studies that either focused on pastoralist mobility (Axelby 2005; Saberwal 1999) or took a particular village and its inhabitants as their unit of study (e.g., Bhasin 1988; Kapila 2003; Newell 1960; Phillimore 1982).

While the Gaddi differ in certain points and stand out as a distinct group of Himachal Pradesh, they are very much Himachali. When I contrast the Gaddi with other parts of the population in the following, I talk about local distinctions, which are quite readily forwarded—that is, distinctions made by Gaddi people as well as their Pahari speaking neighbors in my fieldwork villages in Kangra. These locally made distinctions are mostly based on a fairly intimate knowledge of the other's *rīti-riwāz* (customs). The term *pahari*—literally of the mountains or mountain people—is generally used for inhabitants of the Indian Himalayan states. In Kangra and in the present work Pahari refers to the Pahari-speaking sections of Kangra's population described, for example, in the works of Parry (1979), Narayan (1986, 1997), and Baker (2005).

Notes

1. I am concerned in the following with a specific approach to environment. When I use the term landscape in regard to my theoretical approach, I understand landscape as a network of places (see below, and Casey 2001). For a detailed discussion of the etymology of the term landscape and its reception in anthropology, I refer to Hirsch (1995) and Fox (1997).
2. The colonial gazetteers took it upon themselves to straighten out the classification of Gaddi castes (e.g., *Gazetteer of the Chamba State 1904* 1996: 60) and caste classification has since remained a topic. One example is *The Anthropological Survey of India*'s encyclopedia *People of India* that draws on colonial sources and traditions in listing Gaddi groups separately by caste divisions (Sarkar 1996a, 1996b, 1996c, 1996d). Contemporary local denominations show less emphasis on internal divisions and differences than these older sources suggest.
3. The clan names are sometimes deduced from a village name but also correlate with larger North Indian clan names. Caste and clan divisions matter for marriage. When it comes to socially accepted marriage norms, clans are exogamous, while Gaddi and Gaddi Brahmans are each endogamous groups (see Newell 1960; Phillimore 1982: 99–101).
4. Numbers of inhabitants are taken from the 2001 Census (Registrar General and Census Commissioner of India 2007).

1

The Study of Environment Reconsidered

To take the study of the Gaddi beyond pastoralism does not only indicate a shift in the ethnographic focus to include nonpastoralist practices, but as a program for the present work, its title also implies a going beyond established approaches in a least two further ways: First, to reconsider the definition of environment in terms of a critique of a nature-society dualism. Second, to overcome an interrelated dualism prevalent in the study of pastoralist groups that links a naturalistic understanding of environment with the study of adaptation strategies and a cultural approach to environment with the study of ideological representations.

Rethinking Nature and Society: Toward an Anthropology of Environment

I draw my understanding of the term environment from such writers as Philippe Descola (2005), Bruno Latour (1993, 2004), and Tim Ingold (2000). In a new turn to the nature-culture debate in anthropology, Descola, Ingold, and Latour advocate the study of environment rather than the study of nature. The term nature is rejected for its strong association with a particular Western concept: the dualistic notion of nature as opposed to culture or society.

What is wrong with the term nature? Following Descola, the term nature is problematic because it is strongly associated with a nature-culture dichotomy. The idea that nature is opposed to culture, however, is a historical development within Western societies. Descola locates the establishment of the divide between nature and culture in sixteenth- and seventeenth-century Europe. The idea of a nature that is external to society is linked to developments in the fields of arts and painting, geometry, physics, and technological developments that made the objectification of nature and its examination as an entity dissociated from human society possible (Descola 2005: 96–97).

As these developments shaped the European understanding of nature and society, the West came to accept the idea of a distinct nature, existing in separation from society, as the way the world is. Descola's deconstruction of the nature-culture dichotomy, in addition to being a general critique of dominant ideas in Western thinking, is specifically aimed at anthropologists. According to Descola, the nature-culture dualism is an ontological problem for social anthropology, because the establishment of social anthropology as a discipline is historically tied to the development of the idea of an objectified nature and the correlating idea of culture as an autonomous entity. Anthropology, born out of this dualism, has implicitly built on the assumption that all societies juxtapose nature and culture (Descola 2005: 119).

Other societies, however, have cosmologies that do not differentiate between a physical and a social environment (Descola 2005: 41). Descola draws from examples from his own fieldwork among the Achuar in the Ecuadorian Amazon region to show that the Western worldview is not universal. The Achuar cosmology is characterized by what Descola calls the socialization of nature. The Achuar do not distinguish between culture and nature, but between beings who have speech and with whom communication is possible (even if this takes place through shamans or songs directed, for example, at the spirits of game) and those who lack the capacity for speech or who are too distant to enable communication (e.g., the stars) (Descola 1994). A unity of the physical, spiritual, and social environments as conceptualized by the Achuar is inconsistent with the Western idea of a nature-culture divide. How to come to terms with these different kinds of cosmologies is a central problem for Descola, Latour, and Ingold.

Descola emphasizes that anthropology needs to approach different cosmologies in a monistic way. In other words, it has to overcome its inherent dualism and treat all cosmologies according to the same principle (Descola 2005: 12–14). He treats the nature-culture dualism as one possible cosmology among others (ibid.: 175). Descola maintains a relativistic approach in that his general conviction is that other societies objectify differently, but asserts that possible variations are structurally limited (ibid.:

15). He develops a model that describes basic principles that structure the ideas of human engagement with the environment. He focuses on the relations between self and other—that is, between humans as well as between humans and nonhumans in different societies. He then analyses how those forms of relations are expressed within the respective cosmologies. Descola identifies four basic modes, or schemes of relation, by which relations between humans and nonhumans are conceptualized: animism, naturalism, totemism, and analogism. They differ in their forms of expressing the way in which humans live and perceive their engagements with the external world in terms of perceived inner and physical similarities and differences (ibid.: 175).

By analyzing different ways in which engagements with the environment—its nonhuman as well as human beings are conceptualized—Descola situates the Western notion of the nature-culture dualism within a broader context of possible cosmologies. Western ideas on nature and culture become one of several possible forms of thinking about the relations that humans have with the world. According to Latour, Descola's distinction between (and definition of) naturalism and animism was a breakthrough because it shifted from the nature-culture divide as a background for all studies to studying naturalism as one way of how humans establish relations with nature. "Nature had shifted from being a resource to becoming a topic" (Latour 2009: 1).

While Descola, who is interested in the idea people have of the world and of their relations with their environment, accepts the Western notion of the nature-culture divide as a particular form of conceiving of the world that, too, can be studied, Ingold and Latour fundamentally challenge the nature-culture dualism.

For Latour, too, the nature-culture dichotomy is part of the modern Western ideology that separates the natural from the social, mind from body, facts from values. But as Latour argues, the West has never been modern. The distinction between nature and culture has always been an ideology, situated on the level of ideas, while reality has always been hybrid (Latour 1993). In *Politics of Nature* (2004), Latour builds on his critique of modernism in *We Have Never Been Modern* (Latour 1993) and further applies it to the ideas associated with the term nature. He proclaims the end of nature, stating that there is no such thing as nature out there or at least it is not relevant to social scientists. Everything that we are able to perceive ceases to be external to society (Latour 2004).

Latour criticizes what he calls mononaturalism—that is, the idea of a single nature to which natural science has access. The correlate of mononaturalism's universal nature is a multiplicity of cultures, that are subject to the social sciences, and exist in front of the backdrop of a unified nature that is the same for all (Latour 2004: 48). Equally challenged by Latour is the concept of multiculturalism, which he criticizes for two reasons: First, with multiculturalism each culture can make equal claims to define reality. The consequence of this relativist approach on a theoretical level, so Latour, would be to acknowledge that there is no common world for all (ibid.). Where mononaturalism establishes a world that is essential "because it has to do with the real nature of phenomena," but is emptied of culture, multiculturalism produces a world of values that is only subjectively given and therefore inessential (ibid.). Second, in practice, mononaturalism and multiculturalism coexist in the academic field, so Latour, in their two respective frameworks of the natural and the social sciences (ibid.: 33). The social constructionist approach to nature in the social sciences, while claiming that there is no immediate access to nature, perpetuates the nature-culture divide by reaffirming it within the scientific divide (ibid.).

> When one speaks as a historian, a psychologist, an anthropologist, a geographer, a sociologist, or an epistemologist about "human representations of nature," about their changes, about the material, economic, and political conditions that explain them, one is implying, "quite obviously," that nature itself, during this time, has not changed a bit. *The more the social construction of nature is calmly asserted, the more what is really happening in nature*—the nature that is abandoned to Science and scientists [i.e., natural science]—*is left aside.* (Latour 2004: 33, my emphasis)

By defining nature as an external reality that exists independent of humans, modern ideology has kept the study of nature out of the social sciences (Latour 2004: 17). Following Latour, this is not justified since we have never been modern, and the split into social and natural things has never corresponded to reality. Latour's approach does not only socialize nature, but also, like Descola's approach, points to the influences natural sciences and technological developments have on society—thus not only the term nature, but also the term society have to be replaced or at least reconsidered (Latour 1993).

As Latour states, the modern ideology that claims that science alone has access to nature, disregards the fact that natural facts are socially fabricated. Scientific facts are discovered in laboratories or through technical devices. They change according to changes in scientific knowledge and with innovations and technological developments (Latour 2004). Thus, there is no objective, definite view of nature, but the understanding of nature always and everywhere undergoes changes and modifications. Latour, therefore, does not speak of nature in the singular but of natures in the plural, or rather of involvements of nature and culture, or natures-cultures, which he labels collectives (ibid.: 45).

Latour further advocates the study of what he calls networks.[1] The study of networks is meant to combine the generally separated fields of study that Latour characterizes as naturalization—that is, those concerned with facts; socialization—that is, those concerned with power; and deconstruction—that is, those concerned with discourse (Latour 1993: 5–6). Reality and its description cannot be reduced to one of these dimensions alone: "Is it our fault if the networks are *simultaneously real, like nature, narrated, like discourse, and collective, like society*?" (Latour 1993: 6; emphasis in original).

The image of a network stands for the mutual involvements of these dimensions with each other to create "real situations" (Latour 1993: 4).

With the study of networks and the rejection of the nature-culture dichotomy, Latour proposes what he calls a symmetric anthropology. The problem of anthropology according to Latour is that it is not truly comparative as long as it subscribes to the Western notion of an objective nature and subsequently studies culture as opposed to nature. Science, from this view, is not open to study for anthropologists whereas ethnosciences are (Latour 1993: 94). According to the ideas of natural science, its privileged access to nature via natural science sets Western culture apart from all other cultures (ibid.: 97). Modern thinking thus adds a second divide to its internal divide between nature and society: the divide between modern society (us) and premodern societies (them) (ibid.: 99). Latour, on the contrary, emphasizes the need for anthropology to become truly comparative or symmetric and to drop both divides by studying networks and involvements.

Contrary to postmodern deconstructionist approaches, Latour does not aim at revealing discourses alone that for him amounts to a reduction of phenomena to forms of representation (Latour 1993: 62–63). He acknowledges that there are things out there that very much exist and have effects on others, whether on humans or on nonhumans (ibid.: 5). But, he points out, there is not one objective and definite interpretation of those things. Latour remains rather agnostic about the nature of external reality: Since the environment is never to be objectively known, he advocates the consideration of uncertainty, or an uncertainty about relations—one first has to discover what is part of the network and what is connected to what (Latour 2004: 21–25).

Ingold shares the critique of the nature-culture dualism and its place in anthropological theory with Descola and Latour. For Ingold, the anthropological claim of a "perceptual relativism," that means the assumption that other cultures perceive in a different way, "reinforces the claim of natural science to deliver an authoritative account of how nature really works" (Ingold 2000: 15). The study of cultural constructions of nature according to Ingold's critique involves a double disengagement. First, it suggests that humans live in a culturally constructed world, which means taking a step out of nature or the world of other beings. Second, to regard these culturally constructed systems as cosmologies means taking a step out of culture, in that the observer is looking at other cultures from a position where she or he is not confined by culture herself but has recourse to a more abstract reason (ibid.: 14).

> If it is by the capacity to reason that humanity, in this Western discourse, is distinguished from nature, then it is by the fullest development of this capacity that modern science distinguishes itself from the knowledge practices of people in "other cultures" whose thought is supposed to remain somewhat bound by the constraints and conventions of tradition. In effect, the sovereign perspective of abstract reason is a product of the compounding of two dichotomies: between humanity and nature, and between modernity and tradition. (Ingold 2000: 15)

Here Ingold's criticism of the absolute knowledge of modern science versus culturally framed, limited knowledge of indigenous knowledge matches Latour's contrast between natural science and ethnoscience, and Latour's critique of the divide that this distinction establishes between the modern Western and the other, premodern societies.

Ingold therefore endorses the study of environment instead of the study of nature. He explicitly objects to the term nature, which, according to him, designates the Western idea of nature as a world without human beings, an idea that has also been incorporated into natural science. Ingold defines the term environment, first, as relational—that is, environment exists only in relation to a being (human or animal). The term environment, in contrast to the term nature, implies the idea of beings within a world. Second, Ingold defines environment as incomplete—that is, environments are continually under construction through the activities of living beings, human or nonhuman (Ingold 2000: 20). Environment is thus not a bounded entity, something that is already present and available for analysis independent of the beings it relates to, but rather a process (ibid.). In his 2004 article "Culture on the Ground," he illustrates the idea of environment as a process:

> [T]he forms of the landscape—like the identities and capacities of its human inhabitants—are not imposed upon a material substrate but rather emerge as condensations or crystallizations of activity within a relational field. As people, in the course of their everyday lives, make their way by foot around a familiar terrain, so its paths, textures and contours, variable through the seasons, are incorporated into their own embodied capacities of movement, awareness and response. (Ingold 2004: 333)

What is new in Ingold's approach, in comparison to Descola's and Latour's approaches, is the attention paid to perception as well as to practical experience. Ingold incorporates ideas from Bourdieu's theory of practice into his concept of environment. He values Bourdieu's theory of practice for its focus on people's practical activities (Ingold 2000: 162). In his attempt to overcome Cartesian dualism, Ingold further draws both from phenomenology and ecological psychology in establishing what he calls the dwelling perspective. With the term dwelling, Ingold points out that the world becomes meaningful through being inhabited—in other words, through activities and active engagements (ibid.: 173). He positively evaluates phenomenology and ecological psychology for their emphasis on perception as an action in an environment (ibid.: 166).

Ingold criticizes, however, that especially phenomenology in its emphasis on direct bodily perception remains in a dualistic framework. It merely repositions the body that was formerly "placed with the organism on the side of biology" as a subject and thus on the side of culture, while the organism is conceived as a "biological residuum" (Ingold 2000: 170). Ingold's solution lies in breaking down the distinction between culture and biology. He argues for the need to recognize "that the body *is* the human organism, and that the process of embodiment is one and the same as the development of that organism in its environment" (ibid.; emphasis in original). In addition to being an organism, the body is inseparable from the mind in the "environmentally situated activity of the human organism-person" (ibid.: 171).

Humans according to Ingold are agents in an environment with which they are involved physically and sensorily (Ingold 2000: 171). He emphasizes that humans perceive their environment through sensory experiences by commingling with it (Ingold 2007: 29). What follows from his approach for a research perspective is, according to Ingold, that, since humans are immersed in their environment, "such processes as thinking, perceiving, remembering and learning have to be studied within the ecological contexts of people's interrelations with their environments" (Ingold 2000: 171).

To conclude: Descola, Latour, and Ingold start from common ground—the critique of dualist notions implicit in the terms nature and culture, or nature and society. All three authors link their critique of the nature-culture dichotomy, and its deconstruction as a particular Western idea, to a criticism of the anthropological approach to the study of the social construction of nature. The social constructionist approach is criticized not because the authors claim that there are no cultural constructions but because in practice this approach implicitly reinforces the assumption of an independent entity called nature, and thus implies the very same dualist notions that should be overcome. All the authors link their theoretical considerations to the empirical level. Their aim is to reshape the concepts and categories for writing ethnography and understanding concrete phenomena. Their solutions, however, lead in three different directions. Descola develops a structuralist model of ontologies, Latour advocates the study of networks that differ in scale and the types of connections they make, and Ingold emphasizes perception through physical involvement in the environment.

I value Descola's approach for its starting point of treating different cosmologies in the same manner. A unity of social, spiritual and physical environment, as he describes for Amazonian societies, also does apply for India (cf. Daniel 1984; Marriott 1976; Moreno and Marriott 1989; Sax 1991, 2009). Thus, to move the analysis beyond the nature-culture dualism and the question of how to treat different cosmological conceptualization is of practical importance for my ethnography. Descola's highly systematic model of ontologies answers one specific question—namely, how different cosmologies conceptualize relations between humans, nonhumans, and the external world. Social practice is investigated in Descola's approach: not as the topic of study, but rather as something to abstract from in order to deduce cosmological ideas. Cosmologies, however, are per definition coherent while reality includes contradictions. Furthermore, cosmological frameworks might overlap when people take recourse to different frameworks for making sense of the world. The structuralist model, however, presents cosmological frameworks as neat abstractions from a messy, empirical reality for which the model itself does not account.

For Latour, on the contrary, cosmologies do not carry significance in their own right but are always subject to the particular network within which they come into being. Latour's networks first aim at outlining and describing phenomena on the ground. He argues for the complexity and irreducibility of reality. For ethnographic practice, Latour's agnosticism about the reality to be described—that is, that one does not know from the start what belongs together and which connections are made, is imperative. So is his advocacy of complexity with which he points to the entanglements of seemingly distinct phenomena such as technological and political innovations and social conditions. Paul Robbins (2001) has delivered an example of how to apply Latour's idea of a network connecting social and natural aspects to a concrete example. Robbins analyses the unexpected appearance and spread of a tree species over the landscape through looking at the social and natural aspects making up the network relevant to the tree's distribution.

Describing particular phenomena in networks of involvements, as Robbins does in his case study, seems generally feasible and illuminating, but how to apply Latour to a more holistic ethnography seems less clear. The practical question arises of what has to be taken into account (to use

Latour's phrase) to accomplish a satisfactory description and how to integrate multiple phenomena in this analysis. Annemarie Mol in the conclusion of her study on atherosclerosis points to the practical difficulties for descriptions arising from increasing complexities. She stated that it was possible to describe one disease as a part of the practices in which it is enacted, but "if one begins to study the interferences between the enactments of two or three multiple objects (such as atherosclerosis *and* sex differences), then the complexities start to grow exponentially" (Mol 2002: 151; emphasis in original). Furthermore, the discovery of ever-new networks and connections questions the possibility of abstractions and generalizations that enable comparisons between different networks and societies.

Concerning Ingold's approach, I find his advocacy of the study of practical engagements and emphasis on sensory perception, as well as the processual perspective on environment, intriguing. But, similar to Latour, Ingold does not put forward a cross-cultural, ethnographic application of his method himself. Ingold has been criticized for understanding environment rather narrowly as the biophysical environment and for leaving out symbolic aspects (Guneratne 2010) and questions of power relations (Campbell 2010). Ingold's emphasis on thinking and perceiving as actions in an environment leaves aside the involvements and relations that make up the networks (to speak with Latour) within which the actions—or lived experiences—concerned take place, receive meaning, intentions, and interpretations. I would further like to stress that Ingold's notion of humans mingling with their environment and its ecology is highly androcentric (or organism-centric). It seems too exclusively focused on empirical phenomena and physical objects and leaves open the question of how to include spiritual agents, for example. As a practical application to ethnography, however, the focus on the role of sensory perception, practical experience, and concrete activities as a starting point for conceptualizations, descriptions, and evaluations of the environment seems convincing.

I will not apply any of the three authors exclusively, but rather will selectively draw on their insights for the presentation and discussion of my ethnographic findings when it seems appropriate to do so. What I generally adopt for my writing is their use of the term environment. The term environment, in the above-delineated usage, moves the discussion of human-environment relations beyond the nature-culture divide. The discussion is no longer about what is nature and what is culture. Neither does the term environment imply the existence of an objective truth about nature. The term environment thus directs the focus of attention to how humans establish meaningful relations with the external world and how they conceptualize these relations. The aim is to take a fresh and more holistic look at what has to be taken into account in order to understand how people engage with their environment. The critique of the nature-culture dichotomy in Western thought and academy is particularly relevant to the present work because writings on pastoralist societies, including the Gaddi, largely exemplify this dualism.

Between Adaptation and Ideology: Himalayan Pastoralism in the Literature

The anthropological literature on pastoralism and transhumance in South Asia and more specifically in the Himalayas can be characterized as caught between adaptation and ideology. With this characterization, I point to two trends in anthropological research on pastoralism and transhumance: the interest in resource use and adaptation to the physical environment on the one hand, which I here label adaptation, and the interest in cultural constructions of the environment or pastoralism as a particular worldview, or a focus on ideology, on the other hand.

The physical environment as a topic of studies on pastoralist societies, especially those of mountain regions, has received increased attention during the 1980s and 1990s.[2] The relation between pastoralists and their environment has been discussed by social anthropologists in journals such as *Mountain Research and Development* and *Nomadic Peoples*. Environment is here generally understood as the physical environment. Common terms characterizing the research interest are, for example, ecological (in)stability, fragile mountains environments, risk, degradation (of forests, land, etc.), land use, resource use and management, sustainable development, local knowledge, environmental effects, and, more recently and increasingly, conservation.[3] As Tapper noted, these topics were not constrained to academic debates but were raised in several international forums discussing pastoralist issues that often had an applied outlook (Tapper 2008).

These study and research interests at least partly hinge on definitions of pastoralism, nomadism, and transhumance, which in themselves define directions of research. Before I further engage in a discussion of pastoralist studies, it is therefore necessary to consider the basic terminology used in the field. On a general note, the terms pastoralist, nomadic, and transhumant are often used either interchangeably or in combined expressions such as nomadic pastoralism, pastoral nomadism, or transhumant pastoralism. In distinctions that are more clear-cut, pastoralism is the most general term, signifying a system of production, such as in, "the use of extensive grazing on rangelands for livestock production" (Food and Agricultural Organization of the United Nations [FAO] 2001: introduction, overview). Following the distinctions of the FAO, pastoralism in turn can be categorized according to the degree of movement involved in herding practices from "nomadic through transhumant to agropastoral" (ibid.: introduction, pastoral enterprises). However, "any classification of this type must be treated as a simplification; pastoralists are by their nature flexible and opportunistic, and can rapidly switch management systems as well as operating multiple systems in one overall productive enterprise" (FAO 2001: introduction, pastoral enterprises).

The FAO distinguishes nomadic pastoralism from transhumant pastoralism by the definition that nomadic movements, albeit following established migration routes, vary from year to year in search of pasture. Transhumant movements follow regular routes in the seasonal exploitation of pastures. Transhumance is associated with permanent homes and often some agriculture. It varies from agropastoralism through the latter's definition as the cultivation of sufficient land for subsistence and grazing areas within the reach of villages (FAO 2001: introduction, pastoral enterprises). In the *Encyclopedia of Social and Cultural Anthropology* (Barnard and Spencer 2002), Salzman defines nomadism not chiefly as a form of pastoralism, but rather through the regular movement of the residential group (Salzman 2002a). It is this sense in which I use the term nomadic in the following unless I refer to its usage by other authors. Transhumance in accordance with Salzman, in contrast, is the seasonal use of climatic zones for livestock herding, generally through the exploitation of altitudinal zones in mountains, but independent of the movement or nonmovement of the residential group (Salzman 2002b).[4]

Not all authors agree in their definitions of the terms used, nor do they always apply them coherently. Despite the resulting fuzziness of their usages, on a more general level the terms pastoralism, (pastoral) nomadism, and transhumance are defined by reference to economic systems, their adaptation to ecological conditions, and forms of resource use (cf. Rao and Casimir 2003: 3). Studies on pastoralism and transhumance show corresponding research foci.

Casimir and Rao apply the expression vertical control to the Himalayan context in order to describe the exploitation of different altitudinal zones in their study of what they call the pastoral ecology of the Bakrwal in Jammu and Kashmir (Casimir and Rao 1985). The focus of their study lies on the Bakrwal's system of utilization of pastures in different altitudes through the course of the year and its impact on the mountain ecosystem. Veena Bhasin's study of the Gaddi follows a cultural ecology approach. Bhasin's interest is the cultural adaptation to the physical environment. She aims to demonstrate correlations between socio-cultural systems and ecology whereby her investigation into the impact of ecological conditions on economy (pastoral and agricultural) and social relations displays a strong materialistic bias (Bhasin 1988).

The study of pastoralism and its adaptations to the physical environment has been influenced by Frederik Barth's adaptation of the concept of an ecological niche to human societies (1956). According to Barth, the territorial distribution of different communities in Swat, North Pakistan, has to be understood as the specialization on different ecological niches—that is, the place of a group has to be seen in relation to "the total environment, its relations to resources and competitors" (ibid.: 1079). Transhumant pastoralism and nomadism for Barth are such specializations that exploit ecological niches vis-à-vis the settled, agricultural population. A further example for the interest in pastoralist resource use is Salzman (1971a, 1971b). Salzman in his writings on nomadism in Iran is interested in nomadism and transhumance as distinct systems of resource use (Salzman 1971b). He recognizes that nomadism can be an adaptation to social and political rather than primarily ecological circumstances (Salzman 1971a), a notion already present in Barth's definition of the ecological niche. Nevertheless, he, too, regards nomadism as a form of adaptation.

The studies that I characterize as adaption focused have made important contributions, for example, in emphasizing systems of local knowledge of resources and land use. In examining pastoral practices and their impact on the ecosystem, the studies contributed to the rehabilitation of pastoralists who had often all too readily been identified as the culprits for ecological degradation. They have helped to argue for a place of pastoralists vis-à-vis an alarmist discourse of desertification, overgrazing, land degradation, and its implications for policy making (for the Gaddi, cf. Chakravarty-Kaul 1998; Saberwal 1999). However, in light of the criticism of the Western nature-culture dualism, the adaptation-centered approach represents the naturalist side of the dichotomy in that it analyzes pastoralist adaptation to a physical environment that is more or less objectively given and defined by natural science.

A second strain of research interests, particularly concerning pastoralist societies in South Asia and the Western Himalayan region, is the study of pastoralist ideologies. Studies following the second approach are often driven by a romanticism associated with a pastoral way of life. Both approaches correlate in the sense that they appear to be two sides of the same coin: the coin of nature-culture dualism. On the one hand, there are the more geographically influenced works on resource use and adaptation to the environment; on the other hand, there are studies that treat environment in a social constructionist framework and focus on ideological and cosmological conceptualizations and symbolic representations (cf. Ahmed

1983; Gooch 1998; Parkes 1987; Rao 2000; for the Gaddi, cf. Kaushal 2001a, 2001b).

In criticism of economic and ecologic definitions, Ahmed has argued for ideology rather than ecological conditions as determining for nomadism. In the case of the Gomal nomads in Pakistan, he sees nomadism primarily as an expression of social values rather than as an economic or ecological specialization (Ahmed 1983). That pastoralism or nomadism should not be reduced to economic reasons is also highlighted by Tapper, who points out that there are also many cases "where people pursue pastoral nomadism (or transhumance) for political and cultural reasons" (Tapper 2005: 841).

The focus on cultural reasons for nomadism, however, has in practice often led to the assumption of the existence of such a thing as a pastoralist ideology. Again, pastoralism itself, which in this approach is assumed to be a distinct type of ideology, becomes the research interest.[5] The FAO report *Pastoralism in the New Millennium* nicely portrays a scholarly fascination with pastoralism as a way of life and subsequent research projects:

> The literature on pastoralism is not simply an ordered body of empirical descriptive literature; to read through this material is to become aware of authors writing within a particular context. Although nomadism is viewed negatively within many of the countries in which it is practised, it is as often viewed positively by outsiders. Writers are frequently impressed by the independence of nomads, their ability to survive in extremely harsh landscapes and their cosmopolitan outlook compared with that of neighbouring farmers. The other side of this, however, is the discourse of the "crisis" or "problem." Even from the early period, the literature is rich in articles and books analysing the crisis of nomadism or the problems nomads experience or are said to cause. (FAO 2001: the discourse of pastoralism)

In a more recent publication, Tapper criticizes the exercise of establishing typologies such as nomad, pastoralist, or nomadic pastoralist as it is conducted on the basis of analytical categories that do "not take into account the autonymic self-identities or classifications of the people so labelled" (Tapper 2008: 106). Tapper further argues in the context of pastoralist groups in Afghanistan that an overvaluation of nomadism as a value has led to a generalization and idealization of all nomadic groups. As a consequence, a specific nomadic ideology and distinct identity is attributed even to those pastoralists who do not value nomadism as such but are much more pragmatic about their life and work than the advocates of their way of life, whether academics or political planners (ibid.: 111).

For the Gaddi, too, it has been argued that their "way of life is not dispensable" for them (Kaushal 1998: 76). Shepherding according to Kaushal is more to the Gaddi than a profession. It is a way of life, religiously sanctioned, that they are not inclined to give up. The latter part of the statement sharply contrasts with my findings. In my experience, the practice of transhumance appears very much dispensable to Gaddi shepherds. Many families have given up the practice of shepherding or seasonal migration for practical reasons without much nostalgia for a different way of life. Shepherds as well as their wives frequently describe shepherding as *gandā kām* (dirty work). It is dirty according to the people making this qualification because it is physically hard and depriving. Shepherds need to live in the open in all weather; are deprived of comforts, even of dry clothes or meals in heavy rains; risk their lives on hill slopes; live in proximity to wild animals in the mountains; and spend long stretches of time away from their families. In spite of the fact that shepherding is a respected profession within the community, none of the shepherds I talked to wanted his sons to follow in his footsteps, but rather planned for the their education and later employment in jobs where they could stay at home, have a secure income, and at best a pension after retirement.[6] If an ideology particular to the Gaddi and their way of life exists, one has to look farther than at the practice of transhumance in itself. I thus agree with Tapper in being critical of typological generalizations and deductions from preconceived classifications and his call to give more weight to the study of people's self-definitions.

The two perspectives on pastoralism outlined above are usually treated in separate frameworks.[7] Studies in ecology scarcely inform about cultural meanings in human-environment relations, whereas studies on ideology and cosmological conceptualizations do not engage more deeply with ecological factors. The dual interests in studies of pastoralist societies—adaptation and ecology on the one hand, ideology on the other—fall within the criticism of the nature-culture dualism of Descola, Latour, and Ingold. The adaptation framework understands environment as the physical environment, more precisely as nature. Nature here, as for natural science, is an independent entity to which pastoralists can adapt with their system of resource use. Symbolic constructions of that physical environment are left to be studied in the ideational framework. The focus on ideology as a study of social constructions in practice results in leaving ecological factors to the adaptational perspective.

What is more, after an increased interest in pastoralism, especially concerning land use and ecology, in the 1980s and 1990s, with a change in research interests more recently, attention to pastoralist societies appears to have decreased. As a consequence, adaptation-centered studies on pastoralism have remained standard reference works concerning pastoralism and environment in the Himalayas. Thus, the term environment, with regard to pastoralist groups, remains first and foremost strongly associated with nature, ecology and the physical environment.

However, with Latour, nature and society "do not offer solid hooks to which we might attach our interpretations . . . but are what is to be explained" (Latour 1993: 95). The aim in the following chapters is to move beyond adaptation and ideology—to borrow from Descola's title—in looking at human-environment relations. This means to follow a more holistic approach to understand how Gaddi people establish meaningful relations with their environment.

Notes

1. Latour's approach is also known and further developed as actor network theory (ANT), which has been especially received by sociology and political science (cf. Latour 2005; Voss and Peuker 2006).
2. Previous interest, especially during the 1960s, was strongly focused on the relation between pastoralism or nomadism and the state (see Rao and Casimir 2003; Tapper 2008).
3. For a more detailed discussion and criticism of the discourse on pastoralism and land degradation, see Guneratne (2010) and Saberwal (1999); for land degradation in the Himalayas more generally, see also Smadja (2009a).
4. For a geographical typology of pastoral practices see, for example, Kreutzmann (2004).
5. See also Axelby's critique on the representation of the "nomadic 'other'" (2005: 12).
6. A similar attitude of Gaddi shepherds toward their work has been reported by Axelby (2005: 127–128).
7. At least the separate treatment of nature and culture has been dominant in the literature on transhumant pastoralism in South Asia. This separation is, for example, visible in Aparna Rao's work who has written on resource use and adaptation, as well as ideology, but largely in distinct publications. A stronger emphasis on a combined analysis is supported, for example, by Pernille Gooch (1998) as well as by Irmtraud Stellrecht (1992).

2

The Gaddi in Images

My first contact with Gaddi took place through music video CDs (VCDs). I started my research and fieldwork preparations from Chandigarh, where I lived with a family, themselves from Himachal Pradesh, although they were Pahari speakers and not from the Kangra district. While staying in Chandigarh, I accompanied my hosts on visits to their relatives and friends, most of whom were also Himachalis living and working in Chandigarh permanently, albeit maintaining their connections to Himachal. After explaining that I was preparing to go to Himachal to research Gaddi culture, the hosts in the majority of cases responded by telling me they had something I should see. They switched on their TV and VCD recorders, took out a VCD with Himachali folk songs, and ran it forward to a song with a video that featured Gaddi people. My Himachali acquaintances in Chandigarh were not the only passionate viewers of VCDs with Himachali folk music and dance. Later on, in the initial stages of my fieldwork in Himachal, Gaddi people played the same and additional locally produced VCDs to introduce me to their culture.[1]

The images conveyed in VCDs are significant because VCDs are a widespread and very popular medium in Himachal Pradesh, and throughout India. As Peter Manuel, who studied cassette culture in North India, states, the images transmitted in popular culture matter, because "popular music is inseparable from notions of social identity, and derives much of its appeal from the ways it embodies, however obliquely, encoded ideologies" (Manuel 1993: 6). Since social identities are inscribed in popular music encoded in the ideologies of its producers, the "expression of community identity can depend on the nature of control of the mass media, the ability and propensity of distinct groups to resignify received media content, and, of course, the degree of community self-consciousness" (ibid.: 260). Manuel notes in his book on the spread of cassettes as a new medium (ibid.) that it opened up new decentralized forms of music production and diversification regarding language, region, genre, and performer. Cassettes were comparatively easy to produce and opened up possibilities to record music in regional dialects by smaller companies that catered to regional markets, whereas the recording industry had previously been dominated by Hindi and Urdu recordings that reproduced the popular culture of the mostly urban middle classes (ibid.: 156).

The VCD industry is following in the path of cassettes as a decentralized form of mass media, able to capture regional tastes, languages, and forms of expressions.[2] With the spread of TVs and VCD recorders to village homes, the VCD is today preferred to the cassette in rural as well as urban areas in the wider Himachal Pradesh and Punjab border regions. In the consumption of VCDs, a major stress is put on the video clips made for each song. People enjoy seeing the singers and dance performances in the videos.[3]

As Manuel points out, while on the one hand the "spread of cassettes creates new possibilities of musical and even socio-political discourse, by extending media control and access to an unprecedented variety of groups" (Manuel 1993: 259), on the other hand cassettes—and VCDs—open up a new field of struggles over representation and negotiation of identities. Manuel writes, "in general, the range of hybrid musics now marketed on cassette, whether emergent, residual, elite, or proletarian in orientation, can be seen, in Hall's terms, as 'contested terrain' where dialects of class, gender, ethnicity, age, religion, and other aspects of social identity are symbolically negotiated and dramatized" (ibid.).

This contested terrain of folk music VCD production is thereby to be seen in the context of negotiations of social identities as well as of an overall Himachali identity. Himachal is today widely known in India for its mountains, its apples, and its electricity projects. Development projects such as hydropower projects and investments in infrastructure, whether roads, hospitals, or schools, have raised the basic living standards within the state. A pronounced aim of the state is to establish Himachal Pradesh as the "hydro power state of the country" (Himachal Pradesh State Electricity Board 2006). This goal is coupled with attempts at a relatively ecofriendly development, first and foremost through the generation of electricity from renewable energies. Water power is generated through run-of-the-river technology in small and larger dam projects instead of the huge dam constructions that had previously been carried out in the state at Pong Dam on the Beas River and Bhakra Dam on the Sutlej River (Chhatre and Saberwal 2006: 29). Following Chhatre and Saberwal, the state of

Himachal Pradesh has in recent years "sought to craft a new Himachali identity that is based on environmental values" (ibid.: 28).

The economic and infrastructural development of the state is accompanied by investments in the tourism sector. The Himachal Tourism Department actively promotes the state's image as a tourist destination. Apart from cities such as Shimla, the former summer residence of the colonial government, Dalhousie, and other hill stations that promise a cool retreat during the summer for well-off visitors from the plains, the Himachal Tourism Department is promoting adventure tourism such as trekking, water rafting, winter sports, and paragliding, as well as religious tourism (Department of Tourism and Civil Aviation 2008). *Dev bhūmi* Himachal, the land of the gods (a title Himachal Pradesh shares with Uttarakhand), is advertised for its Hindu, Buddhist, Sikh, and Christian pilgrimage sites (the latter being located in the old colonial hill stations), as well as for the peaks of the Himalayan ranges that, "with its great scenic beauty and aura of spiritual calm seem the natural home of the Gods" (Government of Himachal Pradesh n.d.). For tourism, as for hydropower and apples, the state's capital is its mountains. Himachal Pradesh thereby presents itself as an educated, environmentally conscious, and economically progressing state that promotes the image of its mountains as an untouched spiritual and natural land. Where do the Gaddi figure in this picture of Himachal between *dev bhūmi* and paragliding?

First, the Gaddi are widely known throughout Himachal Pradesh because of their transhumance, which takes them through large parts of the state. Chetan Singh in his historical work on ecology and society in Himachal Pradesh suggests that the Gaddi's practice of transhumant pastoralism had an integrating capacity and was important for the development of a regional identity of the postindependence founded state of Himachal Pradesh (C. Singh 1998: 233). However, if with Singh the Gaddi shepherds' practice of transhumance has contributed toward a sense of belonging together within the state of Himachal, the administrative system of Himachal Pradesh has in turn set the Gaddi community apart from the mainstream population through the scheduled tribe (ST) status.

The category of ST, similar to that of scheduled castes (SC), grants special entitlements and reserved seats or quotas that facilitate access to education facilities, government employment, and welfare programs. It is an instrument provisioned by the Indian constitution that is intended to serve as a form of positive discrimination to uplift the status of economically and socially disadvantaged groups. Which groups are recognized as a scheduled tribe is determined at state and district levels. Among the criteria for ST designation, according to the ministry of tribal affairs, are geographical isolation, distinct culture, primitive traits, and economic backwardness (Ministry of Tribal Affairs n.d.).[4] In the case of the Gaddi, the state and districtwise granting of ST status led to the situation where, while Gaddi living in Chamba were recognized as an ST from the 1940s, in Kangra (formerly part of Punjab) the Gaddi were recognized as an ST only in 2002 (Kapila 2008). In the campaign for ST status in Kangra, the Gaddi based their claim on their distinctive way of life, namely pastoralism and seasonal migration (ibid.).

Since the Gaddi shepherds who move through large parts of the state with their flocks are well known to other Himachalis, it should not come as a surprise that the Gaddi as a group also figure prominently in Himachali music VCD compilations—in the clips as well as on the covers. The question arises how the Gaddi are portrayed in these VCD clips—which popular perceptions and ideologies are transmitted through the images, which identity and place within Himachali society are ascribed to the Gaddi in this medium of popular culture.

Popular Imagery

First, the characters in the video clips are identified as Gaddi through their dress; it is generally women who are portrayed as Gaddi. The typical dress of Gaddi women is called *nuāncarī*. It is a cotton dress with a bodice of a close-fitting, green, blue, or purple blouse and a wide, flowing, red skirt patterned with flowers. The dress is bound round the waist by a *ḍorā*, a long, black, woolen cord. The headscarf worn with the *nuāncarī* is large and wide, reaching to about the woman's knees. The *nuāncarī* is today worn only on festive occasions, such as life-cycle rituals, with the exception of Bharmaur, where some elderly women can still be seen wearing *nuāncarī* on an everyday basis. A woman gets her first *nuāncarī* on her wedding. Girls may wear it only for pictures or cultural days in school. In popular imagery, however, it appears as the general dress of Gaddi women.

The Gaddi dress is the topic of the popular, quite short, rhymed Pahari song *Satarangī Merā Colā Kālā Merā Ḍorā*, whose text is centered around the lines, Colorful is my dress, black is my *ḍorā*, I will become a butterfly and start flying.[5] In the VCD *Satarangī Merā Colā Kālā Ḍorā*, the lyrics to this song are matched with images of young women dancing in *nuāncarī* (Thakur n.d.: song 1). The scene or background of the dancers changes between trees, grass, bushes, and a river. In a song (*Cal Maīye Kesaro*) on the same compilation (Thakur: song 5) two women in *nuāncarī* are contrasted with a young woman dressed in jeans. In the video, the Gaddi women as representatives of the countryside show their jeans and T-shirt-wearing visitor from the city their physical surroundings, and repeatedly point to the mountains, for which two alternating mountain scenes are inserted. In a chorus, the Gaddi women invite the city girl to walk into the mountains with them.

City versus mountains is also the topic of a song portraying a Gaddi woman, to be identified by her *nuāncarī*, on the VCD *Bheṛliyān Carāndī Reshmā* [sic], subtitled Himachali Folk Songs (Panyari and Maity 2004). In the song *Kajo Bhedhliyan Charandi* (Why tend the sheep?), the Gaddi woman is tending a flock of sheep and goats near a river where she is photographed by a man who has come from the city as a tourist. While she is seen walking between the animals carrying a crook, crossing the river with them, and dancing on the meadow next to the river, he is portrayed as the modern town dweller, which is shown by his rather expensive clothes, the hat that appears to be trekking equipment, and the camera with which he is taking pictures of her. In the lyrics he asks her why she would want to be walking with the sheep from hill to hill and invites her to leave the sheep and come with him to the city of Delhi. He points at her clothes and in the corresponding line promises to buy her a sari for Delhi. The next video sequence shows her dancing dressed in a sari instead of the Gaddi *nuāncarī* and the location is shifted from the river bank to a higher meadow below the old Kangra Fort, empty of sheep and goats.

Tending sheep is a common topic of songs that are matched with videos depicting Gaddi. This itself is not surprising, since it is their flocks and traditional occupation as shepherds for which the Gaddi community is known. It is rather the extent to which these images find expression in the VCD production and the straightforward connection of Gaddi with sheep, mountains, and rivers and wastelands that is remarkable. The common setting for these scene shootings is the jungle or wasteland situated between village and river. The very first VCD that was ever played for me in order to show me Gaddi people during my stay in Chandigarh united these clichés. It featured images of a Gaddi woman in *nuāncarī* who is holding a lamb in her arms standing on big rocks in a riverbed with the Dhauladhar range in the background. Similar images figure in the song *Bhedliyān Carādiye O* (Tending sheep) on the VCD *Dhoban* (Paniyari 2006). In contrast to the last clip described above, both actor and actress appear to be Gaddi in this song. The video accompanies a romantic song. It depicts the couple running after sheep, crossing a river, dancing, and pausing on rocks in front of greenery and trees. While her appearance in a Gaddi dress is fairly accurate, his clothes display a mix of different styles, none of which, besides the Himachali cap, can be ascribed to Gaddi men in particular. As Pinney states, however, this should not distract the imagery, since Indian visual imagery is not primarily concerned with authenticity (1997). Moreover, the couple in the VCD, again, can unmistakably be recognized as Gaddi through representation of the woman. More significantly, the "Gaddi" man in the video meets an almost classical stereotype of the flute-playing shepherd. This stereotype exists in the literature as well as in popular imagination, but I could never confirm it in practice.

In sum, in Himachali folk music VCDs the Gaddi are portrayed as "tribals," seemingly living in close proximity to nature, sheep, and the mountains, and thus are placed with the physical environment. This is accomplished first through dress. In the videos, the Gaddi appear in their traditional dress that is opposed to jeans or sari. Gaddi women are thereby contrasted with young women from the city or opposed to the tourist who comes to take the woman back to the city for a better, seemingly modern life.

Dress here marks not only the rural, but also the ethnic distinctiveness and renders the Gaddi's ST status visible. This "tribal" portrayal of the Gaddi is further enhanced by the setting of the videos—the jungle or wastelands, the mountains, and the flocks. The images, on the one hand, play on romantic ideas associated with shepherding and the mountains as, for example, visible by the couple acting to a romantic song and the image of the flute-playing shepherd. But through the wastelands rather than the village, and the traditional dress rather than the sari (which is rather associated with urbanity than with most of Himachal Pradesh) the image of the Gaddi further carries a notion of innocent simplicity and otherness. There are other songs—often on the same compilations—that display town youth, women waiting for their husbands who are in the army, and other images that evoke associations with modern life or a national identity, but in them discernible images of the Gaddi do not figure.

Moreover, there is a gender aspect to the images. The Gaddi are overwhelmingly represented through women. While, among the Gaddi, women in practice do occasionally help with grazing the flocks, men do the shepherding and moving through wastelands and mountains. In the videos, in contrast, it is women who are placed with sheep, mountains, the riverbeds, and locations opposed to city life. Following Osella and Osella, it should not surprise us that Gaddi identity is represented via the dress of women since the symbolism of men's dress has largely been overlooked in popular as well as in academic literature (Osella and Osella 2007); in addition, women are generally more marked in local representations.

This imagery taken together reflects to some extent what Lutgendorf discusses as a tendency prevalent in Hindi cinema, namely the thematic polarities of women, nature, and tradition, on the one hand, and men and modern civilization, on the other hand, or the rural versus the urban, as well as the local, marked in ethnic costume, versus the cosmopolitan (Lutgendorf 2005: 32).

Both, the placement of the Gaddi within the physical environment as well as the representation through women, are paralleled by the representation of other pastoral societies. In Iran, nomad tribes have also been naturalized as part of the environment and "feminized or emasculated. Photographs of nomads taken up to the mid-twentieth century were usually of armed men, on horseback. In recent years, pictures of women have become far more common, doubtless in part because nomad women's dress is usually more colourful than men's" (Tapper 2008: 109). The images of colorful dresses are meant to appeal to tourists and are used in tourist brochures (ibid.). With regard to the Gaddi, Tapper's observation needs to be qualified: their representation, at least from the time of the colonial gazetteer, has never been martial but rather peaceful and friendly (see next section). The folkloristic or touristic aspects of images of female clothing, however, seem to be in place in Himachal as well.

This is not to say that the mountains, pastoralism, or rural scenery carry negative connotations. The Gaddi are depicted as part of an imagery that represents Himachal Pradesh. The mountains, rivers, and green vegetation are in general positively associated with Himachal Pradesh's physical environment and in the official discourse are presented as integral to the state's identity. The mountains with their touristic attractions are what people from the plains travel to Himachal for during the hot season. However, by presenting the Gaddi as part of this physical environment, the image of the Gaddi as a pastoral mountain people as opposed to modern city dwellers is spread. And the Gaddi in the VCDs represent a natural as well as a traditional Himachal—far from hydroelectric power generation and paragliding.

Ethnographic Representations

> The Gaddís are the most remarkable race in the hills. In features, manners, dress, and dialect they differ essentially from all the rest of the population. (*Gazetteer of the Kangra District 1883–1884* 1884: 91)

The visual imagery of the Gaddi in the VCDs has parallels in ethnographic descriptions. The prevalent portray of the Gaddi in the colonial literature depicts them as remarkable through their distinctness from other Himachali communities. The authors show respect for the shepherds' pastoral work and their ability to make a living in the harsh mountain tracks, but thereby describe the Gaddi as simple, undemanding people who are well adapted to the mountains. While the men are portrayed as being strong in the mountains, they are described as peaceful and hospitable in social relations. The women have the reputation of being beautiful (*Gazetteer of the Kangra District 1883–1884* 1884: 91; *Gazetteer of the Kangra District 1897* 1899; Rose 1980).

The stereotype of the Gaddi as friendly and peaceful, hardworking, cheerful, simple, beautiful, and above all distinct from the other population is still found today in postindependence census literature, handbooks on Himachal Pradesh (Balokhra 1998), as well as in several academic publications (Handa 2005; Verma 1996). The romanticized idea of the Gaddi as remote mountain dwellers has thereby proven so pervasive as to tempt authors to give ecologically unsound descriptions of the Gaddi such as "shepherds of the snowy ranges" (Chakravarty-Kaul 1998: 6). Balokra in a compendium on Himachal Pradesh even depicts the Gaddi as representing a better stage of society, where moral values are still upheld, mutual help is extended, and life is simple but happy (1998: 25).

The similarities in representations of the Gaddi in colonial and present accounts lie in the picture of the Gaddi as a peaceful mountain "tribe." The stereotypical picture of the Gaddi as a distinct community transmitted in the literature to some extent seems to be replicated by the uncritical acceptance of earlier accounts. It moreover lacks detailed information on how the Gaddi, in fact, differ from their neighbors apart from external characteristics and generalizations of character traits. The image created of the Gaddi thus remains superficial.

As a matter of fact, these general descriptions contrast with writings on the Gaddi, for example, by K.P. Sharma, who treats the Gaddi as an integral part of the larger Chamba society (2001, 2004; K.P. Sharma and Sethi 1992), as well as with publications of the vernacular literature, for example, Khushi Ram Sharma who integrates the Gaddi into his description of "The Culture of Kangra and Life of its People" (K.R. Sharma 1974). Both authors do not exclusively write on the Gaddi, but on the region of Chamba and Kangra, respectively. They name the Gaddi as a group and highlight Gaddi-specific practices, festivals, dances, dress, and so on, but treat these as variations of broader regional patterns rather than as markers of a fundamental ethnic distinctiveness.

The preoccupation with the Gaddi as transhumant pastoralists, on the contrary, reduces their collective identity to being shepherds who adapted to the ecological conditions of the mountains. Here it matches the imagery used in VCDs insofar as both the literature and VCDs equate the Gaddi with sheep and goats and with the mountains and more generally the physical environment of Himachal Pradesh. Both media further inscribe on the Gaddi an ethnic distinction. Popular imagination and ethnographic representations assign mountains and jungle to the Gaddi as their niche and thus place them on the nature side of the nature-culture dualism.

Being imagined as belonging to nature and as a socially and ethnically distinct group, the Gaddi thereby emerge as what Latour calls natural-social hybrids.

Evaluation of Popular Representations

In my experience of watching folk music videos together, Gaddi people in my fieldwork villages did not oppose the image created of their community in the local VCD productions. On the contrary, several Gaddi people explicitly used these folk music VCDs (as well as productions of devotional songs) to introduce me to their culture. From the credits on the folk song VCDs, it is not evident if members of the Gaddi community were involved in their production, since the names in the credits are representative of different communities in Kangra including the Gaddi. With some productions, this might well be the case, with others this is rather unlikely. On a general note, the Kangra productions are fairly accurate in their depiction of Gaddi people.

The local competency in Kangra-based compilations becomes obvious when contrasted with productions from outside the district. A negative example in this context that shows major inaccuracies in depicting the Gaddi is a VCD from a Mumbai label titled *Gaddan*, the female form of Gaddi (Rana 2008). Without engaging in ethnic or racial theories, it can be asserted that the dancers in traditional Gaddi dress are either Tibetans or from the district Lahul and Spiti. The jewelry of the musicians is also decidedly not Gaddi but from the inner Himalayas. Above all, in one song a woman in *nuāncarī* is portrayed shamelessly dancing through a village followed by two instrument-playing men. This is in absolute contrast to the usual image of the chaste Gaddi women and a rather offensive depiction in terms of a woman's code of conduct and moral standing. It does, however, match ideas about the Himalaya as an erotic topos both in its associations with divine play and, more literally with the pictures in the video, in its associations with an "abode of human communities who practice a deviant social code that affords more sexual agency to women" (Lutgendorf 2005: 32). The images in this Mumbai production thus cater to fantasies of Himachal or better the Himalayan mountains in general as, for example, expressed in Bollywood imageries (ibid.), which are, however, not backed up by actual knowledge of the region and its inhabitants.

The Pahari compilations in contrast convey a local competency in portraying the Gaddi, despite the use of stereotypes. This is not surprising for they address a local audience, of Gaddi and Pahari speakers alike, who as consumers identify with the portrayed imagery of the region. That Gaddi people participate in the consumption of the VCDs points to the fact that, on the one hand, the images created in the VCDs, at least to some extent, must fit Gaddi self-presentations and that, on the other hand, Gaddi people themselves identify with the larger Himachali culture as presented by the VCDs.[6] This is not to say that the representation of the Gaddi in VCDs and Himachal literature is unproblematic. But, if the equation of the Gaddi with sheep and goats and mountains is not really contested by self-descriptions, a straightforward criticism of these images as outsider perceptions is not convincing. Instead the task is to investigate how the Gaddi themselves use these images.

A look at family photo collections reveals similarities between Gaddi representations in the VCDs and self-presentations of a Gaddi identity. Most women own one or several pictures of themselves dressed in *nuāncarī* and typical jewelry. Often these are single pictures, sometimes of groups or couples, for example of sisters or spouses. It is not uncommon to enlarge these pictures and display them on the living room wall. Less frequently than women, but not seldom, are men photographed in the characteric Gaddi outfit. For men, the "traditional" dress is called *colā*. It is a long, wide shirt made of white sheep wool that, like the *nuāncarī*, is tied at the waist with a black woolen *ḍorā* (cord).[7] Alternatively, men also pose in sheep wool jackets or at least with a Himachali cap. People take pride in their pictures in "traditional" dress. I was often asked to photograph them dressed accordingly. Moreover, it was insisted on several occasions that I had to have my picture taken in a *nuāncarī*.

But not only the "traditional" dress figures in visual references to Gaddi identity in photography, but also—as in folk music VCD representations of the Gaddi—more strictly pastoral motifs are popular, too, and people commonly pose for pictures with sheep and goats. Again, I was shown many of these pictures in family albums and was asked to photograph people accordingly. Shepherds asked me to photograph them with their flock for which they in some instances singled out a large he-goat to stand in the foreground with them or picked up a sheep. Parents also like their children to be photographed with goats and sheep. In the case of shepherding families, of course, this would be with their own flock; for others, also with a domestic goat or sheep. What is more, posters with the pastoral motif of a couple leading a flock on migration, which are available at local markets, is a common living room decoration in many Gaddi homes (see figure 2.1). One motif shows a scene with a woman in a *nuāncarī* type dress in the foreground and a mountain range in the background.

Since at first sight the Gaddi seem to identify with the stereotypical images of their community—pastoralism, traditional dress, mountains—that are created in popular perceptions and in parts of the literature, it could

Figure 2.1 Framed poster with a pastoral motif next to an image of the god Krishna on a living room wall. Photo by A. Wagner (2008).

be claimed that the Gaddi have taken over the images that have been projected of them into their own identity constructions. But a closer look reveals multiple dimensions of meaning behind images with reference to Gaddi identity as they are used by the group concerned. While *nuāncarī* as well as *colā* serve as markers of Gaddi identity, both have ceased to be everyday clothing.[8] On festive occasions, in turn, *nuāncarī* and *colā* are worn selectively, and are thereby ascribed certain functions such as highlighting kinship relations—for example, the mother's brothers' wives of the groom wear *nuāncarī* on the first day of a wedding and the in-married women of the family on the second wedding day. The garment is taken off immediately after a certain function in the ceremony has been fulfilled. Furthermore, not all festive occasions imply that people will wear the traditional dress. It is rather restricted to life-cycle rituals such as weddings, ceremonies following a death, and retirement functions.[9] Other social and religious events, however, even some perceived to be specifically Gaddi, do not involve the wearing of traditional dress. The dress thus is selectively put to use as a marker of and referent to Gaddi community identity (see figure 2.2).

The selective usage of traditional dress hints at a negotiation that is taking place about when and how recourse to a tradition or traditional way of being is appropriate. This play on the presence and absence of traditional features in self-representations and local practices reminds me

Figure 2.2 In-married women of the groom's family dancing in *nuāncarī* at the groom's house on the morning of the day they will welcome the young bride into her new home. Photo by A. Wagner (2007).

of what Mark Liechty described in his study of the middle class in Kathmandu (2003). Liechty points out that to be a modern Nepali is not about overcoming what is seen as traditional in favor of what is considered to be modern, but rather is about the balance of and negotiation between the two. The balance between being modern and keeping traditions becomes further obvious when one considers that in their self-understanding people make a difference between the perception of a collective identity—that is, what being Gaddi stands for—and their self-perception as a shepherd, government employee, or college student. Identifications with representations of a collective Gaddi identity further involve negotiations and contextual shifts between an emphasis on own cultural distinctiveness as a community and emphasis on a broader regional or national identification, for example, in the form of identifications with Kangra or Himachal. Still, in producing, collecting, and displaying photographs, posters, or VCDs depicting traditional dress, sheep and goats, and the mountains, people actively promote a Gaddi mountain link in their self-presentations of a collective identity.

That the Gaddi themselves identify with representation of their community as belonging to the mountains indicates local understanding of these images. The characterization of the Gaddi as a mountain people in the literature, however, often has stopped at their general association with sheep and goat herding and the seasonal exploitation of different altitudinal zones. Thereby the mountains are assumed to exist as a physical fact to which the Gaddi are linked. Local understandings, however, should be expected to stem from actual practices through which the mountains come into being. It is time to uncover the engagements that Gaddi people themselves have with the mountains and their environment instead of contenting oneself with preconfigured images of transhumant identities.

Notes

1. The lyrics of these songs are in Pahari dialect. Accordingly, melody, rhythm, and dance are in the style of Pahari music, some with Punjabi influences. Language as well as melody, rhythm, and dance in these songs differ from typical Gaddi music. I have not come across Gaddi *lok gīt* (folk songs) on VCD. The Pahari dialect and music still dominates the genre of folk music. Gaddi language, music, and dance recordings exist, however, in the genre of *aincalī*, which are *dharmik* or religious songs. Here notably Gaddi men in traditional dress figure alongside women in the videos.
2. VCD culture has not received the same scholarly attention as cassettes so far and Manuel's *Cassette Culture* (1993) remains the authoritative work on the subject of popular music production and consumption in North India.
3. This was brought home to me when I took a CD recording of German folk songs to India. I had repeatedly been asked about German songs on my previous visit. In every household where I played the CD, people were disappointed at only hearing songs without seeing visual images. In contrast to India, audio CDs are the usual media for the distribution of music in Germany.
4. The administrative category of ST is not related to anthropological definitions of tribal societies, which focus on forms of social organization. The Gaddi fall into the administrative and not the anthropological category.
5. Here, *colā*, which is also the term for a woolen gown (that can be either a men's or a women's clothing), is used for the women's *nuāncarī*.
6. A deeper discussion of the latter point is beyond the scope of this section.
7. I am concerned here with references to dress as encountered during my fieldwork, including the visual media. Dress traditions have been traced in more detail and with attention to ornaments and headgear for men and women by K.P. Sharma and Sethi *Costumes and Ornaments of Chamba* (1997).
8. There are indications that *nuāncarī* and *colā*, among others, have actually been worn as everyday clothing in the past. This is suggested by reports of the elder generation as well as by photographs showing Gaddi men and women, for example, by the photographer Nowrojee who documented festive occasions as well as daily scenes in and around McLeod Ganj from the 1950s (private collection by the photographer). How far both clothing items have undergone changes and changing fashions in themselves is a different question. The

clothes connected with the Gaddi, however, in turn match the wider regional dress traditions.
9. Celebrating the retirement, which here always means the retirement from government service, is currently widely practiced in Himachal Pradesh as a social event. As such, it requires the invitation of family and colleagues and the exchange of gifts, mainly cloth and money. On the occasion of accepting the gifts, the retiring person and his spouse may dress in *colā* and *nuāncarī*.

3

A Sheep for Shiva

The god Shiva is highly important for the construction of a Gaddi identity and religious practices. The Shiva narrative can be seen as an overarching mythology both in respect to identity constructions and to conceptualizations of place since Shiva in local understanding is intimately connected to both the Gaddi community and the region of Bharmaur. The god Shiva is one of the great Hindu gods who, together with Brahma and Vishnu, is commonly considered to form the Hindu trinity. Shiva is generally known for his ambivalent or dual character. In her examination of the Puranas, Wendy Doniger O'Flaherty calls "the paradox of Śiva the erotic ascetic" the central paradox of Shiva mythology (Doniger O'Flaherty 1973: 4). In the classical texts, Shiva is at the same time the preserver and the destroyer, the ascetic and the erotic. Today Shiva is for the most part worshipped as a peaceful god (cf. Michaels 1998: 239). It is important to note that there is not one single form of worship nor one conceptualization of Shiva, as Michaels has pointed out. Shivaism is rather a term under which different theist strains and sects are subsumed (ibid.: 237). Michaels further notes a historical dimension to the image of the god Shiva as well as differences between textual and various local traditions. Thus, it is important to ask how Shiva is depicted in Gaddi narratives and imagery.

Living Like Śiv-ji: Shiva and Gaddi Identity

The worship of Shiva is central to Gaddi religious beliefs. In everyday language, Gaddi people usually refer to their god Shiva as Śiv-ji—that is, by adding the suffix *ji*, denoting respect, to his Hindi name Śiv. Among his many other names are Manī Māheś, Śankar, Bolenāth, Śāmīān, Bholā, Nīl Kaṇṭh, Jaṭā Dhārī, Trinetr, and, in Gaddi dialect, Dhuṛū. In the common pictures displayed on living room walls, the god Shiva is generally portrayed as an ascetic but householder. Typically, Shiva is shown sitting in meditation at Mount Kailash, with a leopard skin around his waist, a snake around his throat and bare breast, and the River Ganga falling from his matted locks. Further symbols are his *triśūl* (trident) and his vehicle, the bull Nandi. Often, in these pictures Shiva is accompanied by his wife Gaura (Parvati), and their two sons Karttik and Ganesh.[1] In Shiva temples, the *Shiv ling* (a phallus) is the most prominent representation of the god, but statues with the imagery described above are also erected. A statue of the bull Nandi is usually placed opposite the temple entrance.

The god Shiva is central to constructions of Gaddi identity in several ways. It is Shiva who is said to have made the Gaddi into shepherds, and following the religious legend the work of herding sheep was assigned to the Gaddi as a divine task (cf. Axelby 2005: 123; Kaushal 2001b: 33; Noble 1987). Moreover, the link between the Gaddi as a community and the god Shiva is also understood in geographic terms. There is a spatial union between Gaddern, the land of the Gaddi, and Śiv Bhūmi, Shiva's realm. Just as the state of Himachal Pradesh is called Dev Bhūmi or land of the gods, Bharmaur subdistrict in Chamba district, also known as Gaddern, is referred to as Śiv Bhūmi. Mount Kailash, Shiva's seat, is understood in northwestern Himachal to be Mount Kailash, situated in the middle of Bharmaur subdistrict.[2]

An annual pilgrimage, the Mani Mahesh Yatra, takes place from the town of Bharmaur to the Mani Mahesh Lake beneath Mount Kailash. The last thirteen-kilometer climb up to the Mani Mahesh Lake that is situated at about 4,100 meter altitude has to be managed on foot. The pilgrimage is accomplished by a bath in the holy lake of Mani Mahesh; women also bathe at Gauri Kund, a holy lake assigned to Shiva's wife Gaura (Parvati). The bathing at Mani Mahesh, for the Gaddi, stands in relation to the bathing in other holy lakes connected to Shiva and *nāg* (serpent) deities on both sides of the Dhauladhar on the day of *nhauṇ* (see chapter 6 for details). The Mani Mahesh Yatra starts from Janmashtami (the god Krishna's birthday), the eighth day of the dark half of the Gaddi month Bhaḍom (August–September), and lasts for fifteen days until *nhauṇ*, which coincides with Radhashtmi (Krishna's consort Radha's birthday).[3] The Mani Mahesh Yatra draws not only Gaddi pilgrims, but also pilgrims from other parts of Himachal Pradesh, Punjab, and the wider region. For 2008, the Hindi newspaper *Panjāb Kesrī* reported around 400,000 pilgrims and the inauguration of a helicopter service from Bharmaur to Gauri Kund, beneath the main lake (Vikās 2008).

In addition to living in spatial proximity to Shiva's seat Mount Kailash, the Gaddi can be said to live like Shiva or, as my informants sometimes phrased it, Shiva lives just like a Gaddi. Shiva is said to reside six months of the year up in the mountains on Mount Kailash and six months down in the plains. He migrates to the plains on Janmashtami in the month Bhadoṃ (August–September) and returns to Mount Kailash six months later on Shivratri (Shiva's night), the darkest night of the month Phāgūṇ (February–March).[4] On Shivratri Shiva, also known as the lord of the beasts, is said to release the snakes that he keeps with him during the cold half of the year. Thus, his upward migration is associated with warm weather and the appearance of snakes in the fields and villages in Kangra.

The seasonal migration of Shiva matches the seasonal migration of the Gaddi people. Molly Kaushal takes this correspondence literally when she writes that the "seasonal migration of the Gaddis coincides with the migratory period of Shiva, prominently marking their annual calendar with two important dates. . . . From Janamashtami onwards he [the shepherd] and his flock begin to look toward Jandhar, the lower valleys of Kangra and on Shivratri, he starts moving upwards to Gadderan" (Kaushal 2004: 188).[5] This linkage between the said migration of Shiva and the dates of the shepherds' transhumance was already established by the colonial gazetteers (*Gazetteer of the Chamba State 1904* 1996: 181).

I doubt that festivals like Shivratri and Janmashtami, which are determined by a lunisolar calendar and thus variable within limits, can serve as such exact anchor points for transhumant movements. A collective activity on those dates coordinating the shepherds' movements is conspicuous by its absence. As a matter of fact, shepherds themselves, when describing their pastoral cycle to me, never referred to Shivratri or any other festival. They described their movements mostly by counting the days they stay in one place or spend on the move. Shiva's migration on Shivratri and Janmashtami should therefore not be taken literally as dates but as reference points for the timeframes of Gaddi transhumance.

More important, however, the Gaddi do not only refer to the shepherds' transhumant movements when they describe themselves as *chemahīne* (six months), but they also refer to the traditional seasonal migration of families between their summer home in Chamba and their winter residence in Kangra, and thus to the life-style of the Gaddi community as a whole.[6] This interpretation contrasts the common transhumance-focused explanation in the literature. The question whether the migration of the god Shiva is linked to transhumance or to seasonal migration (or to both) is significant because it carries a gender aspect. The former establishes a link between constructions of a collective identity based on male practices, while the latter is an inclusive account that draws attention to patterns practiced by women, children, elderly, and nonshepherding men. It is significant that the latter interpretation was put forward in conversations I had with both women and men.

All this suggests that, for the Gaddi, Shiva is an accessible god with whom they as a community have a very personal relation and who in some respects even serves as a role model for their own lifestyle. He is predominantly conceptualized as a benevolent and protective god. By characterizing Shiva as an accessible god, I refer to the way of interaction with him. In contrast to gods like Vishnu and Ganesh who feature, for example, in life-cycle rituals but with whom communication is usually mediated by Brahman priests, Shiva can be grouped with other intrinsic Gaddi deities, like local goddesses, serpent deities, and even Shiva's son Karttik (Kelang in Gaddi dialect), as well as other local and family gods who are addressed by their devotees at a much more direct level.[7] Shiva's accessibility is also shown by the fact that he possesses *celā* (oracles) and thus is considered to interact and speak directly to his devotees. Kathleen Erndl similarly noted about the figure of the goddess in the Serānvāli Mata cult in Northwest India:

> The goddess Śerāṅvālī is like the great gods Viṣṇu and Śiva in terms of her degree of power, purity, and universality. At the same time, she shares characteristics such as accessibility, immanence, and intimacy with the lesser deities and saints. While the great gods of the Hindu pantheon do not generally possess their devotees, the lesser godlings do. (Erndl 1993: 111)

With regard to the Gaddi, it is Shiva who is simultaneously the great god and a god with which the devotees stand in an immanent and intimate relation. This is further shown by the fact that an animal is given to Shiva in sacrifice. The element of animal sacrifice in the *nuālā* ritual is somewhat exceptional in the South Asian context. *Bali* (Hindi for animal sacrifice), less common to the North Indian plains but not foreign to the Himalayas, is usually known to be connected to so-called smaller deities or to the goddess in her wild form of Kali. The Gaddi practice stands out in that the sacrifice is offered to Shiva, one of the "high" gods. One of my interview partners, a Gaddi Brahman priest from the Bharmaur area, recognized this discrepancy in relation to the orthodox traditions when he explained that, although the Gaddi sacrifice sheep for Shiva, Shiva himself would not eat the meat but would pass it on to his entourage. Overall animal sacrifice in my fieldwork area in western Himachal, in contrast to reports from other regions, for example, in the case of Uttarakhand (Sax 2002: 199), is neither the subject of passionate local debates nor is it notably targeted by Hindu nationalist movements. Sacrifice is rather considered a normal part of Gaddi rituals. It seems to be taken as a matter of fact, as the Gaddi way of doing things.[8] Since, as argued above, Shiva is seen as a Gaddi god, it is not surprising that he receives animals. For rituals performed for Gaddi deities, the interesting question is not whether an animal is offered in sacrifice, but rather which type of animal is given. The discussion of sacrifice in this context should be redirected not to ask "if" but rather "what": a sheep or a goat, a young or a mature animal.[9]

Why is a sheep offered to Shiva? On the one hand, there is a gender aspect to the classification of sacrificial animals. Among the Gaddi, goddesses typically receive goats and gods typically receive sheep. This applies to other male gods besides Shiva, for example, *nāg devtā* (serpent deities), too, although some male *nāg devtā* receive a goat as well. On the other hand, there is a pronounced connection between Shiva and sheep. Shiva is generally known to be fond of sheep. Talking about Shiva's flock of animals, my partners in conversation usually mentioned sheep first. The white wool used for the flower garland in the *nuālā* ritual is referred to as Shiva's wool. Another hint why Shiva likes sheep can be found in the stories of his wedding to Gaura (Parvati).

In one of the songs about Shiva's wedding, which is also sung during the *nuālā* ritual, Gaura is asked by her *māmā* (MB) what she wants from him as dowry.[10] The MB in general, as in other parts of North India, is the person obliged to fulfill the wishes of his sister's children. Furthermore, he plays an important part in the marriage rituals. The *māmā* of Gaura is Himraj, the ruler of the snow.[11] Himraj offers to give Gaura everything she wants in dowry: pots and a potter, sheep and goats and a shepherd, cows and a cowherd. Gaura in response states that all those things will not last: The sheep and goats will be eaten by tigers, and so on. All she wants from her *māmā*, the ruler of the snow, is snow. So much snow that the *barāt* (the groom's marriage party) will not be able to cross the mountains. Her wish is granted by Himraj. The story continues that Shiva on his way to his bride's house for the marriage ceremony sees the snow that threatens to make the crossing of the passes impossible.[12] He summons a flock of sheep and instructs them to walk in front of him and his party. With the sheep paving a way through the snow, Shiva is able to arrive at Gaura's home and the wedding can start. Sheep are actually considered to be good at walking over snow and are sent ahead of the goats when the shepherds cross passes and icy stretches.

The story of Shiva's and Gaura's wedding does not only hint at the connection between Shiva and sheep, but also an important part of Shiva's wedding story is enacted in the Gaddi wedding ceremonies. This happens at two prominent points of the wedding ceremonies: first, during the sacred thread ceremony, a Hindu life-cycle ritual for twice-born castes, and second, during the circumambulation of the sacred fire. As in other parts of Himachal Pradesh with castes that practice the sacred thread ceremony as part of the wedding rituals, the Gaddi groom is made into a yogi and sent begging during his wedding. This takes place after he is presented with the sacred thread and before he is dressed as a groom. The groom is dressed in a yellow loincloth, with a black *ḍorā* (sheep wool rope) draped around his torso. His body is powdered with flour. His earlobes are pierced and golden earrings that support small round bread loaves are fixed to his ears.[13] He is then sent begging in front of his house—in the courtyard among his female relatives—three times. His elder female kin stand to the left side of the door and hand him coins and pieces of *pūrī* (fried bread). His *bhābhī* (elder brothers' wives; eBW), stand to the right of the door, hit him with twigs on his way back inside, and try to pull off his loincloth the third time he passes. For the guests this is one of the most exciting and most closely watched parts of the ceremonies for the groom. After sending him begging three times, the priests asks the groom what he wants to become in life, an ascetic or a householder. He answers householder, and is subsequently bathed and dressed in the red gown of a Gaddi groom. The explanation given for the groom becoming an ascetic is that a man has to pass through the different stages of existence during the course of his life, including that of the renouncer. Moreover, whereas people in the lower and more southern parts of Himachal speak of the groom becoming a yogi, in Gaddi weddings he is identified explicitly with the ascetic Shiva. As the Gaddi express it, "*Lāḍā Śiv-jī bantā hai*" (the groom becomes Shiva) (see figure 3.1).

Figure 3.1 A groom on his way to "beg." Photo by A. Wagner (2007).

What makes Gaddi people say that they marry like Shiva, however, is the Gaddi variation of the *sāt phere*, the seven rounds around the sacred fire.[14] In Gaddi marriages, bride and groom walk around the fire four times at the bride's home. After arriving at the groom's home the couple circumambulates a *ghaḍā* (water pot) three times, bringing an end to the wedding rituals that have been performed by the priest. The circumambulation of the water pot in the groom's house was interpreted by several interview partners, including young unmarried men and a Gaddi priest as the completion of the *sāt phere* (seven rounds) that the bride and groom have to walk together for the marriage to be completed. The splitting of the seven rounds between the bride's and the groom's place is considered to be the reenactment of Shiva's and Gaura's wedding story.[15]

Shiva, it is told, walked away from his wedding ceremony after completing four rounds around the fire. Gaura had to run after him and caught up with him right at Mount Kailash where they then completed the seven rounds. Gaura as can be seen from the song quoted above was not in favor of this marriage and hoped to stop it by blocking the passage with snow. Another fragment of a song that is also part of the *nuālā* repertoire tells how Shiva and his party are treated at Gaura's home:

जानीऐं जो डेरा कुन्थू दैणा अम्मा मेरीएं माऐ।	Where shall we place the groom's party's camp, oh my mother?
जानीऐं जो डेरा सुक्कै वागे धीएं लाड़लीएं।	The groom's party's camp is in the dry woods, beloved daughter.
सुक्कै वागे होई वो हरियाली अम्मा मेरीएं माऐ।	The dried woods are greening again, oh my mother.

The groom's party is not hosted at the bride's house but rather is allotted a separate *ḍera* (camp) at a short distance. The camp of Shiva's marriage party as told in the song is placed in the rather inhospitable dried woods. When the leaves of the woods turn green again, it was explained to me, Gaura realizes that her groom is not an ordinary man but must be a god. From this point, she rejoices in the fact of marrying him. But the ill treatment of the groom did not go unnoticed. My Gaddi informants, in this case young unmarried men, interpreted his running away as Shiva's annoyance with and revenge for his bride's critical stance toward him. Gaura thus has to prove herself by following him all the way up Mount Kailash. This episode is reenacted in Gaddi weddings with the four circumambulations of the sacred fire, and the three circumambulations of the water pot at the groom's home. Gaddi thus say they marry like Shiva. The Gaddi groom, of course, does not run away and the bride does not have to beg him to complete the marriage, but is rather conventionally carried in a palanquin to her in-laws' house.

Concerning place-making, it is important to note that, since Mount Kailash is in Bharmaur and Bharmaur is Śiv Bhūmi, Gaura does not simply run through an abstract or mythical mountain environment to Kailash Parvat. But the very real mountains of the Dhauladhar range are imagined as the place of this story. Thus, there exists an intimate and very practical connection with the mythical landscape. The environment of everyday activities — the landscape Gaddi people live in and move through, worship their deities, graze their animals, collect their firewood, plant their crops, and visit their relatives — is the environment of Shiva's abode. The place is one and the same.

With regard to place-making, there is, however, an even more explicit connection between constructions of Gaddi identity, the identification of the community with the god Shiva, and the physical Mount Kailash in Bharmaur. Again, this connection is made through practices performed at life-cycle rituals albeit here not at marriage but in connection to the death of a person. After a death and the cremation of the body, a part of the ashes is brought to Haridwar in Uttarakhand and immersed in the Ganga. Water from the Ganga is brought back to be used in subsequent rituals. In addition to the journey to the Ganga, Gaddi people often journey to the Mani Mahesh Lake below Mount Kailash in Bharmaur to fetch water from Shiva's lake, which they mix with the Ganga water. Thus two connections are established, one as customary in North India to the Ganga and its purifying water, the other to the water connected to the god Shiva and Bharmaur's local landscape.

A Sheep for Shiva: The *Nuālā* Ritual

When I started my fieldwork among the Gaddi, I was repeatedly told by my interview partners and hosts that if I wanted to learn about Gaddi culture there were two things I had to see: a Gaddi wedding and a *nuālā*. *Nuālā* is the name of a night-long Shiva worship during which the devotees invite Shiva to their home. It starts in the evening and lasts until dawn. Shiva is worshipped with the sacrifice of a sheep, singing, dancing, and a night vigil. Throughout the night, professional musicians and singers perform songs dedicated to Shiva. Shiva usually comes over his oracle(s) during the night and is said to speak through them to the audience. A *nuālā* is always an event. It is performed with a large audience. The guests can easily add up to more than a hundred people.[16] Expenditure for a *nuālā* includes the sheep to be sacrificed, a fee for the musicians, fee and gifts for the priest, as well as food and drink for the guests, thus making it a quite costly affair. Hosting a *nuālā* is also a prestigious act. Taking part in a *nuālā* means worshipping Shiva through dancing and singing, but also means drinking, meeting relatives, and enjoying. Performing a *nuālā* can further be interpreted as a performance of communal identity by which not only a link to the god Shiva, but also to the region where the Gaddi live is established. The literature on the Gaddi, starting with the colonial gazetteers, rarely fails to mention the *nuālā* ritual as a distinct trait of Gaddi culture. The *Gazetteer of the Chamba State* published in 1904 reports, "Animal sacrifice, called *niwāla*, is a common feature of Shiva worship" (*Gazetteer of the Chamba State 1904* 1996: 181). Yet the descriptions of the *nuālā* remain rudimentary.[17]

The Gaddi consider the *nuālā* to be a special ritual. It is special in two senses. On the one hand, the *nuālā* is said to be a genuine Gaddi ritual for the worship of Shiva that is not performed by other people.[18] On the other hand, it is a ritual that is staged only for Shiva, and it differs in elaboration as well as the meaning attributed to it by Gaddi people from rituals performed for other deities. During my fieldwork, a *nuālā* was always a promptly accepted and unarguable reason to leave for another place.

The term *nuālā* is a word from the Gaddi dialect and denotes, on the one hand, the whole ritual, the Śiv-jī *kā pūjā* (worship of Shiva)—that is, the offerings, singing, dancing, and night vigil—and, on the other hand, the *nuālā* or Śiv-jī *kā mālā*—that is, the garland of wool and flowers that is hung above a mandala and supposed to serve as a seat for Shiva during the night. The meaning of the term *nuālā*, sometimes mentioned as *navala*, *newala*, or *niwala* in the literature, is commonly explained as new house in the literature (see, e.g., Basu 2000: 30). In my ethnography, there is no link to the rituals connected with the building of and moving into a new house. On the contrary, a house can serve as the location for a *nuālā* only after the family has inhabited it for some time, for about six to twelve months according to my informants.

The occasion for performing a *nuālā* is always a joyful event. It can be staged as a thanksgiving ritual—for example, someone might promise a *nuālā* to Shiva in exchange for the recovery from an illness or the birth of a son. It can be a more general way of pleasing Shiva and thanking him for the well-being within one's house, for example on the occasion of a retirement, employment, or education of the children. And it is usually performed during weddings, when the bride is welcomed at the groom's house. Performing a *nuālā* at one's son's wedding is not a prerequisite but is considered good. The bride's parents might stage a *nuālā* if the day of the bride's departure falls on an inauspicious day, for example, a Tuesday, when one does not send one's daughter to her in-laws' house. To make up for this coincidence caused by the auspicious date for the wedding and to make Shiva nonetheless happy, one can perform a *nuālā*.

The conventional day for staging the *nuālā* ritual is Monday, Shiva's day of the week. But this is the ideal, for in combination with a wedding or a second ritual it takes place on other days of the week as well. Again in theory, the two months associated with Shiva, Māgh (December–January) and Sauṇ (July–August), are the months to perform a *nuālā*. From my observations, though, the highest incidence of the ritual does not occur in Shiva's months but is connected to the passing of the flocks through their home villages in Barsākh (March–April) and Kātī (October–November). As for weddings and other religious functions, there are certain dates that would be inauspicious for the performance of a *nuālā* due to astrological constellations. Therefore, the family priest is consulted on fixing the date for the ritual.

To stage a *nuālā* nine people are needed. These are, on the one hand, professional specialists and, on the other hand, people who are designated to take over a special task for the time of the ritual. The professional specialists are the *kul purohit* (family priest), a Gaddi Brahman, and four musicians. One musician is the lead singer, three sing and play the *thālī ghaḍā* or *ghaṇṭāl* (brass plate and clay pitcher), and one or two play *dholkī* (small barrel-shaped drums).[19] The musicians are themselves Gaddi, who perform only for *nuālā* rituals. They are part-time musicians who do not earn their living by performing. They are usually called upon from within their local region. A few groups have become professional in the sense that they record songs for sale on VCD and even bring technical equipment like microphones and speakers to performances. This, however, has not become the rule yet. The role of the *kul purohit* (priest) in the *nuālā* appears at first sight odd, since rituals involving animal sacrifice as such do not demand the presence of a priest. Why does the *nuālā* need a priest? The first and in my interpretation most important task of the priest for a *nuālā* is the drawing of the mandala: the priest is needed to create the temporary ritual space for the *nuālā*. The priest moreover recites mantras during the *nuālā* that only a Brahman can utter.

Next there is the *jajman* (patron) of the ritual, also called the *gharvālā* (householder). I will in the following use the term host. The term host conveniently covers two meanings: the host of the ritual and the host for the invited guests; it thus points to a religious and a social function. Two men out of the invitees are assigned a special task during the ritual. They are called *botwāl* and *kotwāl*.[20] The former's task is to hand out the *prasād* (consecrated food offerings). The latter is supposed to keep the other people from falling asleep. In effect, the host, priest, musicians, *botwāl*, and *kotwāl* are the persons who have to stay awake all night. As a sign of their function, these people wear reddish scarves around their necks.

The ninth person is the *celā*, the one through which Shiva speaks. Although he can be seen as a specialist for his vocation of being the oracle of a deity, he neither has to be designated as a *celā* for the *nuālā*, nor is he specially invited. Rather someone belonging to the house of the host or to the invited relatives is known as a *celā*—as having the god come over him. In the case of Shiva, this is always a man. Quite often more than one *celā* will be present. The people who become possessed by the deity do not differ from other guests. They simply start what is referred to as playing: shaking and speaking. There is no initiation or subsequent restrictions that would set them apart in everyday life.[21]

Invitations to attend a *nuālā* are issued to all *khās riśtedār* (special relatives).[22] First, this includes the *ghar ke log* (people of the house), the descent group: the host's father's brothers, if alive, his own brothers and sons, with their respective wives and children, as well as his unmarried daughters.[23] Furthermore, the descent group's out-married women—married daughters and sisters of the host—with their parents-in-law, husbands, and children belong to the category of *khās riśtedār*. Moreover, it includes parents, brothers, and sisters of the in-married women of all generations, all with their spouses and children. In short, the patrilineal descent group and its affinal relations of all generations are invited. In addition, neighbors are invited, depending on the closeness of the relation. Usually this includes all Gaddi households in the neighborhood (if not part of the first category already) and in the same village. The invitation might be extended to non-Gaddi neighbors as well. In addition, special guests may be invited such as unrelated friends and colleagues of the host, or anthropologists. The latter—non-Gaddi—category of invitees depends purely on personal relations.

On the afternoon of the *nuālā* ritual when the guests have started to arrive, the *nuālā mālā* (garland) is made. The *nuālā mālā* consists of a thread of white sheep wool referred to as Śiv-jī *kā ūn* (Shiva's wool). Marigolds, seasonal flowers like bougainvillea, leaves of the *balpatr* tree, and the paper-like bark of the *bhojpatr* tree (birch) are knotted into the thread.[24] The *nuālā mālā* is made by some of the guests, usually close relatives of the hosts. Elder women and girls often sit together to prepare the garland, but it can be made by men and boys as well. The whole garland is about twenty meters long. When completed, it is stored until the evening.

For the *nuālā* ritual the family priest, the *kul purohit*, has to be called in. The whole ritual takes place outside the house, on the veranda and in the courtyard. The *pūjā* (place for the worship) is prepared by the *kul purohit* who first draws a mandala on the veranda.²⁵ The mandala consists of thirty-two squares, or houses, outlined with wheat flour. The squares are filled with rice, walnuts, flowers, and *balpatr* leaves. *Mān kī dāl* (urad beans), rice, flour, and white unspun wool, along with a small *lotā* (jug) with water and a *diyā* (an oil lamp) are placed beside the mandala. A *mīṭā makkī kī rotī* (flat, sweet maize flour bread), later used as *prasād*, is baked and put next to the mandala as well (see figure 3.2).

Throughout the night, the *kul purohit* sits next to the mandala seated on a Gaddi *pattu* (homespun woolen blanket).²⁶ Next to him—or depending on the space available—close to the mandala the four musicians are seated in a straight line.

About dusk, the *nuālā mālā* is installed above the mandala. An L-shaped fork of a branch is hung from the ceiling of the veranda and the garland is laid in eleven loops around it. The garland hangs down between one and a half to two meters touching the mandala on the ground. Because the fork of the branch often remains in its place after the *nuālā* ritual, one can detect at which house a *nuālā* has taken place. Instead of being looped around the branch, the threads alternatively can be attached to rings made out of twigs to keep a distance between the threads. The garland is also described in this way by K.P. Sharma and Sethi (1992). In both cases, the garland is built into a triangular shape atop the usually squared mandala.

Figure 3.2 *Nuālā* mandala. Note that here the priest drew thirty-three instead of thirty-two houses. Photo by A. Wagner (2007).

The mandala with the flower garland on top can be interpreted as having the conventional shape of a Hindu temple, which is considered a representation of Mount Kailash.

Before putting the garland in its place, the *kul purohit* calls on all *ghar ke ādmī* (men of the house) to touch it collectively. The *ghar ke ādmī* include all male members of the descent group, regardless of their actual living in a joint house cluster or not. They lift the garland shouting, "Śiv-jī *ki jai*" (victory to Shiva). After this, one of them loops it around the branch. The collective touching of the object to be installed by the male members of the descent group parallels the touching of the *sehrā* (head-dress) of the groom before adorning the groom with it during his wedding. In the latter case, only the married men of the descent group touch the object, whereas the *nuālā mālā* can be touched by unmarried sons, too. Thus, the men of the host's descent group are united and physically participate in the installation of the seat into which the god Shiva is invited during the *nuālā*.[27]

The *kul purohit* then covers the upper part of the garland with a light-colored cloth (in yellow, light pink, or white). The garland is covered to keep it from direct view. Shiva is invited to join the ritual and this protected place in the garland is the place created for him. Some of my informants described the making and covering of the garland as the building of a nice home, or as creating a space for a guest—as creating a place where Shiva will feel comfortable and inclined to seat himself. A Gaddi priest remarked, concerning the significance of the flower garland, that it was the garland in which the Gaddi people worshipped Shiva.

The offering of the sheep and as such the practical start of the *nuālā* ritual takes place after dusk, at about 9:00 p.m. The sacrificial animal, a mature ram, is brought into the courtyard and let loose in front of the *nuālā mālā*. Men surround it to make sure it does not run away, but leave enough space for it to move freely. The host of the *nuālā* comes forward and sprinkles water and flowers over the back of the animal, and water on the mouth and on all four feet of the sheep. *Dhūp* (incense) is lighted and offered to Shiva, held by someone or fixed to the sheep's horns. The offerer then steps back and everybody watches the animal. People are waiting for the sheep to shake its body—a shiver has to run through his whole back and head. This is the sign that Shiva has accepted the animal offered for sacrifice.

When it has shaken, the ram is led away, accompanied by shouts of "Śiv-jī *ki jai*" (victory to Shiva) and "*jai ho*." This is the point when, as one informant explained, "the *nuālā* can begin." The musicians start performing and the first people dance. At the same time, at the side of the house the animal is decapitated. One man able and willing to cut a sheep stands with *drāt* (Gaddi for a type of axe) raised above the animal's head, while another man holds its hind leg. When the sheep holds its head straight, the neck is cut from above, preferably with a single stroke. The head and one foot of the sheep, and sometimes, after skinning, the fleece, are placed on the ritual space beneath the *nuālā mālā*. A bloody handprint, a common sight on temple but also on house walls after offerings, is made on the wall behind (see figure 3.3).

If the *nuālā* ritual forms part of the welcoming of the new bride, the couple will perform a *pūjā* in front of the mandala before the garland is put into place. The bride, however, can enter her in-laws' house only after the offering of the sheep has been accepted (the shivering, not the butchering, being the crucial moment). If this is adhered to, the bride will in the meantime wait on the veranda. The marriage rituals, which take place inside the house, are continued after the offering.

What if the sheep does not shake? If the sheep does not shake after the host has offered it, other members of the *ghar ke log* (descent group) step forward and repeat the procedure of offering. This is usually, although not necessarily, in strict order, first the oldest son, then the host's wife, the host's brother, the brother's wife, and so on. The offering is repeated by additional members of the category of *ghar ke log*, or by previous offerers who perform the act a second time.[28] In between two acts of offering, the spectators stand quietly, folding their hands (in *namaste* position), they light incense, and watch the sheep move in front of the *nuālā mālā*. If it wanders off too far, it is picked up, carried back and placed or even thrown in front of the consecrated ritual space again. Shouts of *"jai Śivjī"* may break the silence (the silence applies only to immediate spectators, groups of people who are sitting at a distance will go on chatting). Although the music starts only after the acceptance of the offering, the musicians might start to play and sing the line of the opening song, saying "Take, o Shiva, your offering."

A nonshaking sheep also draws responses from the deity. Shiva will come over one of his present *celā* either spontaneously or voluntarily induced, for example, through the inhalation of incense and playing of a rhythm on the drums. The *celā* now delivers Shiva's message. He states the reason for the refusal of the animal, calls on the audience to show more patience, or calls for a certain member of the family to do the offering.

Reasons for a sheep not being fit for sacrifice are among (many) others: it has some physical fault (an intact animal has to be given); it has been used as a scapegoat before, thus having some stigma attached to it; or it has not been paid for properly. A sheep that does not shake can also point to a problem with the host's motivation for the ritual. This leads to the interpretation that he is not carrying it out with a pure heart and therefore Shiva is rebuking his intention.

A Sheep for Shiva • 53

Figure 3.3 *Nuālā* ritual space after a sacrifice, here with a fashionable light-adorned garland. Photo by A. Wagner (2007).

When I inquired what would happen in the case of sheep not shaking at all, people assured me that it would surely shake—but that if this takes too much time "it spoils the fun." A nonshaking sheep might lead guests—especially the not closely related neighbors who often do not plan to stay for the whole night anyway—to leave. I was told that the *nuālā* will not be called off, but rather continued without a sacrifice. An animal will never be killed without shivering—that is, without the visible sign of acceptance by the deity. The shiver has to run through the whole back of the animal, a partial shaking of the head is not recognized as a sign of acceptance.[29]

I have witnessed both the replacement of an animal by another ram and waited for one and a half hours for a sheep to shake. I have never heard of a *nuālā* being called off nor have I attended one that was started without the sacrifice.[30] I came across a case during a different ritual where only one of the designated two sacrificial goats shook and therefore only one was killed but there was one sacrifice, after all. As people repeatedly assured me in the case of the *nuālā* ritual, the sheep will shake eventually but waiting spoils the fun.

1. कुनीऐ परोथे तेरा मंदल जे लिखियां
कुनीऐ ता शिवा मेरे कुनीऐ ता गुंदी फूल माला ओ
कुला रे परोथे मेरा मंदल जे लिखियां
मालणी ऐ गुंदी फूल माला ओ

1. Which *purohit* has drawn your mandala? Who has woven your garland of flowers, Shiva?
The *kul purohit* (family priest) has drawn my mandala, the garland weavers have woven my flower garland.

2. बत्तीस कोठे तेरा मंदल लिखियां चौले माऐ कोठे भरे ले वो शामी शिवा मेरे ले वो शामी अपना उधारा ओ

2. Thirty-two houses make up your mandala and rice and *mān* (urad bean) fill the squares. Take oh Śāmī, my Shiva, take oh Śāmī, your offering.

3. इक अरज मेरी होर सुणे औतरा रे घरे पुत्र दे भोलेआं शामीयां

3. Listen to one more request of mine: Give sons to houses of barren women, Bholeā Śāmīyān.

4. दूई अरज मेरी होर सुणे कोडीयां दे कुष्ट चुका भोलेआं शामीयां

4. And listen to my second request: cure lepers from their troubles, Bholeā Śāmīyān.

5. तेरी अरज मेरी होर सुणे अंधे जो लो दे भोलीआं शामीयां

5. And listen to my third request: give light to the blind, Bholeā Śāmīyān.

Opening song

A fragment of the opening song of the *nuālā* is given above. I collected this version in 2007 around Dharamshala. During the night, two types of songs are performed: *nuālā* songs and songs classed as Śiv *vai*, Shiva's wedding. Both fall into the category of *aincalī*, which are *dharmik* or devotional songs in Gaddi dialect. While the wedding songs retell the story of Shiva's marriage to Gaura (Parvati) the *nuālā* songs comment on the happening during the ritual: for example, the opening song in which the drawing of the mandala by the *kul purohit* and the making of the flower garland are described. Depending on the repertoire of the musicians, other *aincalī* might be performed as well.

When the musicians begin to perform, they start by playing the instruments and shortly afterwards they begin to sing. They grow gradually louder, but they will never be the sole nor necessarily the loudest voices, since conversations do not stop. People start dancing, usually two to four at first, then more depending on the mood of the audience. There are two styles of dancing: either on one's own, or in pairs of two. Although groups of women and men, respectively, tend to form for dancing, especially at the beginning, generally women and men both dance together (for details on dances see K.P. Sharma 2004).

The musicians halt their performance regularly to take some rest, smoke a *bīṛī* (a leaf-wrapped cigarette), and drink a cup of tea. At one *nuālā*, of which I made a complete audio recording, the musicians' performance was split into eight parts during the night. The first breaks were comparatively shorter and singing lasted longer, while near dawn the pauses became longer and the musicians' performances were shortened to only one song at a time.

The *kul purohit* performs his worship parallel to the singing and continues when the musicians stop. He remains seated next to the erected ritual space throughout the night, and recites mantras and performs offerings at garland and mandala. It is the *kul purohit* who calls on the man in the function of *botwāl* to distribute the *prasād* among the guests. Several kinds of *prasād*—which are first offered to Shiva on the garland—are handed out during a *nuālā*. At first *kaṛā* (Hindi: *halvā*, a sweet dish) is distributed, then banana pieces. *Bhedu* (sheep), the fried heart of the sacrificed ram, is distributed usually around 1:00 a.m. The last *prasād*, the distribution of which is the final step in the ritual, is a piece of the *nuālā mālā*.

When the musicians pause, women may start to sing *nuālā* songs. Dancing and singing interrupted by episodes of rest continue during the night. People might sing along, repeat some lines, or shout with joy when the atmosphere draws them in. Drinks are being passed both among the men and among the women. Tea is served every now and then. Brothers and sisters, women of different generations (both out-married like FZ and BD or related through the female line like MZ and ZD) as well as partners in joking relationships (foremost *jījā-sālī*, ZH-WZ, and *bhābhī-nanand*, BW-HZ) meet. They enjoy a great deal. At the same time more distant relations leave early, for example, neighbors might come over only for the start of the ritual. Guests go to sleep on mats spread on the floor inside the house. The later it gets, the fewer the people who actively take part in the *nuālā*. As noted above, in effect the specialists (priest, host, musicians, *botwāl*, and *kotwāl*) have to stay awake.

Shiva, on the one hand, is understood to be present in his seat in the covered part of the garland during a *nuālā*. On the other hand, the god also visits his human oracles, "he comes over someone" as it is expressed in Hindi. This happens as described above in case the sheep does not shake. It is also expected to happen during the night as people are dancing. According to my informants, this possession might occur any time during the worship of Shiva or, as they expressed it, "when god's name is taken." Although in discussions of the ritual the coming of Shiva to his human oracles was almost always mentioned as a part of a *nuālā*, at two *nuālā* rituals that I saw there was no possession at all, at least not until I went to sleep, which in one instance happened after only a few very inebriated dancers were left.[31] Still people talked of these *nuālā* rituals as successful events.

The possession of the *celā* is referred to as *khelnā* (playing). The gods are said to play in their human oracles. This is consistent with the terminology used in other parts of Northwest India (Berti 2001; Elmore 2006; Erndl 1993; Sax 1991, 2009). The following sketch shall illustrate what these instances of possession look like.

The playing starts with one of the dancers—usually someone known to be a *celā*—whose hands and arms, fists clenched, start to tremble. Then the whole person appears to be vibrating rather violently. This is followed by heavy breathing and sometimes utterances or shouts. The spectators generally halt their dancing and form a circle around the *celā*. From my observance, there are mostly two *celās* who become possessed in a row. That means one person starts to tremble and after that a second one, the latter typically more violently than the first. It is usually the second one to whom people pay more attention and who then proceeds to speak or who gives out blessings. The *celā* usually will take off his shirt, and is handed a *sangal* (iron chain). He hits himself with the chain and holding it with both hands lays it around the neck of the host and those standing next to him (often the host's B, S, FB, or W). People come up front to be blessed by the *celā* in this way. The *celā* might then continue to play by trembling and dancing or by continuing to speak. He usually asks for water or vermillion to bless the audience. He hands out blessings to participants in form of a *ṭīkā*—that is, by applying an auspicious mark of red or orange powder (vermillion), sometimes also of flour taken from the mandala, to the forehead of the participants who hurry to step in front of him to receive the mark. The voice of the *celā* is said to be Shiva speaking to his devotees. The god communicates whether he is pleased with the procedure of the *nuālā* and the intention of the host. People converse with him and those facing a problem, for example, an illness, ask for advice.

The god playing in his *celā* does not necessarily have to be Shiva or Shiva alone. Different gods can start playing together. The participants usually know which god is coming to which *celā*. In addition, the gods communicate their identity. Besides Shiva *kul devtā* (family gods), for example, a *mātā* (here a local goddess), Kelang (a Gaddi deity from Bharmaur region, also identified with Shiva's son Karttik), a *nāg devtā* (serpent god), or Baba Balak Nath (a famous Himachali yogi) might start to play. When asked about the *celā* and gods playing during a *nuālā*, a Gaddi *purohit* with whom I conducted an interview on the *nuālā* replied,

> [H]e [Shiva] has to come, then it will be pure, it becomes auspicious, it becomes good. . . . [H]e comes, sooner or later he comes, to someone or the other he comes, sometimes, somewhere it even happens that it becomes really a lot, he comes to as many as four or five together to play, Shiva comes, or to someone their own [family] deity comes.[32]

The episodes of playing might last anywhere from a few seconds to about twenty minutes or even more. The acts of blessing, speaking, and dancing alternate. Participants praise Shiva by shouting "*jai*" and one of his names. The musicians react to the actions of the *celā* by either halting their songs when he speaks, picking up the drumming, or by chanting song lines commenting on the occasion, such as "*Bolenāth āyā*" (Shiva has come). The possession ends with the *celā* being lifted up by another person, often the one who became possessed first. Typically, someone gives the command to do so when he notices that the *celā* stopped playing. The two hug each other and the possessed *celā* is lifted a few centimeters off the ground and put down again. The playing of the *celā* generally ends the respective sequence of the performance and is followed by a break before the musicians start their next session.

Shortly before dawn, the last break of the *nuālā* takes place. The *nuālā* ritual that has emphasized the musicians, *celā*, and participants throughout the night, ends rather like a typical *purohit* ritual with the focus of attention shifting to the action of the *purohit*. When he rings his bell for a last *pūjā*, the host, his wife and children, and other *ghar ke log* step in front of the *nuālā mālā*. Then *āratī* is performed. A lighted oil lamp is placed on a brass plate and waved by the priest in front of the *nuālā mālā* accompanied by an *āratī* song dedicated to Shiva. The host couple, their children, and other participants hold their hands over the flame and then touch their face and forehead to transfer the blessing of the divine from the flame to their body. Afterwards the participants—also those who had gone to sleep—step in front of the ritual space facing the *nuālā mālā* one by one to perform a personal *pūjā*. Children are woken to get a *darśan* (view) of the deity, or as it is called in Hindi, *mātā dekhnā* (to see the mother).[33]

As at the beginning of the *nuālā*, there is a specific song that is sung as the last of the *nuālā* songs. It is sung after the *āratī* at approximately 4:00 a.m. when it starts to dawn and the first birds begin to sing. With this song, the performance of the musicians ends. The song figuratively asks Shiva to leave:

1. उड़ाया वो भमीरूड्यां होई गाईयां भयागा री बेला हो	1. Fly away o night-bird[34], it is dawn.
मूं वो कीयां करी उड्या मेरे पंख बड़े सीयाणे हो	How shall I fly away? My wings have become very old.
पंखा तेरे जो चाँदी मां मड़ाली ओ उड़ी वो समाणा जो जाणा हो	I will frame your wings in silver. And flying you will go up to the sky.
2. उड़ाया वो भमीरूड्यां उड़ी वो समाणा जो जाणा हो	2. Fly away o night-bird. Flying you have to go up to the sky.
मूं वो कीयां करी उड्या मेरे पंख बड़े सीयाणे हो	How shall I fly away? My wings have become very old.
पंखा तेरे जो सोने मां मड़ाली ओ उड़ी वो समाणा जो जाणा हो	I will frame your wings in gold. And flying you will go up to the sky.[35]

The garland is then ripped into small pieces and handed out as the last *prasād* of the ritual. The receivers of the *prasād* attach their piece of the garland to their head, either by knotting it to their hair, earrings, or necklace for women, or sticking it in their *topī* (cap) for men. The *kul purohit* then unties the cloth that covered the upper part of the garland. With this gesture, Shiva is sent back home.[36]

The subsequent morning meal served to the invitees includes a meat dish. At weddings, the meat of the sacrificed sheep is served at the midday *dhām* (feast), which is also the *baṛā dhām* (feast given for the bride's relatives and the village).

Identity and Performative Creation of Community

Concerning oral epics in India, Stuart Blackburn and Joyce Flueckiger have stated that what makes epics special is "the relationship epics have with the community in which they are performed, a relationship acknowledged by performers and audiences in many parts of India when they call an epic 'our story'" (Blackburn and Flueckiger 1989: 5–6). Oral epics, in other words, "help to create and maintain that community's self-identity" (ibid.: 11). I argue that the same applies to the *nuālā* ritual—last but not least because the Gaddi call it "our Gaddi Śiv-jī *kā pūjā*" (Shiva worship).

William Sax (2002) has shown how ritual performances create selves and communities, thereby negotiating power, authority, and an individual's place within the group. In contrast to the *pāṇḍāv līlā* of Garhwal that Sax describes, the *nuālā* is not a public, village level ritual. It is not a village event that articulates the inclusion and exclusion of certain groups and factions and therefore negotiates questions of power and authority. The *nuālā* is an individually organized family event. Everyone invited is considered part of the same group. This can be seen by the group of invitees that include, if ever, only very few non-Gaddi neighbors and friends. In contrast, usually all Gaddi families from the village as well as friends are invited to wedding feasts. Although the touching of the flower garland by the men of the patriline and the offering of the sheep by the descent group, for example, emphasize certain kin groups, hierarchies or internal differences within the group of participants are not symbolically acted out in the ritual as they are, for example, in marriage ceremonies.[37] In worshipping Shiva all invitees can equally take part, dance, sing, and be blessed by the god through approaching the *celā* and receiving *prasād*. I argue that the *nuālā* is performed among a group of people who by participating confirm a common practice and identity vis-à-vis those who do not—that is, most non-Gaddi neighbors. And thus the *nuālā* stresses sameness. Its most prominent features are its inclusive capacity and its celebration of community.

That performing the *nuālā* marks the Gaddi community also came to the fore during a conversation I had with a group of college students, the sons of the family I was staying with and their neighbors' sons and daughters, early in my fieldwork. We were sitting around the kitchen fire chatting one night after dinner when I inquired about the drumming and singing that was heard from across a distance through the neighborhood. There was a wedding going on in one of the other castes' house cluster in the village; that house belonged to a Pahari speaker. The singing came from a *jāgrātā*. The *jāgrātā*, one of the young men explained, was like the *nuālā*: both were night vigils and both can be performed during marriages, only the *jāgrātā* was performed to the goddess.[38] And, he continued, the *nuālā* was celebrated by Gaddi people whereas the *jāgrātā* is celebrated by the Pahari-speaking castes: "We do a *nuālā* and the other people do a *jāgrātā*." This comparison was approved of by the other listeners.

The distinction between the Gaddi and Pahari communities according to the rituals they perform, in this context drew a fine line between the groups it distinguishes rather than pointing out fundamental differences. At the same time as they were aware of how the neighborhoods can be told apart by their ritual performances, the young people emphasized a broader commonality in placing both rituals side by side as comparable religious practices. This general commonality is embedded in the Gaddi's involvement as one of the population groups of Kangra, with integrated Gaddi and Pahari villages, friendships, shared educational and professional experiences, or hobbies such as cricket or hockey games. The everyday shared experience for most people, however, ends regarding the occasion that had triggered our conversation: society disapproves of marriages out of one's group and caste, although they occur as individual cases. So the question whether one does a *nuālā* or a *jāgrātā* can shift from being a comparable ritual in terms of a mutually intelligible way of doing things to becoming a major distinction.

As shown above, the cultural identification through Shiva that distinguishes the Gaddi in self-representations is not only present in the *nuālā*, but also the relation with the god Shiva is enacted at Gaddi weddings, it is part of the oral narratives, and explains the Gaddi way of life. Shiva hereby is an inherently benevolent and an intrinsic Gaddi god. But the answer to the question about Shiva's identity is not only about Shiva, but also essentially about who the Gaddi are. The Gaddi here are not any worshippers of Shiva: they are Shiva's people, made into shepherds by him, and coming from his land in Bharmaur, the land of his seat at Mount Kailash. Through the worship of Shiva in the *nuālā*, Gaddi identity is lived and celebrated. I argue that it is the performance of cultural identity and community that makes the *nuālā* a special ritual for the Gaddi, and is the Gaddi ritual par excellence.

Cultural identity is hereby closely linked to place. The Gaddi, Shiva, and the Dhauladhar are intimately linked through the threefold connection of the Gaddi and the god Shiva, the Gaddi and their perceived ancestral land Bharmaur, and of Shiva and Mount Kailash, the peak within the Dhauladhar range. The connection to Shiva is therefore also about place-making: about the concrete environment of the Dhauladhar mountains. It is not only about who the Gaddi are, but also about where they live.

While the strong connection between the worship of Shiva and the Dhauladhar region has been emphasized in this chapter, it is neither fixed in its constellation nor timeless, as one small example from my field impressions illustrates. During my first visit to the region in March 2006, the conceptual integration of the region was shown by a noticeable distribution of temples. The number of Shiva temples within the Dhauladhar range stood in contrast to a striking prevalence of temples to the god Hanuman in the lower-altitude regions of Kangra and adjacent areas of western Himachal Pradesh. Comparable regional distributions of temples and patterns of worship within Himachal Pradesh, foremost for the deities Mahasu and Gugga, have been noted by the historian O.C. Handa (2004). On my visit to Bharmaur in August 2008, however, I noticed several new temples and statues to Hanuman along the way to Bharmaur town. It appeared to me as if Hanuman, whose statues were shining in a bright orange color, had started moving up into the mountains of the Dhauladhar. In the Bharmaur village where I had started my fieldwork, too, there was a newly erected statue of Hanuman in front of the temple of the village deity. The suggestion to put up this statue, I was told after asking my former host about it, had come from one of the ascetic renouncers who visit the village and stay at the temple during the warm months. The villagers had approved the idea and collected money for the creation of the image of Hanuman, thus adding one more deity to their village and allotting Hanuman a place in Śiv Bhūmi Bharmaur.

Notes

1. Karttik is also identified as Kartikeya or Skanda. The Gaddi further identify Shiva's son Karttik with Kelang, a local deity from Bharmaur.
2. Mount Kailash as Shiva's seat is not unequivocally or better uniquely linked to Bharmaur subdistrict. The most famous Mount Kailash associated with Shiva by Hindus is situated in China (Tibet), also known as Kailash Mansarovar. For Himachal Pradesh there is a further peak named Kailash in Kinnaur district in the eastern part of the state.
3. In Kangra and Chamba, the *purnimata* system is followed in the calendrical arrangement—i.e., the dark fortnight of a month precedes the bright fortnight (see Fuller 1992: 264). Throughout this work, I use the Gaddi names of the months.
4. Both Janmasthami and Shivratri are religious festivals that are celebrated in Northwest India. For the Gaddi, Shivratri and other festivals such as Diwali or Holi are more pronounced as festive days than is Janmasthami (apart from the dates of the Mani Mahesh Yatra). Shivratri itself is not considered special to the Gaddi, as it was severally pointed out to me in conversations. As one

young man put it, Shivratri is not special to the Gaddi, it is what all people in Kangra celebrate. What he considered to have a special character in marking Gaddi culture but also in terms of religious importance was the *nuālā* (see below).
5. The term *jandhar* is often used to refer to the plain or winter area as such. It might be derived from Jalandhar, a town and its surrounding region in the Punjab plains and Shivalik hills. This interpretation is also put forward by K.P. Sharma and Sethi (1997: 47).
6. *Chemahīne* (six months) refers to people living six months up (in the mountains) and six months down (in the lower regions).
7. For more on the expression Gaddi deity and the associated deities, see chapter 6. It is noteworthy that among the Gaddi, Shiva—as an accessible great god—is worshipped in the form of Shiva and not as Bhairava, where Shiva appears as a village deity or family deity in other regions of India as well as in the scriptures (Fuller 1992: 39). In Garhwal there is a local deity called Bhairav that is similar but not identical to the Bhairava mentioned by Fuller (Sax 2009) but strikingly different from the Gaddi Shiva worship described here.
8. Although I know Gaddi who oppose sacrifice, the opponents I have come across do so quietly—in other words, they do not sacrifice in their own home, but at the same time do not hesitate to attend other people's sacrifices. Some of these persons are vegetarians, others eat meat but oppose the practice of sacrificing animals as not the right way to communicate with the gods.
9. While adult male animals are usually given in sacrifice on occasions involving the invitation of a large number of guests, lambs or kids, for example, are offered at the temples of the family deities at the shepherds' houses when the flocks are passing through the village. Most shepherds I know practice this. The wife of one shepherd, however, told me that her husband had stopped sacrificing sheep and goats after the birth of their first child, saying that he did not want to take the life of any being's child.
10. The complete version of this song that I collected is given in the appendix.
11. Note the regional variations of Shiva's and Gaura's wedding story: In Garhwal (Sax 1991) as well as in the classical texts (Doniger O'Flaherty 1973), Gaura is the daughter of Himraj and not his sister's daughter.
12. I was not able to record the full song text, but severally told the following sequence as a story. I take this version of the story of Shiva's reaction from my field notes, as related to me by one of my hosts. In my second fieldwork village, I heard another version in which brown bears and not sheep were employed to pave the way through the snow for Shiva and his marriage party. The motif of sheep paving the way through the snow over a pass appears in the literature as the reason of why Shiva created sheep (Axelby 2005; Kaushal 2001a; Noble 1987). In the literature, this is not connected to the story of Shiva's wedding, however.
13. Nowadays wearing earrings in everyday life has become old-fashioned for men. But older men may still be seen wearing a pair of golden earrings and certainly all have their ears pierced for their wedding. As I was told, one used to be able to tell a man's wealth by the size of his earrings.

14. I thank Anne Keßler for pointing out to me that the seven rounds are a rather new image that transposed the seven steps around the fire into the number of circumambulations. *Sāt phere* (seven rounds) has become a synonym for the Hindu marriage, however, as it is also indicated by a popular Hindi soap opera by the same name. My informants related their tradition to the idea of a sevenfold circumambulation. As Kusum Lata informed me, at Rajput weddings in the Hamirpur district of Himachal Pradesh the couple also walks four rounds around the sacred fire.
15. The following account is a summary of the versions of this story I was told during my fieldwork.
16. As with other functions (ceremonies involving the invitations of guests), the number of guests varies according to the financial means of the family, its social status, but also the weather conditions and competition with other events, especially during a marriage season.
17. The most extensive account is the one by K.P. Sharma and Sethi (1992: 57–59).
18. The *nuālā* ritual is also practiced by the non-Gaddi population in the Chamba district and Chamba town. Chambiyali people used to sacrifice a sheep to Shiva, too, but the sacrifice of the sheep has been replaced by the offering of a coconut in the last generation (K.P. Sharma personal communication). In Kangra district, the *nuālā* ritual is to my knowledge only performed by Gaddi people.
19. For a description of the musical instruments, see K.P. Sharma and Sethi (1992). One of the two *dholkī* might be a replacement for a *ḍaggā*, a male *nagārā*, because Sharma and Sethi describe the *ghaṇṭāl*, *ḍaggā*, and *dholkī* as the *nuālā* instruments. Sharma and Sethi mention the *ḍaggā* as one of the instruments played with narrations called *ainchalī* under which *nuālā* songs can be subsumed (ibid.: 27).
20. 19. K.P. Sharma and Sethi talk of *batwal* and *kutwal* (1992: 57) for *nuālā* in Chamba district. *Kotwāl* is also the term for police officer, and might thus been seen as having the connotation of someone in the role of a supervisor. According to K.P. Sharma, the god Bhairon who is guarding the entry to Mount Kailash in Bharmaur is said to perform the duty of a *kotwāl* for Shiva (2001).
21. I therefore hesitate to call this type of *celā* specialists. They differ from Gaddi *celā* specialized in ritual healing or those being explicitly chosen by a deity as the oracle of their temple. All types of Gaddi *celā* I have come across differ in appearance from the oracles in the *gur* tradition in neighboring Kullu district described by Daniela Berti (2001, 2004) who undergo a change of status by becoming an oracle; among other things, this status is made visible by their uncut hair.
22. For a detailed analysis of Gaddi kinship including specific terminologies and corresponding subcategories of kin and affines, I refer to Phillimore (1982). In this section, I use the vocabulary employed in everyday usage, which in part corresponds to, but in other parts and specifications might differ from the description given by Phillimore.
23. Formally, it is always the father, if alive, not the married son who hosts the ritual, although the ritual might, for example, be conducted for the son's child.

24. *Balpatr* are leaves that are more widely used in connection with Shiva among the Gaddi and in India.
25. In case the house happens to have a Shiva temple in the courtyard, the mandala alternatively can be drawn inside or in front of the temple.
26. Gaddi people generally use their homemade pure wool *pattu* (blanket) as a seat during rituals.
27. In one case, which I witnessed, the women of the family were called to touch the garland as well. Thus the whole descent group, *ghar ke log* (people of the house), was united before installing the seat for Shiva. This observation is in line with the relatively unpronounced gender differentiation among the Gaddi.
28. Animals are offered by all descent group members, also by unmarried children, sons as well as daughters, if the act of offering of the adults is not successful, even if the children are still small. In one case, I observed how a married daughter was called to perform the offering as well.
29. For a discussion of this visibility as evidence in Himachal Pradesh, see Elmore (2006).
30. A different case was a *nuālā* without a sacrifice, the reason being the hosts' opposition to animal sacrifice altogether.
31. Moreover, it is said that deities and gods do not appear between 12:00 a.m. and 4:00 a.m., which is a time when only *bhūt*, ghosts, possess humans.
32. My translation, from an interview with a Gaddi priest recorded in July 2007.
33. The expression "to see the mother" is commonly used to refer to the religious act of stepping in front of the deity for a *darśan* (view), although in this case the deity, of course, is not a mother (a way to refer to the goddess) but the male god Shiva.
34. Night-bird is my translation of *bhamīrūḍūyān*. *Bhamīrūḍūyān* is the name of a local night-active bird. I am not aware of its Hindi or English name.
35. Note that in a version of this song published on VCD the line "go up to the sky" is substituted by *kailash ko jānā hai* (go up to Kailash), thus directly identifying the bird that is sent away with Shiva (J.K. Sharma 2004, song 6).
36. The unveiling of the garland's upper part is in this way similar to the erasing (wiping) of the mandala drawings that is done after other rituals to send the deity back.
37. During the latter groups are marked (within as well as between the respective side's of bride and groom) inter alia by dress (see above), performing certain functions or actions (e.g., dancing, eating), or receiving certain gifts.
38. The performance of the *jāgrātā* ritual in the Punjab and Himachal region of Northwest India has been described and analyzed by Erndl (1993), although Erndl worked in an urban rather than in a village setting.

4

Doing Kinship, Doing Place

Kinship plays a crucial part in guiding people through the landscape of the Dhauladhar—that is, through their specific network of places. By enacting kinship relations, people also enact places. In emphasizing the connection between social relations and place-making I am concerned with notions of belonging and conceptualizations of place as well as the practical activities through which these human-place relation come into being among the Gaddi. Specific to the Gaddi is the practice of seasonal migration.

Seasonal Migration and Ancestral Villages

Gaddi people often comment that what characterizes being Gaddi is being *chemahīne* (six months). Being *chemahīne* refers to the life-style of seasonal migration, of living in both of one's places of residence for six months of the year. In spite of the setting apart of the Gaddi from other communities of Kangra and Chamba with their description as *chemahīne*, it is acknowledged that this is a life-style associated with the Gaddi community but not practiced uniformly. As a matter of fact, several women and men explained the distinctiveness of their community by reference to the six months as the old or traditional life-style, while they themselves had only one place of residence and did not practice seasonal migration.

The Bharmaur subdistrict of Chamba—also called Gaddern—where the summer villages lie, is considered to be the homeland of the Gaddi.[1] Virtually all Gaddi families relate to an ancestral village in Bharmaur or in adjacent subdistricts of Chamba, whether they still migrate seasonally, or their families settled in Kangra on a twelve months' basis several generations ago and they do not own property, land, or houses in Bharmaur anymore. Seasonal migration has been in a state of transition for at least the past 150 years. Gaddi people as landowners and year-round settlers in Kangra have been reported as far back as in the *Gazetteer of the Kangra District 1883-1884*:

> [The Gaddi] hold lands on this side and also in Chamba, and in former days were considered subject to both States. At the present day the hold of the Chamba chief over them has materially relaxed, and many continue all the year round on this side of the range, acknowledging no allegiance whatsoever to Chamba. (*Gazetteer of the Kangra District 1883–1884* 1884: 91–93)

While this quotation from the gazetteer establishes a historical trend for the Gaddi of settling in Kangra, the statement that those families who settled in Kangra hold no allegiance to Chamba "whatsoever" appears unlikely. Most probably, the compilers of the gazetteer took only legal or administrative allegiances into account but left out religious and other nondocumented ties (see below).

According to Axelby, legal changes introduced by the British in the second half of the nineteenth century and subsequent land transfers from the *rājā* made the purchase of land for the Gaddi possible. The Gaddi were classed as an agricultural caste and thus were eligible to buy land under the new colonial land settlement regulations, and could benefit from the newly created land market, because their flocks gave them the financial means to acquire land (Axelby 2005: 263–264). Following Axelby, the advantage of buying land in Kangra for shepherding families lay in the acquisition of rights over adjoining wastelands for grazing (ibid.: 265).

Concerning my fieldwork area around Dharamshala, the colonial gazetteer's report on the shift of the British administrative capital from Kangra town to Dharamshala and the hill station of McLeod Ganj testifies to Gaddi land ownership in the Dharamshala area from the middle of the nineteenth century onwards: "Most of the land within the limits of the municipality is owned by Gaddí peasants, whose cottages in places dot the hill-side. It is from them alone that new land in the station can be acquired" (*Gazetteer of the Kangra District 1883–1884* 1884: 251).

What are the state of seasonal migration and land-owning patterns among Gaddi families in Kangra today? I base my description on the findings from my fieldwork area around the town of Dharamshala. Gaddi seasonal migration still exists and coexists with various forms of settling in Kangra, as it already did in the times of the first colonial gazetteer. Seasonal migration, although given up by some families generations ago, is still practiced by others. The situation today shows that the process of making the Kangra home the sole place of living is gradual, and a process taken by individual couples rather than by joint families, descent groups, or villages. A range of individual arrangements coexist. It is common to find brothers who split the two homes between them, with one staying permanently in Bharmaur and the other in Kangra. Moreover, families from the same village in Bharmaur, being of the same or of different local descent groups, often bought land in different villages in Kangra, and at different points in time. The result is that people from different villages in Kangra recognize the same ancestral village in Bharmaur. In the following, I outline practices of seasonal migration, residence, and land ownership current in my main fieldwork area.

Seasonal migration today is practiced in several ways that vary according to age and gender. There is no one form of seasonal migration but rather multiple practices among and within individual families. By seasonal migration, I mean the movement between two villages, in each of which a family owns a home. This leaves out for the moment seasonal movements to visit relatives—for example, of a woman to her natal home—even if time and place coincide with those of seasonal migration and the people concerned spend a substantial time at someone else's home. Before I proceed to outline practices of seasonal migration, a few comments on definitions of home and inheritance rules are necessary.

A home is characterized by the existence of a *cūlhā* (separate hearth). All members of a joint family cooking and eating on the same *cūlhā* are considered to belong to one family (cf. Bhasin 1988: 126; Phillimore 1982: 235). Descent is patrilineal and residence virilocal. With the marriage of each son, the new daughter-in-law is assigned her own sleeping room in the family house. The couple remains part of the joint family as long as they share the kitchen with the husband's parents. There is no explicit rule as to when a joint family will split up. However, if there are several married brothers, a couple with children above the age of ten rarely shares the *cūlhā* with the husband's brothers. When a joint family splits, it is generally the older brothers who establish their own kitchen. The youngest son and his wife generally remain with the parents. Splitting from the joint family does not necessarily mean moving into a separate building. The significant indicator for the separation is the establishment of a separate hearth that can simply be a separate kitchen room within the main house. Thus, when people talk about having their own *ghar* (house or home), they refer to the ownership of a *cūlhā*. A house as a building might unite several *cūlhā* and single-family homes under one roof.

If brothers separate their hearths, they also divide the up-to-then jointly cultivated land between them. Each son inherits equal shares of the father's land unless the sons have different mothers. In the latter case, the property can be divided equally between the wives and then among their respective sons. If, for example, a man remarries after the death of his first wife with whom he has three sons and fathers one son with his second wife, then the first three sons would have to share 50 percent of the inheritance assigned through their mother (the first wife) and the fourth son would get a 50 percent share of the father's property through his mother (the second wife). However, this system of inheritance—called *cūndāvand*—is not necessarily followed and equal shares might be given to all sons, which is referred to as *mundāvand* (cf. Bhasin 1988: 127; Phillimore 1982: 244).[2]

What Gaddi people explained to me to be the "traditional" pattern of seasonal migration—that is, to spend six months of the year in Bharmaur and six months in Kangra—is practiced today by only few people, although several middle-aged persons remember shifting residence on a six-month basis in their childhood. Employment in the labor force and schooling results in a differentiation in migration practices according to age as well as to gender. The elder generation, without dependent children and beyond retirement age, generally shift their residence in a six-month pattern. Those in employment or caring for school-going children adjust their movements to vacation times. Here, also, gender plays a role. Women working chiefly in subsistence agriculture and caring for the children are able to take part in a shortened seasonal migration together with their children during the school vacations, which coincide with the agricultural break. Men in employment usually stay all year round in one place of residence apart from short visits to their other home. An example will illustrate how these mixed arrangements of seasonal movements work out in practice.

Ammā (grandmother) is a widowed woman in her late seventies or early eighties, and a mother of five married sons. She owns property, houses and land, in three places: in a village in Bharmaur, in a village close to Dharamshala, and in a third village in western Kangra, close to the Punjab border. The ownership of houses in three different villages is not the rule among Gaddi families in Kangra. In one of the villages where I lived during my fieldwork, however, several families of one Gaddi *śarik* (local descent group) owned homes and land in three places, the third village being situated close to the shepherds' winter grazing grounds. Ammā says she has three homes. While she owns a room and separate *cūlhā* in all three places, she migrates only between two of them. From Kātī (October–November) to Jheṭ (May–June) she lives in her village at Dharamshala. In the month of Jheṭ, one of her sons will accompany her to the Bharmaur village where she stays until the months of Kātī, when she moves back to Dharamshala. Ammā enthusiastically defends seasonal migration, saying that she cannot stand the heat in Kangra in the warm season. "In summer up, in winter down. One lives well like this." This appraisal is shared by others, especially women and men from the elder generation.

Ammā's five sons all own separate hearths in the Bharmaur village home. The two eldest sons are shepherds. They have only two homes. In Kangra, they live in western Kangra, without a separate *cūlhā* at Dharamshala. Both wives migrate to Bharmaur in the summer. They are not restricted to vacation times since their children are beyond school-going age. Her two middle sons stay at Dharamshala. One of them has three homes with a *cūlhā* in western Kangra but goes there only for visits. Both of the Dharamshala based sons are employed by the government. Their wives and children, however, go up to Bharmaur for about four to six weeks during the Dharamshala school vacations in July and August. This coincides with the slack agricultural period in Kangra. They have leased out their land in Bharmaur, and during the summer visits, they collect their share of the crop from the sharecroppers.

Ammā principally shares a *cūlhā* in all three villages with her youngest son and his wife. Since the son is employed year-round, he himself does not migrate to Kangra in the winter but stays in the Bharmaur home. The son's wife and their two children, both in elementary school, migrate to Kangra during the Bharmaur school vacation in December and January and stay for about two months. It is the generation of Ammā's children in which the change has taken place, from a full six-months' migration to a short visit of the second home, as in the case of her sons, or a school-timings-adapted migration, in the case of her sons' wives and children. Although Ammā's sons and daughters-in-law do not describe themselves as *chemahīne*, they still consider themselves to be migrating, going to Bharmaur. They speak of having two (three) houses. The *cūlhā* is the material sign of their separate homes. The ownership of a *cūlhā* implies the paying of a so-called *cūlhā tax* (a per household levy). This also means being registered in two places, which might become important, for example when applying for a job for which the government regulates access by district affiliation.

In contrast to Ammā and other members from the generation of elders, the generation of her grandchildren who have grown up in Kangra and did not migrate to Bharmaur on a regular basis or only during school vacations does not ascribe to the six-months' pattern as a life-style. The young women and men with whom I discussed this topic take pride in having a home in Bharmaur and a home in Kangra. They further recognize the practical climatic advantages of seasonal migration. But they envisage Kangra as their place of residence, which for them is not only where they have grown up, but also is less remote and better equipped in infrastructure and connected to the bigger towns of the region.

In spite of many young people's preference for Kangra, there are certain economic pull factors for keeping up seasonal movements between

Kangra and Bharmaur. The seasonal migration, besides being a way of life and showing the ongoing connection to the Bharmaur village, also can have an economic motivation. While wheat and rice are grown around Dharamshala depending on the season, pulses, especially a variety of *rājmā* (red kidney bean) and *mān kī dāl* (urad bean), both prized for their taste, are cultivated in Bharmaur. The most important cash crop of Bharmaur, however, is apples. In addition to elderly seasonal migrants like Ammā, seasonal migration is practiced by some couples, where both or either of the spouses, who are not bound by wage labor or school-going children, cultivate the land in both places. In contrast to Ammā's sons' wives, these families have not rented out their land in Bharmaur, but migrate between their villages in order to cultivate land in both. Movements between both sides of the Dhauladhar are thereby easy. Only shepherds still cross the passes on foot to get to Bharmaur; for all others there are several direct bus connections between Dharamshala and Bharmaur every day.

In contrast to families who still practice seasonal migration in one or another form, there are those families that settled in district Kangra about five or six generations ago. These families say that they have only *ek ghar* (one single home), which is their Kangra village. In general, they do not have a house or own land in Bharmaur anymore. Still, they all know their *purānā gām̐v* (ancestral or old village) in Bharmaur by name and location. I will give an example of how links between Dharamshala and the old village in Bharmaur are kept up below. In short, these links remain important through the family deities and their respective temples in the old village or other important places in Bharmaur.

There are no statistical data available on how many Gaddi families own only one house in Kangra. As a rough estimation, at least half of the Gaddi families in the Dharamshala area have ceased to practice seasonal migration, and families with only one place of residence can be considered to form the majority of Gaddi families. Many of the families whom I interviewed about their settling in Kangra did not remember any details of this process other than that it had taken place more than four or five generations ago. In one case, the family remembered a fight about three or four generations back after which two brothers had split their property in Bharmaur and in Kangra between themselves, which led to a permanent settlement in the respective places. In another case, a woman told me of having lost her family's land in Bharmaur only recently since the tenants who had rented it had legally registered it in their own name. Most families, however, simply do not trace their migration stories. This is also visible in the case of the inhabitants of two villages in Kangra who both trace their clan name to the same Bharmaur village. While the inhabitants of one village still practice seasonal migration, those of the other village left

Bharmaur generations ago. People from both villages recognize the same ancestral village and clan name without further relating to each other. The split took place so long ago that they do not form a common local descent group.

Having one or two houses—in other words, practicing migration or not—shows a heterogeneity within the Gaddi community. However, these forms of living are not mutually exclusive in the sense that people practicing migration and those who do not form distinct groups. For marriage arrangements, for example, the number of homes or practice of migration per se is not a criterion; other criteria like the family background, education, and job are much more important. As a consequence, a woman might start or stop seasonal migration after her marriage. It cannot be said to be regarded as old-fashioned or modern to migrate or have one house. While seasonal migration is considered the traditional life-style, shepherding is considered the traditional occupation of the Gaddi. Both, however, do not necessarily go together. The shepherding families I knew and lived within Kangra do not practice seasonal migration, while none of the seasonal migrants in my fieldwork area owns sheep. What seems more significant, in spite of the coexistence of various individual patterns and arrangements, is that virtually all families, including those who settled in Kangra generations ago, recognize a certain named ancestral village in Bharmaur.

In addition to seasonal migration between Bharmaur and Kangra, a second form of seasonal migration exists at Dharamshala. There are families who have left their Bharmaur village several generations ago but who own land in two Dharamshala villages that are situated at notably different altitudes. Although these families have permanently settled on the Kangra side of the Dhauladhar, they have carried the practice of seasonal migration with them. They practice a seasonal migration without crossing the Dhauladhar range, having their summer village on the upper slopes and their winter village farther down toward the Kangra Valley. To my knowledge, this localized seasonal migration has not been reported in the literature on the Gaddi in Kangra, nor in the literature on other groups in Kangra. Axelby, however, mentions Gaddi families owning summer and winter homes at different altitudes within one valley in Chamba (Axelby 2007: 44, fn. 24).

One example of this localized seasonal migration is a small village not far from McLeod Ganj (the Dalai Lama's place of residence), where every family has a house in a second village situated at a distance of about fifteen kilometers by road and about nine hundred meters in altitude in the valley below. The families change their place of residence between summer and winter. Commuting between both homes takes two to three hours. The families simultaneously grow rice in the valley and maize and potatoes in the upper village in summer as the *kharīf* (monsoon crop). The *rabī* (winter) crop in the valley is wheat, while in the upper village there is no winter crop due to the cold and snowfall. Cultivating land in both places increases their range in homegrown foods. Often, for example, a daughter-in-law stays mainly in the lower village where her children go to school and looks after the rice plants, while her parents-in-law and husband's unmarried siblings move to the upper village, so that both of the family's fields are taken care of. The small village is recently experiencing increased financial investment by its inhabitants as well as by the local authorities. The construction of a motorable road up to the village was under way in 2008. Also, several inhabitants have started to rebuild their wooden houses using concrete. There is thus no sign of people giving up living in their upper village.

The system of seasonal migration without crossing the mountains was also practiced from at least two other villages in the valley to a farther village in the proximity of McLeod Ganj. The families who still own property at McLeod Ganj have often either rented out their house to people working in the tourist sector, which is mushrooming around McLeod Ganj, or are themselves building hotels on their land. Or if they themselves stay in the upper village, they rent out the lower-altitude house, which might be financially attractive if the village is close to Dharamshala town. Agriculture around McLeod Ganj in general is practiced on an increasingly smaller scale. Here, in contrast to the first example, the fields have given way to tourist hotels and the second home to rentable rooms.

The Dharamshala-centered form of seasonal migration, although likely to be a locally restricted case, could be an indicator for arguing that there is a special ideology connected to the seasonal migration that led people to carry this practice from Bharmaur to Kangra. Apart from purely economic reasons for cultivating land at two altitudes, migrational movements characterize a life-style whose rhythm is adapted to seasons and climate. As in the evaluation of the elderly seasonal migrants mentioned above, spending the hot season in the mountains and the cold season in the Kangra Valley is described as a good way of life. Especially regarding villages in Bharmaur and Kangra, to ask which place is better is the wrong question, as one eighty-year-old woman, fed up with my repeated inquiries, corrected me. The question of importance, as I was taught, is not which village is the better or nicer place, or which one someone likes better. The question has to be rephrased adding a temporal aspect and an emphasis on altitude: when is it good to be in the upper and when in the lower village? The reestablishment of the practice of the seasonal shift of residence in Kangra shows a persistence of the idea that the hot season should be spent at higher and the cold season at lower altitudes.

In spite of the value attached to the seasonal movements as a life-style and adjustment to ecology, there seems to be no nostalgia attached to it. One man in his sixties who had told me about his childhood, when the family used to shift between two homes in Kangra, said he never missed the cooler weather in the upper village after they had settled in the lower home, since one gets used to the place where one lives. Women often make comments that are even more pragmatic. Two woman in Bharmaur, who both migrated to Kangra until their marriage, remarked that one does what one has to do (i.e., what one's in-laws do), adding that after all, one home was easier to manage than two.

Although an overall tendency to stop the seasonal migration connected to schooling and wage labor and so on can be seen, the decrease of the practice of seasonal migration is not a straightforward development: there are women with only one natal home who start seasonal migration after their marriage. Furthermore, men, or couples, who stopped migrating due to their jobs take up seasonal migration after their retirement to cultivate land in both places. So people adjust their life-style according to the family's circumstances and to different stages in their life. While seasonal migration is decreasing, it is not disappearing, and various arrangements continue to coexist.

Belonging to Multiple Places

The combination of pastoralism and seasonal migration is quite common in the Indian Himalayas (Gooch 1998; Hoon 1996). When looking at engagements with place, not only the pattern of seasonal migration and questions of ownership described in the previous section are of interest, but also expressions of belonging in forms of engagements of people with places apart from or in addition to the ownership of a hearth as defined above. From the literature on communities practicing seasonal migration it appears that, in spite of cyclical movements between two villages, often only one village is the place that defines belonging. Following Gooch, the transhumant Van Gujjar families, who move between their summer and winter settlements in Uttarakhand, are identified by the place they stay in during the winter months (Gooch 2004: 129). These families themselves speak of belonging in terms of the site of their winter camp (Gooch 1998). In contrast to the Van Gujjar, for the so-called Bhotiya of eastern Uttarakhand, who also practice a seasonal migration, the summer areas are considered to be the land of the Bhotiya. It is also the summer village from which the family name is derived (Hoon 1996: 105). This leads to the question whether there is also an up–down, summer–winter distinction prevalent in notions of belonging around the Dhauladhar. The Gaddi are associated, similar to the Bhotiya, with their perceived ancestral land in Bharmaur, Gaddern. However, this representation is a view that draws on historical and mythological narratives rather than on people's (current) self-definitions of belonging. The question we need to ask, therefore, is, Which village do Gaddi families engaged in a seasonal migration consider to be their place of belonging?

At first sight, the identification of the own village depends on the context of the question. While people talk, on the one hand, about having two or even three houses, they do, on the other hand, answer the question "Where are you from?" or "Where is your home?" by naming only one village. Further questions and discussion, however, reveal that in responding to questions about belonging people usually answer the easiest way by naming either the place locally closest to them at the time of answering, the place closest to the topic of conversation, or the place closest to the assumed understanding of their counterpart. A middle-aged teacher living in Kangra did not move to Bharmaur due to his work but owned a home in Kangra and in Bharmaur. As he put it, "When I am asked where I am from in Kangra, I say x [the Kangra village]. When I am asked by someone from Bharmaur, I say y [the Bharmaur village]. But it's both. I belong to both places."

It is the latter aspect that is important in the context of identifications with place. In spite of contextual identifications with either one or the other village, in terms of belonging, all my respondents strongly argued that they belonged equally to both places. A common way to put this double allegiance to a place is to say, "Our home is here and it is also there." People thus quite simply have multiple places of belonging. This is equally true for people migrating between Dharamshala and Bharmaur, as in the example quoted above, and for people involved in a smaller-scale migration between two Dharamshala villages. Women whose natal family practices (or used to practice) seasonal migration similarly claim two places as their *māykā* (natal home).

That one person can belong to multiple places as such is not surprising. Women in the North Indian region generally identify and keep up connections with their natal as well as with their marital place (cf. Polit 2006; Raheja and Gold 1994; Sax 1991). But the notion of multiple places of belonging among the Gaddi shows that not only women, but also men can identify with multiple places of belonging. Thus, the notion for identifications with multiple places among the Gaddi is not gendered. However, while the identification with summer and winter homes as one's own village extends the space perceived as one's own to two villages for men, this space is even larger for women, who do not only identify with two places, one marital and one natal, but also possibly with multiple marital and multiple natal places.

In a general statement concerning place and local hierarchies in Garhwal, Sax has noted, "[p]ersons who have no 'place' or those who, like women in this virilocal society, move from one place to another, are devalued. With no particular place to contain and constrain their actions, they are regarded as low, impure (too 'mixed,' in Marriott's terms), unpredictable, and volatile" (Sax 1991: 74).

Among the Gaddi, belonging to multiple places is not devalued but rather is a positively emphasized marker of Gaddi identity in characterizations such as being *chemahīne*, or in ideas of the seasonal movement as the good way of life. Neither is it the case that the Gaddi have no place, nor that they emphasize summer or winter village over the other. Rather they have identifications with multiple places.

The notion of multiple places of belonging is not an abstract way of identifying with place, but is acted out in social practices: The relationship between a person and his or her places of belonging is performed through the practices following the death of a person.

Following a death, the body of the deceased is cremated on the same day, or, if the death occurs at night, on the following day. A period of *sog* (ritual pollution and mourning) starts. Death pollution affects all members of the deceased's *śarik* (the local descent group), and if the deceased is a woman, her natal descent group, too. On the twelfth or thirteenth day following a death in the deceased's village, and on the eleventh or twelfth day in a woman's *māykā*, a *kriyā* (ritual of obsequies) takes place.[3] This *kriyā* ends the period of death pollution. Further *kriyā* are performed after three months, six months, one year, and four years. It is the first *kriyā* with which I am concerned in the following.[4]

For the *kriyā* the affines of the deceased's family visit the deceased's home and bring a goat. The goat is brought by one of the affinal relations, which might be a daughter and her husband, a sister and her husband, and so on. The goat is sacrificed and subsequently fed to the members of the descent group that have been affected by the death by their affines. This is referred to as *bakrī khīlānā* (to feed a goat). The descent group thereby is purified from the pollution of the death and can subsequently recommence normal interactions with others, significantly interdine, and can serve food to others at their home.

But what is more important here, the *kriyā* is performed in all villages of belonging. The *kriyā* for a deceased man takes place in each of his villages of belonging on the same day. If he used to migrate between Bharmaur and Kangra, families in an affinal relation, most properly different persons, will bring a goat to his Bharmaur home and one to his Kangra home.

In case of multiple homes in Kangra, a *kriyā* will be held in each village simultaneously. In case of a woman's death, the *kriyā* is held in both her *sasurāl* and one day earlier in her *māykā*, as mentioned above. If she relates to multiple *sasurāl* or *māykā*, there will be multiple *kriyā* held in each place. Thus for a woman who has two marital homes, one in Bharmaur and one in Kangra, and one natal home in Bharmaur, the *kriyā* will be held in three places, organized by the closest relatives and their respective affines in each place. The performance of the *kriyā* in a woman's *māykā* is another indicator for the above-mentioned ongoing connection between a woman and her natal family as well as her natal place.

One of my informants attributed the fact that the *bakrī khīlānā* (*kriyā* ritual of feeding the relatives) is performed in all villages of belonging to the fact that the deceased's kin in the other village are affected by the death as well, and thus need to be ritually purified, too. In the case we discussed, however, the relatives from the Bharmaur village immediately traveled to the deceased's Kangra home on the news of the death. In spite of their visit to Kangra, they went back to Bharmaur to perform a *kriyā* in their Bharmaur home on the twelfth day. Since the physical distance can be, and actually is, bridged on the news of a death, performing the ritual in both villages simultaneously is not convincingly accounted for by reference to the physical distance and the necessity to purify the whole *śarik* alone. The fact that the *kriyā* is performed in both villages of belonging reveals more than ties between humans. In addition to marking kin relations, the performance of the *kriyā* in multiple places also points to the connection between the deceased and his places of belonging. As Sax has argued for Garhwal, "[T]he biological, social, and moral relationships in a house or a village are not only among the people who live there but between them and the place, house, or village itself; all are parts of complex, biomoral wholes; all are related through place" (Sax 1991: 125). The practices of performing the *kriyā* among the Gaddi show that here these relations extend between a person and several homes, as well as to the natal home of a woman.

To sum up, I initially asked how—in the light of the practice of seasonal migration—belonging is conceptualized. One answer is that Gaddi people do not emphasize just one but rather identify with multiple places of belonging. In this the findings from my fieldwork contrast with writings on other pastoral and seasonally migrating communities in the Indian Himalayas who have been described as defining belonging in relation to either the summer or the winter settlement. In contrast to the Van Gujjar and Bhotiya, Gaddi people who are involved in seasonal migration do not recognize one village to be primary. Instead, people identify with both or even multiple villages. Belonging to multiple places as such is thereby not gendered. Although women, in identifying with their marital as well as with their natal places, relate to even more places than their husbands, men, too, identify with multiple places of belonging.

However, the Gaddi community is not homogenous. Those families who ceased to practice seasonal migration several generations ago and who do not own a house or even land in Bharmaur anymore do not relate to their Bharmaur village in terms of belonging but rather in terms of descent. The Bharmaur village in this case is referred to as the *purānā gāṁv* (old or ancestral village).

Ancestral Villages and Family Deities

When people whose ancestors have stopped the seasonal migration talk about belonging, only the Kangra home is mentioned. Still, the Bharmaur village appears to be an important reference point, although not as *apnā ghar* (one's place), but as *purānā gāṁv* (one's old village). If the tie to the ancestral village remains even in the absence of the ownership of *cūlhā* (hearth), land, or *khās riśtedār* (close relatives)—a *śarik* (common local descent group) is generally recognized—what does this link consist of? How is it expressed, acted out, kept up?

Social relations are only in a very narrow definition constrained to relations between humans. It is significant that relations expressed through kinship in the Indian Himalayas are also relations with deities. Important activities that engage families with the ancestral villages are visits to the family deities' temples there.

The *kul devtā* (family deity) is a deity whose worship is common to the members of a family. The *kul* (a social unit) is smaller than the *śarik* (the local descent group). *Kul devtā* are recognized by the patrilineal descent group. Sons inherit the *kul devtā* of their father. Thus, brothers share common *kul* deities. However, families generally worship more than one family deity. A family can acquire a further *kul devtā* through the continued worship of a deity. Thus, a *kul devtā* can be common to a set of brothers, to brothers and their father's brother's sons, and even to a local descent group.

Families with homes in Bharmaur and in Kangra who are engaged in seasonal migration regularly visit the temples of their *kul* deities in Bharmaur to worship them. Once families give up their Bharmaur home to settle in Kangra, they will usually bring their deities down later. The expression for transferring a deity to Kangra is *nīce lenā* (to take down) the deity. For this to take place, first the deity has to ask to be taken to Kangra through his/her oracle. Then a *pūjā* is performed at the Bharmaur temple after which the deity is taken to Kangra in the form of one of her or his signs; depending on the deity this can be a *triśūl* (trident) or a *sangal* (an iron chain), for example. This sign is then established in a newly built temple at the Kangra home. The deities thus multiply their places. But unlike Gaddi people, the deities are not *chemahīne*. Neither do they leave their Bharmaur temple, nor do they migrate seasonally between both places.

In spite of the fact that several deities have been taken down to Kangra, from time to time a pilgrimage to the temple of the *kul devtā* in Bharmaur is performed. That families who have long settled in Kangra do go back to their old village at certain points emerged only later during my fieldwork, when my hosts invited me to join them on a *jāgrā* to their ancestral village in Bharmaur (for a description of a *jāgrā*, see chapter 6). This invitation not only gave me the opportunity to participate in and observe the occasion, but also triggered further descriptions from other families of when they last went to Bharmaur or plan to go next, in spite of their former claims of not going to Bharmaur anymore. People go back to their old village in Bharmaur even if they stopped migrating because, as one of my hosts put it, the deities have stayed behind. These pilgrimages back to Bharmaur do not necessarily occur on a frequent or regular basis, but might happen only once in ten years. As described in chapter 6, there is a certain season for undertaking pilgrimages and visiting deities in Bharmaur. I shall be discussing reasons for taking a *jāgrā* to one's *kul devtā* in chapter 6. Here, I would like to emphasize a different aspect of these journeys, namely that not only a deity whose only place is in Bharmaur is visited at their temple, but also deities who have been taken down to Kangra.

The example of a village deity in a village in the Bharmaur subdistrict shows an occasion for a family to undertake the journey to Bharmaur. This Bharmauri village is a village in which families of several *śarik* live. In the center of the village is an old *nāg devtā* (serpent deity; see chapter 6) temple that is at the same time the village deity and a family deity. The rules connected with this temple and its deity are of interest here. First, the temple has to be visited by the eldest son of each family that recognizes the place as their present or old village: he will go there together with his wife after their marriage. They will circle the temple together and give a *jāgrā* to the deity. The eldest son of a family in each generation, thus, has to go back to the old village to worship its presiding deity on the occasion of his marriage. Second, if a family goes back to the village to hold a *jāgrā* at the *nāg* temple, the *jāgrā* has to start from a house of the same *śarik*. This means that the *prasād* (food offerings) are prepared at the house, the family members holding the *jāgrā* bathe there, and the procession to the temple departs from this house. This implies that a family from Kangra, which does not own a house in the village anymore, has to relate back to their *śarik* members in order to perform their ritual. Thus through the worship of the family deity in Bharmaur links to the ancestral village, as well as to one's descent group, are kept up.

In sum, the connection to the old village is kept up by performing the relation to the family deities. By visiting and worshipping the deity in the Bharmaur temple, people reconfirm their link to their old village, too. The relation to the deity thereby establishes rights in the place. When going back to worship a family deity, one does not come as a tourist, traveler, or pilgrim to one's old village, but as someone with a legitimate link to the place. I do not mean to deny that the motivation for these pilgrimages is religious, but there is more to these pilgrimages than the obvious religious aspect. Tracing gods also means tracing social roots, and claims to the ancestral place.

Kinship and the Inside Space

Social relations not only include relations within the own patrilineal group, but also importantly with one's affines. It is the role of notions of kinship in relating to places and their performances—or acts of "doing" kinship, as acts of making place—with which I am concerned in this section. In short, understanding kinship is a key to landscape and place.

A first indication for the importance of kinship for the conceptualization of place is that relations to place are commonly expressed in kinship terms. When people converse about places, phrases like the following are commonly heard: "Ah, Bhagsu. My *māmā* (MB) is in Bhagsu," "My sister is married in Bharmaur," or "Yol? You know who lives there? X's *mausī*'s (MZ's) daughter." In short, kinship relations are a common—and maybe the most common—way of relating to, talking about, and personally knowing places.[5]

Moreover, in the language employed when talking about people and place there is a strong identification between a person and her or his place of residence. The place itself is not only a designation, a name, but also is a relationship: people are linked to their place of residence in such a way that there appears to be a unity between people and place. Rarely would someone say her or his *mausī* lives in place x. Rather, the expression is, "*x merī mausī kā ghar hai*" (x is my *mausī*'s home). The *mausī* from village x is the *xvali mausī*. Furthermore, a woman is spoken of as having married in such and such a place ("*x men shadi kī*") and not as being married to a certain man (see also Sax 1991: 77).

The meaning of *ghar* (home) is thereby more than house—it denotes a whole place. That kinship-place vocabulary interconnects with spatial vocabulary has also been pointed out by Karin Polit:

> Everyday matters such as work, family, behaviour, and interaction with the other villagers ... are often described with spatial vocabulary. *Ghar*, literally meaning house or home, is used to refer to the village area, including the fields and the forest surrounding it. *Ghar* usually refers to a woman's *sauryas*, her home where her main responsibilities lie. But the term *mait* is a similarly spatial term. It does not only mean family and people, but also a woman's natal place. (Polit 2006: 159)

That in India people and place form a unity and are interconnected through mutual involvements has been extensively discussed in the literature (Daniel 1984; Marriott 1976; Polit 2006; Sax 1991, 2009). I want to point to a different aspect of place-making here, namely that kinship relations guide people through the landscape. They constitute an inside space that regulates and stimulates movements between places.

In their analysis of women's movements and the observation of purdah in Pind, Pakistan, Mumtaz and Salway (2005) note the importance of social categories for interpreting space. According to those authors, social categories thereby do not only define an abstract social space, but also stand in direct relation to concrete places, and thus lead to places being perceived as a social inside or outside: "The identity of the people who share a space at a particular moment in time determines whether the space is classified as *'baar'* (outside) or *'ander'* inside space. Presence of *biraderi* members, both women and men, creates a socially acceptable 'inside' space, while the presence of a non-*biraderi* man, or even a woman, creates an 'outside' space" (Mumtaz and Salway 2005: 1758).

Among the Gaddi, too, the concept of an inside space—referred to as *hamārā ilakā* (our area) or *apnā ghar* (our home)—exists. Inside relations are thereby defined—that is, acted out, in a broader way or narrowed down, depending on context. In its most narrow sense the inside refers to the own village or villages in case of two homes. For women, the inside includes both, their *sasurāl* and their *māykā*. But more often than not, the inside includes more than the relations with one's own places of belonging described above. Inside relations are generally kin relations and thus places included as inside are the places of one's kin. Our home and our area then denotes the homes and places of one's kin and affines.

The idea of certain places constituting an inside space has very practical consequences: movements between places are guided by kin relations. Visits to places almost always occur within kinship circles. This is not to say that people do not go to places for reasons of business, shopping, medical care, and so on. However, to enter a village in order to meet someone in the absence of a kinship relation almost invariably would be linked to a very concrete and justifiable purpose. For kin relations, however, the kinship link is reason enough to visit.[6]

What are the kinship relations that make up the inside space and how do they come into being? Phrased more pragmatically, Where does one go? Where does one visit? The answer is quite simple: to all the houses of one's kin and affines.[7] These findings are quite exceptional, in that they contrast not only with Parry's description of Kangra, but also of kinship relations within the Himalayan Pahari region, for example, in Garhwal. Following Parry's description of the Rajput castes in the Palampur region of Kangra, relations between wife-giving and wife-taking affines are hierarchical. While wife-givers will be treated unceremoniously or even with contempt, wife-takers are treated as honored guests (Parry 1979: 300–301). In Garhwal, even among Dalits, where affines are of equal status, a man has reservations toward staying at his wife's natal place, which does not become an inside place for him (Polit 2006: 160-161). What is more, among high castes in Garhwal married sisters will not visit each other's places without invitation; doing so would be considered shameless because the sister belongs to someone else's house (Sax 1991: 124).

To understand why the Gaddi visit all their kin and affines equally, a short look at the characteristics of the Gaddi kinship system becomes necessary. In contrast to the Rajput system of hypergamy described for the district of Kangra by Parry (1979), marriages among the Gaddi are symmetric. Neither does a difference in status exist between the bride's and the groom's side, nor are marriages asymmetric alliances between groups. Marriages are framed as marriage by exchange. Within the same and adjacent generations, marriages between descent groups take place in both directions. Patterns of *bartan* (gift exchange) as well as hospitality on formal occasions and during informal visits show a system of status equality and reciprocity between affines. As Phillimore remarks in his study of Gaddi social organization (1982), there are no inhibitions to visit or eat at a daughter's or sister's house: "The very idea of hospitality being asymmetric struck most of my informants as bizarre and at worst insulting" (Phillimore 1982: 412).

Sibling relations are strong and valued. The brother–sister relation is worshipped during annual festivals, but from my observation the sister–sister relation is no less important. Not only do brothers visit their sisters' homes, but also married sisters visit their sisters' homes. It is even expected of a sister to visit her sister's place if she is passing nearby. If a woman has gone to her sister's place, even if it is close by, no one in her home shows surprise if she stays overnight. Also, sisters invite and help each other during rituals and weddings at their home. One has to give a set of clothing to one's siblings' children at least once in their infancy. Women are the agents in this exchange; it applies equally to the children of a woman's siblings and to the children of her husband's siblings.

In the same generation, with the exception of the avoidance relationship between a woman and her HeB, all relations are either sibling bonds or joking relationships. The locally most commented-upon joking relationship is the one between *jījā* and *sālī* (ZH and WZ, respectively). In addition and as a counterpart to the avoidance relationship between a woman and all elder male relatives of her husband, *bhābhī* and *devar* (eBW and HyB, respectively) also stand in a joking relationship. More pronounced than with her HyB, however, a woman will joke with her *nanand* (HZ).[8] One could argue that the joking relationship between *bhābhī* and *nanand* is possible because marriage relations are symmetric and HZ and BW meet on equal terms, each relating to the other's husband as her brother. Unlike the Kangra Rajput logic that "the affine of my affine is my affine" (Parry 1979: 304), for the Gaddi the affine of my affine is my brother or sister. Less pronounced, but still recognized, is the joking relationship between *jījā* and *sālā* (ZH and WB, respectively). Joking is a central feature of all occasions where relatives of the same generation meet.

In general, two categories of kin relations exists: on the one hand, the *ghar ke log* (patrilineal descent group, comprising about three adult generations) who as a wider group merge with the *śarik* (the same clan with a common place of belonging), and, on the other hand, *riśtedār*, which include all affines.[9]

To rituals at one's home such as the *nuālā* or *kathā*, and *jātar* or *jāgrā* (pilgrimages), all *khās riśtedār* (close relatives; comprising about two generations), are invited. This includes out-married daughters of all living generations with their respective husbands, children (including in turn married daughters), and parents-in-law, on the one hand, and the in-married women's parents and brothers, as well as sisters with spouses and children, on the other hand. The *ghar ke log* in principle being present in the house and village already are included among the invitees and will be invited along for pilgrimages.

In addition, informal visits between kin are frequent. A mother might just stop over at her daughter's place when it happens to be on her way. The same is true for a woman's brother, daughter, and even daughter's husband's mother or a sister's husband. There are many occasions when visits are expected, in addition, as in the case of a birth, death, or on the news of an illness of a relative.

The inside—talked about as our—is at the same time a social and a spatial concept, and more than that not an idea that exists in the abstract, but that—as the next section will show in more detail—comes into being through enactments of kinship. But where is the boundary of the inside? As mentioned in the beginning of this section, the inside space is not fixed. It can be contextually extended or narrowed down. While the absence of kinship relations clearly marks a distinction between inside and outside, within kinship networks the boundary is more flexible. However, the boundary is well known to those concerned, who then often express insecurity about being in a place that is not their own or not fully of their own relations. The notion of one's own usually breaks down where the inside is defined through women. The MZ's place, on the one hand, belongs to one's inside space, since the MZ and MZH are included within the kin group. The MZHB and his affines, on the other hand, are *dūsre log* (other people). The same applies to the FZD's place. It is at the boundary of the inside where fights might break out, for example, during celebrations when "own" and "other" meet. Especially men often can be heard commenting that, for instance, when going to a certain place they will not drink alcohol (a seldom-kept promise that would also conflict notions of hospitality and socializing). One does not know what will happen, because one is not in one's "own area" and one does not know the "other" people in that place (i.e., one does not relate to them in kinship terms). In other contexts, however, the MZ's place is very much considered part of the inside.

How Children Do Kinship and Place

Children learn early and very practically how to make kinship and place. They get to know places by physically traveling through the inside. During school vacations, children are invited to the places of their maternal and paternal relatives. It is common to meet five- to ten-year-olds performing kinship by traveling. Not only small children, but also young women travel. In the latter case, they are invited by relatives until their marriage. While a child might spend a few days at a relative's place any time during the year and for different reasons, during school vacations these visits take place on a large scale. Suddenly a couple with four children might remain alone while at other houses two or three children are visiting. The children are invited equally by relatives in sibling relation to their parents as well as by siblings of their grandparents. It is noteworthy that it is not always the closest kin of the children who invite them to their place: a woman might invite her FBSD as much as her BD. Moreover, siblings are not necessarily invited together but often leave for different places.

After a few days or a couple of weeks the children are sent back home with the gift of a new set of clothes. This is another example of how social relations are enacted through gift exchanges. The gift of clothes is a unidirectional gift in this case without direct reciprocation. The clothes given vary according to the financial means of the givers. The basic gift for a girl is a new suit (*salvār-kamīz*), the expensive version is a dress or even jeans and T-shirt and might even include shoes. In this context, it is important to note that children are not sent on vacation by their parents but are invited to come by their relatives, and in principle the relatives decide if they want to host a child.

However, these invitations are not free from expectations, especially toward relatives who are financially well off. One woman who is regularly busy inviting children in her various roles as FZ, MBW, and MMZD explained clearly that she does this not only out of affection—that she definitely shows for some children—but also because the children's parents expect her to do so; they surely would like to send them to her place. Those who can afford the invitation are also expected to extend it. Among women, it is often pointed out who—with the means to do so—does not invite children and who does so in spite of little financial means. A lot of emphasis is put on if someone recognizes and values a relationship by inviting a child.

Children themselves often make plans for their vacations. They thereby follow different strategies. A twelve-year-old girl who was looking forward to the next school break told me her aim was to spend the full vacation at her FZ's house, since she really liked the place and was very attached to her FZ. Her only worry was that her mother would oppose a long absence, since she was expected to help with some daily chores at home. A seven-year-old girl who told me about her plans was more concerned with visiting as many different places as possible. She explicitly wanted to spend her vacation *ghūmnā* (traveling; literally to go round or about, to travel), as travel at one's pleasure is called. She had already been invited by her FMZ and was very eager to go, since she had not been to that place before. Knowing that this trip would at most amount to two weeks, she also imagined that she needed to talk to her FeZ who had invited her the previous year and might do so again. She declared that she would first visit her *dādī* (FMZ) and then her *bhūā* (FZ) and then maybe somewhere else, but she still had to decide where that might be. She ended up spending two full weeks at her FMZ's place and then being invited spontaneously to her FyZ for another week, while her FeZ invited the girl's FFBSD.

Mothers will frequently tease or pretend to scold their children for thinking about nothing but *ghūmnā* (traveling). But regardless of what mothers say, they actively encourage and approve their children going on vacation. The mothers themselves fondly remember where they went on vacation as a child.

In my understanding, children on vacation perform kinship by visiting, thus getting to know their inside and thereby experiencing places, as outlined above, along kinship lines. Vacations are not the only situation in which children go to stay at other places independent of their parents. It is not uncommon to send children, generally girls, to live with their MM or MZ if she is either temporarily alone or if she is childless. In addition, boys and girls are frequently sent to stay with relatives for educational purposes, for example, for access to a better school. But in contrast to the latter examples of stays at relative's homes, the emphasis in inviting children during their vacations is on short-term visits and *ghūmnā*. Here the visit to the place and to one's relatives is the explicit purpose. This form of travel is an approved way for children to get to know places and explore social relations. Children thus build their own networks of kinship and places.

Kinship, Place, and Habitus

Practice, as Bourdieu has shown, embodies objective meaning. Practices are produced by a habitus, the "systems of durable, transposable *dispositions*" that are predisposed to function as "principles of the generation and structuring of practices and representations" (Bourdieu 1977: 72; emphasis in original). Practice also means a bodily *hexis:* "A permanent disposition, a durable manner of standing, speaking, and thereby of *feeling* and *thinking*" (ibid.: 93–94; emphasis in original). The habitus generates a certain body hexis that varies from place to place according to the conceptualization of that place. People thus acquire a sense of place that is embodied, and in its most direct sense matched by a corresponding body language. Places are experienced through their corresponding practices by actors, and place-making becomes visible to the observer through body language.

The connection between kinship, place, and habitus in the North Indian context has been most noted in regard to women and their relation to their natal and marital homes. One prominent example is Gloria Raheja's account of her fieldwork experience: Walking through her fieldwork village, she mocks the practice of veiling among the women walking with her. While her jokes are verbal these women, being married into the village and accordingly covering their faces, joke with her, the anthropologist and daughter of the village. When she starts to imitate their veiling by pulling her shawl in front of her face, the women immediately sanctioned her behavior. Not even jokingly does a woman veil in her natal village: "To veil implied a sexuality that needed protection; in one's natal village no issues of sexuality ought to arise, for one is daughter and sister to all" (Raheja and Gold 1994: xxiii).

A woman's scarf plays an important role for indicating the relation to a place among the Gaddi as well. A woman traveling between a place of her husband's relatives and her own relations will at some point of the journey very casually rearrange her *dupaṭṭā* (headscarf), allowing it to fall down over her shoulders when traveling toward her natal relations, or pull it back over her head when traveling toward her husband's relatives or marital home. This rearranging of the headscarf is a common sight, even on buses. A woman knows exactly when she passes from a village closer to her marital relatives, where she must be prepared to veil in front of men senior to her husband, to a place that is not marked by either kin group, or to a place of her natal relatives. The former implies she can drape the scarf rather casually around her head or neck, the latter allows her to pull it down off her head and wear it over her shoulders and breast. When I refer to habitus and bodily hexis according to kin relations, I mean these changes in dress code, but also changes in body language—the way women walk, sit, talk, laugh, and where she goes, eats, or how she interacts with others. The social perception of places is thereby not only visible in people's actions, but also is explicit in the way people talk about place.

In line with the general North Indian ethnography, the difference between a woman's *māykā* (natal place) and her *sasurāl* (in-law's place), which is the place where she takes up residence after marriage, is emphasized and a common topic of conversation. The opposition between *hamārā beṭī* (our daughter; Gaddi *diū*) and *hamārā bahu* (our daughter-in-law; Gaddi *nu*), translates, as women pointed out to me, into being allowed to sit down and chat, or being made to work. Married daughters on visits also may and are even expected to sleep longer in the mornings than the other women. In spite of what people say and contrary to Garhwal (Polit 2006), however, Gaddi daughters do join the other women in domestic work when visiting their *māykā*.

Details on the tension between *māykā* and *sasurāl* have been described elsewhere and the case of Gaddi women does not deviate significantly from the general picture (see Narayan 1986, Polit 2006, Raheja and Gold 1994, Sax 1991). However, there are three aspects I want to point out. First, her *ghar* (her home) is her *sasurāl*. With her marriage the *sasurāl* becomes her home and is not merely her in-laws' place (see also Polit 2006). When she goes to work in the fields, she describes them as "our fields," not as her in-laws' fields. Second, men also have a *sasurāl*. This has been largely overlooked since studies on gender are still mostly studies on women. Gaddi men visit their *sasurāl*, at times even without their wife, and are reluctant neither to eat nor to stay overnight there. By himself and by others, a man's wife's parents' place is referred to as his *sasurāl*. Third, the most notable place-related change in behavior besides that of a woman from *māykā* to *sasurāl* is the behavior of couples, especially young ones, toward each other depending on the couple being in his or her natal home.

Writing on a daughter's behavior in her *māykā,* Raheja observes, "[W]hen Babbli's husband came to fetch her back to her in-laws' home, she resumed before our eyes the posture of a shy and reticent wife" (Raheja and Gold 1994: xxiii). This is unlikely to happen in a Gaddi family. The open interaction between husband and wife changes from her *sasurāl* to her *māykā* as well. Their communication in front of others is much more intimate in talking but also in terms of physical proximity in places belonging to her natal relatives such as her *māykā* and her sister's place, than it is in their conjugal home, the latter being characterized through the showing of a formal distance in front of others, which is not expressed in her natal home.

These examples of how kinship relations are performed also show that the space conceptualized as the social inside is not uniform. As established in the previous section, both *sasurāl* and *māykā* belong to the inside space of a woman, and his home and his *sasurāl* are imagined as the inside space for a man. At the same time, both places go with a different body hexis. While habitus strongly shapes gender-related practices, the change in body hexis is performed by both men and women, and importantly influences their mutual interactions.

Extending Networks, Accessing New Places

Khudlā pāṇī pakhlā māṇū o ḍar lagdā (turbid waters and strange people cause fear) (line from a Gaddi folk song)

What do you do in a place where you cannot resort to kinship ties—that is, where you have no prior relations? As in the song line quoted above, strangers are feared or at least not to be trusted. Since only inside relations are considered to be reliable relations, the means to extend one's social space in the absence of prior ties is—in accordance with the value of kinship—to create fictive kinship relations.

Since the sibling tie, whether between the same or the opposite sex, is highly valued among the Gaddi, it should not be surprising that when one wants to establish relations with someone, this occurs within one's generation and is done by becoming a brother or a sister: *dharm bhāī* or *bahin*. *Dharm bhāī, dharm bahin* (brother or sister by religion) refers to a fictive kinship tie—a sibling tie that has been created through a ceremony that transforms two persons into siblings. This is referred to as *bhāī/bahin bannā* (to become a brother/sister).[10]

The *dharm bhāī, dharm bahin* relationship falls in the same category as *sakhā bhāī* or *sakhī bahin* (real brother or real sister). To become a brother or sister is a question of *bahin/bhāī mānnā,* of regarding someone as your sibling. This subsequently implies that she or he is integrated into the social network: becomes a relative to one's relatives, is included in ceremonial exchanges such as *bartan* and invitations to weddings, and also in the mutual giving of sets of clothes to one's children that happens between siblings. A fictive sibling will also follow the brother–sister holidays such as *rakshā bandan*.[11] Fictive kinship is thus much more than regarding a close friend just like a brother or a sister, and it is notably distinct from *bhāī* as a term of address casually used in North India for a man of the same generation as oneself.

The fictive kin relation of *dharm bhāī, dharm bahin,* although not unique to the Gaddi, is here particularly emphasized. Fictive sibling ties are very common. They are formed on both formal and informal occasions. Usually this involves visiting a temple and feeding each other water and sweets and exchanging a gift of money and a piece of cloth. The two paradigmatic occasions for establishing fictive kinship ties are during one's marriage and on the occasion of a child's first haircut.

The establishing of brother or sister ties at a wedding is not particular to the Gaddi. It is performed through the opening of the protective thread that is tied to the groom's and bride's wrists during the beginning of their respective marriage rituals. The groom's thread is untied by someone from the bride's side, and the bride's by someone from the groom's side. Although the untying of the protective thread establishes fictive kinship, during my fieldwork the fictive kinship established at weddings was more commonly referred to as *mitrā/sahelī bannā* (to become a friend/girlfriend) than as *bhāī/bahin bannā*.

I take the fact that the first haircut of a child is an occasion for creating brother or sister ties to be an indicator of the importance among the Gaddi of fictive kinship ties in general and of sibling ties in particular. Whoever cuts the child's hair becomes the brother or sister of the child's mother. Unlike the case of German *Taufpaten* (godmother/godfather), this does not result in responsibilities toward the child, other than the giving of a set of clothes, which is consistent with the general exchanges among siblings. The primary kinship tie established through the cutting of the hair is between the adults. As one of my informants explained, a woman will necessarily make someone into her sister or brother when going to cut her child's hair for the first time. *Bhāī/bahin bannā* is consciously connected to the hair-cutting ritual. The question asked when hearing that a child's hair was cut is, "Who cut it?"[12]

With whom to establish this bond is the choice of the child's mother. There is no rule as to whether it has to be a man or a woman, a Gaddi or non-Gaddi, friend or relative of a previously different category. As in other cases of becoming a *bahin/bhāī*, it is the sibling bonds that are valued irrespective of gender. It enables one to extend one's social network and adds new places to one's inside places.[13]

The fact that fictive kinship is employed to establish links to outside places is exemplified by the Gaddi shepherds. Shepherds usually stand in fictive kin relations to the local population in their winter grazing grounds (see also Saberwal 1999: 33). My first contact to a Gaddi family during my research was made through their fictive kin at their winter grazing grounds. My argument that fictive kinship opens access to new places while giving security by creating inside space is supported by Saberwal's interpretation of the shepherds' *dharm bhāī, dharm bahin* relations with the local population in their winter grazing grounds: "Support for the herders within the wintering areas derives from individual rather than community-based networks, and as a result, each herder needs to develop these relationships" (Saberwal 1999: 34).

Not surprisingly many herders establish fictive kinship relations in the winter grazing areas, commonly referred to as Punjab, and not in the summer grazing grounds. The Punjab, the plain area, is imagined as the other—or the non-Gaddi other. The winter grazing grounds are other people's places as can be known from the way shepherds talk about Punjab (see chapters 6 and 8). They are not accessible per se, in spite of yearly visits and land-use contracts. The quotation above from Saberwal moreover shows that this way of forging relations is about building networks. Ideas about inside and outside relations are metaphorical ways of talking about place. While these notions are important for thinking about places, making a brother or a sister is a practical activity that does something: the establishment of *dharm bhāī, dharm bahin* relations creates kinship ties and transforms other places into places that can be included in one's network of inside places. Similar to children's vacation travels, fictive kinship is an action of building and extending a network of relations. These networks join a collection of concrete places (and persons) that vary from individual to individual.

The Landscape of the Dhauladhar: From Metaphor to Practice

I have argued that actions of doing kinship and doing place are often one and the same. Thereby one's own and one's kin's places are understood as inside places, as one's own area. On a broader level of identification, the most inclusive inside is equal to what is perceived as Gaddi area. Gaddi area is opposed to the outside, or places of other people (Pahari or Punjabi). What comprises the Gaddi area? From much of the literature as well as popular perceptions of the Gaddi, one would suppose that Gaddi area is Gaddern (Bharmaur), the place of the summer villages that is the region north of the Dhauladhar range and not Kangra to the south. The distinction between Kangra and Chamba can be traced in administrative practice. The Gaddi have historically been classified as foreign herders outside of the Chamba district by the colonial forest department (Chakravarty-Kaul 1998: 9). My findings on local engagements with place, however, reveal a different picture. There is a discrepancy between the Gaddi homeland Bharmaur—the mythical place of belonging—and both sides of the Dhauladhar or the mountains as enacted Gaddi places. These places thereby come into being through activities through which people build, keep up, extend, or deepen their individual place-networks. Seasonal movements between Kangra and Bharmaur villages, performing death rituals, and visiting relatives and family deities all are activities that act out social relations and make place.

To illustrate how the building of networks and ideas about the inside work together, I will briefly cite from a conversation I had with a nine-year-old girl. We had gone on a pilgrimage to the family's ancestral village in Bharmaur. Their small children were going to Bharmaur (Gaddern) for the first time in their lives and had been telling me for weeks about how they imagined Gaddern. The following is a reconstruction of the conversation between me (A) and the nine-year-old (G) from my field notes:

G: How do you like it here?
A: I like it. And how do you like Gaddern?
G: Don't know.
A: Why don't you know?
G: I haven't seen it yet.
A: But are we not in Gaddern?
G: But no. This is *our* x [name of village]. This is our old village.
A: So where is Gaddern?
G: Don't know. Somewhere else.

I do not intend to dwell on how children's perception of places works. But I take the girl's answers as an illustration of how place comes into being through enactments. Through the visit to the ancestral village, the ancestral village has become "ours" for the girl. When the children talked about their imagination of Gaddern while in Kangra, the family's ancestral village belonged to Gaddern. After physically getting to know the ancestral village, however, it is added to the girl's network of inside places—and the word Gaddern to which the nine-year-old cannot relate in a meaningful way is distanced as being somewhere else. Thinking about the landscape of the Dhauladhar as a place-network helps to understand how this environment comes into being. While notions of places as inside or outside, own or foreign, exist among the Gaddi, these notions do not exist independent of concrete places and of actions carried out in those places.

Notes

1. This is notwithstanding migration stories of the Gaddi as a community from Rajasthan, as well as diverse migration stories of individual families. In two independent cases, men who had tried to trace their family history, one from Bharmaur and one from Kangra, told me that it was remembered that their ancestors had come to Bharmaur (and in one case subsequently to Kangra) from Uttarakhand.
2. Daughters might receive a share of their parents' land if the family is wealthy, but generally do not because their share is given to them as dowry. Unless a couple has no sons, or there are no sons from the girl's mother in case of multiple marriages, then daughters will inherit, too.
3. For Gaddi Brahman, the period of death pollution lasts eleven to twelve days. The time span of one day for the ritual is because on Maṅgalvār (Tuesday), Birvār (Thursday), and Itvār (Sunday) the *kriyā* cannot be performed and thus will be postponed for one day.
4. The three-month *kriyā* is called *trimaihanī*, the six-month *kriyā* is called *chimaihanī*, and the four-year *kriyā* is called *cārbaukh*. While I have observed the *chimaihanī*, the one-year *kriyā*, and the *cārbaukh*, I draw my information on the first *kriyā* chiefly from three in-depth interviews that I conducted on the *kriyā* and other rituals following a death. My three interview partners were not connected to one another: one was a woman from Kangra, one a man engaged in seasonal migration, and the third a Gaddi Brahman man from Bharmaur.
5. This contrasts reference to places where people, mainly men but often their wives, too, lived because they were employed there. To a place that one knows because one has a relative there, a social relation is established and expressed when talking about that place. A place where one is stationed for work or used to work might be described as a nice, big, crowded, polluted and so on, place, but there is no lasting meaningful connection expressed to it.
6. During my fieldwork, I experienced this way of moving between places in reactions to my own movements. I was always encouraged to visit the houses of relatives of my hosts. I needed to explain why I had gone to other people's houses, however—research interests were not per se understood to be a reason—while leaving out a sister's house that had been on the way needed justification.
7. I neglect gender differences for now, which do exist but rather concern behavior at certain places than as to alter the general conception of an inside space. Outside the perceived inside space, as common in North India, men certainly are freer to move than are women.

8. The joking is always present in the relationship between *bhābhī* and *nanand*, but it is more pronounced between married women since it is mostly sexual joking. The joking between *bhābhī* and *nanand* culminates in a sort of generalized joking between women at a young man's marriage when all women related to the groom meet and engage in jokes, gossip, dancing, and skits on each other's sexuality.
9. *Jātī* (the same clan) refers to anyone having the same clan name, whereas *śarik* carries the sense of a common locality, although this might be the common ancestral village, not necessarily the place of residence. Phillimore reports the terms *gharet* and *khāndān* for agnates (see also Parry 1979), and *riste* or *riśtedār* for non-agnatic relatives, with a further distinction among the latter into *riste* (consanguines) and *nāte* (affines) (e.g., ZH, WB) (Phillimore 1982). Parry (ibid.) reports *srik* as referring to the narrower descent group.
10. Although the expression *dharm bhāī/bahin* is recognized, fictive siblings are usually referred to simply as brother or sister, with the qualification of having become a brother or sister if the need for specification arises.
11. Also known as *rākhī,* a North Indian holiday celebrating the brother–sister relationship.
12. The person to cut the hair is chosen by the mother of the child (the father might not be involved at all). The first haircut is always performed at a temple, often at the temple of a *kul devtā* of the child's mother's family. It is important to note that in local understanding there is a difference between the first haircut, referred to as *bāl kaṭnā* (to cut the hair), and the *mundān* ceremony. The first is done for every child, girl or boy. It involves the visit of a temple, but necessarily includes only mother, child, and the person chosen by the mother to cut the child's hair, which is done by symbolically cutting off one curl. The latter is generally performed for boys and only if promised to the deity, for example, in exchange for the birth of a boy. A *mundān* is a large social event, involving not only a priest, to perform a *havan*, a barber to shave the full head of the child, but also a *jātar*, a pilgrimage to the temple and the sacrifice of a goat or sheep. It is an occasion to which all *khās risthedar* (see above) are invited and sets of clothing are exchanged between all invited relatives and the mother of the child. In both cases, however, the person cutting the first tuft of hair in the temple becomes the brother or sister of the child's mother through the subsequent ritual as described above.
13. It has to be noted that fictive kinship is not restricted to sibling ties. *Gode mem lenā* (adopting children) is another possibility of creating kinship ties. This can be done, for example, by performing the marriage ceremony for a young woman. The adopted daughter will show kin relations, however, notably in relation to her new brothers and sisters.

5

Walking

In chapter 4 I have shown that enactments of kinship and place often lead people to move through their environment between summer and winter or residential and ancestral villages, between natal and marital homes, or between houses of relatives. Chapter 6 extends the idea of doing kinship and place to include places of deities and respective movements for visiting these places. Through these visits and further activities, place-networks are created and extended. Since practices of visiting places often involve physical movement in the mountains, it is through walking that place-networks come into being. Accordingly, chapter 5 briefly reflects on the significance of walking as an activity.

At first sight, it might not be a surprise that walking as an activity is given significance in a community that is strongly linked to transhumance and a seasonal migration that in former times meant crossing the mountains on foot. Shepherds from this point of view, of course, do walk and need to possess the skills to do so. This utilitarian perspective, however, falls short of an understanding of the significance of walking apart from its being a response to environmental conditions and economic necessities. Walking as a social practice carries significance in its own right (see also Lye 2008; Rival 2002; Widlok 2008). Walking, as Thomas Widlok pointed out, is not necessarily opposed to driving and other forms of locomotion, but rather to staying in place (Widlok: 54–55). Walking can be analyzed as a technique, as a form of or attitude toward mobility—that is, part of the habitus, and as an active engagement with the environment.

Walking as a body technique was already described by Marcel Mauss in his classical essay *Techniques of the Body* (1973/1935). A technique of the body as defined by Mauss refers to the way in which people in different societies know how to use their bodies (ibid.: 70). Mauss stresses that body techniques are not naturally given, but rather are learned—in other words, acquired by education. Body techniques such as ways of walking, running, dancing, giving birth, carrying babies, sleeping, sitting, or squatting are thus social phenomena as much as they are biological phenomena, or, according to Mauss, "[W]e are dealing with biologico-sociological phenomena" (ibid.: 86). Concerning walking, Mauss remarked, "[T]here is perhaps no 'natural way' for the adult," for already "the fact, that we wear shoes to walk transforms the positions of our feet: we feel it sure enough when we walk without them" (ibid.: 74). The social nature of body techniques is described by Mauss as a specific, socially influenced habitus (ibid.: 73): "These 'habits' do not just vary with individuals and their imitations, they vary especially between societies, educations, properties and fashions, prestiges. In them we should see the techniques and work of collective and individual practical reason" (ibid.: 73).

The collective reason refers to the education in techniques of the body by society. Society for Mauss acts as the collective entity that shapes the way humans make use of their bodies. Body techniques are thereby, as he notes, not uniform within one society but vary, for example according to gender (for Mauss, sex) and age.

The attention paid to body techniques reappears in Bourdieu's definition of body hexis. Body hexis—that is, body posture or gesture (body language), "speaks directly to the motor function, in the form of a pattern of postures that is both individual and systematic, because linked to a whole system of techniques involving the body and tools, and charged with a host of social meanings and values" (Bourdieu 1977: 87). Bourdieu, like Mauss, stresses that body language is learned; for Bourdieu it is even one of the earliest learning processes (ibid.: 90). The body moves in space and thus embodies the structures of the world—its spatial organization and symbolism. This in turn enables the appropriation of the world by the body in what Bourdieu calls the "dialectic of objectification and embodiment" (ibid.: 90). Body hexis then is an expression of the habitus—here in Bourdieu's sense as the unifying principle of practice (ibid.: 83). It is the embodiment of structures and principles and a disposition for the generation of practice.

Understood as a social practice and part of the habitus, walking, then, more than a technique is an idea or a disposition toward mobility. As Widlok states, it is the opposite of staying in place—and, as such, about creating and choosing paths (Widlok 2008: 54; Lye 2008: 23) and, I add, also about a readiness to set off.

Ingold (2004) as well as Ingold and Vergunst (2008) go one step farther in the significance they attribute to walking. More than as a social practice,

Ingold and Vergunst stress walking as an activity through which human-environment relations and social life itself come into being. Basic to this idea is the contention that actions such as thinking and feeling are not subjective states performed vis-à-vis an external world made up of objective material conditions but rather that the external world is formed in activities (Ingold and Vergunst 2008: 2). Ingold argues that walking is an "intelligent activity" whose intelligence is not exclusively a state of mind, but also is to be found in the field of relations of the human being in the world (Ingold 2004: 332). Not only, then, is walking a cultural or social activity, but it is moreover a process through which the lived experience of humans as actors in an environment is enacted:

> However to hold—as we do—that social life is walked is to make a far stronger claim [than saying that walking is social], namely for the rooting of the social in the actual ground of lived experience, where the earth we tread interfaces with the air we breathe. It is along this ground, and not in some ethereal realm of discursively constructed significance, over and above the material world, that lives are paced out in their mutual relations. (Ingold and Vergunst 2008: 2)

Accordingly, Ingold and Vergunst propose to embed "ideas of the social and the symbolic within the immediate day-to-day activities that bind practice and representation" (Ingold and Vergunst 2008 : 3). Walking is an activity through which environment as a processual space unfolds and acquires significance, and thinking as well as feeling come together in lived experiences. This perspective enables us to move the significance of walking beyond its straightforward explanation as a functionalist adaptation to economic and ecological conditions. Of course, we can expect walking to be imbued as a practice with significance in a society closely linked to transhumance. But how does walking become meaningful, when, where, and for whom?

Doing fieldwork among the Gaddi, I was reminded that walking is a learned practice, in Mauss' sense of a body technique, and children, as well as anthropologists, have to learn how to walk correctly. Walking correctly means, first, not to trip or slip, and—as I had to learn—always to put down the whole foot to get a steady grip on the ground. Adults usually treated my occasional slipping foot with concern, telling me to be careful, watch the ground, walk slowly, and not to fall. They also immediately corrected me when I was not putting my whole foot on to the ground, for example, when walking up the slope of a driveway or stepping on rocks. I was laughed at and treated with ridicule by small children (who otherwise treated me quite respectfully) when slipping or tripping, for example, on walks together to fetch water from a spring. (I actually rarely fell or really lost my balance.) Children among themselves also expressly ridicule each other for slipping or tripping. Children's mistakes or missteps in walking generally draw reactions from adults, especially their mothers, who, in contrast to the concern they displayed toward me, often scold their children for not being able to walk correctly. Walking mistakes appear to be treated as misbehavior caused by carelessness rather than as accidents, and moreover are sanctioned more than, for example, spilling or dropping things. Children are expected to walk long distances from a certain age, usually about six years. Smaller children are encouraged to walk, even longer distances, but are not expected to be able to do so and are cared for if tripping and are carried if they are tired or unwilling to walk.

The emphasis put on walking skills goes with a certain readiness to walk to rather remote places that are often in the mountains. This is not to say that people would not complain about long distances, steep slopes, and dangerous paths. They do, but in my experience this does not interfere with the perception of the mountains or jungle (wastelands) as being principally accessible. Walking in and into the mountains is positively valued among the Gaddi, whether men, women, girls, or boys. On the contrary, for many Pahari speakers, who usually associate with the valley, walking in the mountains seems difficult and dangerous; these walks require long planning, and are rather discouraged. This different attitude toward walking in the mountains struck me from the very first when I came to Dharamshala. My driver and assistant for a week, a young Himachali from the Punjab border, displayed his anxiety when he realized that I had intentions to visit the mountains, telling me not to go. "Why not, it is *acchā* (good)!" was the immediate response from our host, a former shepherd, with whom I had inquired about the view from the mountain pass. Two Pahari-speaking neighbors of the family with whom I stayed in one village, an elderly woman and her daughter-in-law, further exemplified this skeptical attitude when they told me that they were not able to walk in the mountains since the paths are too steep for them—literally too steep for their legs to walk—and that they would not go into the higher mountains because the perpendicular hillsides frighten them.[1] My Gaddi acquaintances in contrast never questioned the goal to visit the mountains, cross the pass, but merely pointed out the right season, weather, occasion, or people to go with.

During the warm season and early monsoon, in the months of Barsākh (April–May), Jheṭ (May–June), and Hāṛh (June–July), the hillsides on the southern slopes of the Dhauladhar are highly frequented by (Gaddi) people. One usually runs into several other people on seemingly remote mountains paths. People are up in the mountains for various reasons: visiting temples, grazing cows, moving between village and flock to transport salt or grains, visiting shepherds, or collecting wild edible plants such as *luṅgerū* (fern tips). Furthermore, activities are combined in movements through the mountains. A man visiting his brother with his flock, or a group of women returning from a temple, will collect fern tips to cook at home, or a shepherd coming down from his grazing place to join a ritual at a temple will take salt back up to his flock.

Walking back from a visit to a small temple high up on the southern slopes of the Dhauladhar, after a six-hour walk through steep terrain and one more hour to go, my companion, a woman aged thirty, made the following remark:

> You people [you foreigners] are different. We always have a reason for going into the mountains. We go to a temple or something. Those foreigners who come as *tourists* just go to see the mountains. *Trekking hī ke liye jāte hain* (they simply go for trekking). They enjoy to do trekking and look at the mountains, that is why they go. We go because we have some *kām* (work), we do not go just like that. (From interview notes, translated by author)

I first agreed with this observation, which seemed to me a valid description of cultural differences in movements. However, the declaration that local people walk into the mountains with a specific reason while foreigners go simply because they enjoy trekking in itself is not that easily upheld, as a second instance shows.

Returning from a short stay in Bhagsu Nag to visit a family in the village, I met a group of four to five young unmarried men, college students in their early twenties. They were getting off the jeep I was boarding to go to their village. They were on their way up the mountain to Triund, a scenic place on top of the ridge overlooking the Kangra Valley at approximately three thousand meters. A minute after my jeep had left, my mobile phone rang. It was one of the boys who asked me not to mention having met them to their families. They had been to Gūne Mātā, a well-known temple in the mountains, for which they had asked permission from their parents. But then they decided to camp a night up in the high mountains. They had told their families that they went only to the temple *mātā dekhnā* (to see the mother)—in other words, it was a religiously inspired trip. They did not want their families to know that they went *ghūmnā*—or (purely) to enjoy themselves, afterwards. However, back in the village the mother of one of the boys and several neighbors, in casual gossip about news and happenings, told me the boys had gone up to the temple of Gūne Mātā the day before; since they had not returned, it was suspected that they had moved on to Triund to camp up there. People neither disapproved nor were surprised by this, which indicates that camping in the mountains is rather normal for a group of young men to do. This excursion as well as the reaction to it moreover show that a concept of going to the mountains for enjoying high altitudes does exist among the Gaddi, too. While for married women, and to a lesser extent also married men, going into the mountains will most probably be connected to the visit of a temple or some economic activity, similar to unmarried young men, unmarried young women and to a lesser extent recently married women also report going to the mountains with friends to enjoy the cool climate in summer. Unmarried young women further go to spend a couple of days or a week with their shepherding fathers and the flocks, on the southern slopes of the Dhauladhar as well as in the winter grazing areas.

As Ingold and Vergunst state, walking can be seen as a lived experience through which the environment comes into being. Walking thus opens up the space of the mountains or the jungle, which processually unfolds as it is walked. Apparently, Gaddi movements enact the mountains, whereas these activities are not common in Pahari practices. Thus, many Pahari speakers in Kangra perceive the mountains as inaccessible. If the environment is understood as coming into being through walking, however, this environment is not the same for everyone. Rather, walking means individual actions of creating and extending (person-centered) networks.

The idea that the environment is walked relates to reflections on path creation. Through walking, certain paths are chosen over others and, as Widlok has shown for the San of Namibia, going somewhere is turning away from somewhere else (Widlok 2008: 54). For another hunter-gatherer society, the Batek of Malaysia, Lye has argued that walking is about creating pathways in the forest (Lye 2008: 23). The emerging of paths is also central to Ingold's thinking on wayfaring. Since most maps are rarely drawn on paper, their narration is about being able to retrace a walk (Ingold 2006: 27). The notion of tracing paths fits the way Gaddi shepherds talk about their routes through the mountains.

In closing, I come back to my fieldwork experience. When I first interviewed shepherds about their transhumance routes, I received only very general answers, in the form of "we walk up the mountain, then cross the pass, walk down the hillside, cross the river, walk up on the other side," and so on. While the shepherds told me exactly how many days they spend at each halt and on each stretch of walking, they did not give me details of the places on their route until they learned that I had been to the mountains. On hearing that I had visited the temple of Gūne Mātā, Triund, and other places, they started giving place names and explained from which place they walked to the next and how these are situated vis-à-vis the places I had been to. The mountains suddenly became a chain of place names and interlinking paths. This perspective, however, emerged—or was considered to be meaningful to me, too—only after I myself had walked the mountains.

Notes

1. The old woman, too, made this as a general remark and not with reference to her age, also stating that she had never been to the mountains—at least she did not seem to recall this during the conversation, which reinforces the depiction of the perceived inaccessibility of the mountains by Pahari-speaking villagers.

6

Visiting the Deities, Enacting the Mountains

In this chapter, I turn to places, deities, and religious practices that lead people into the mountains. I take up Ingold's perspective on environment as processual—or as coming into being through activities—and accordingly look at movements in the environment inherent to religious practices.

Religious aspects of the environment have often been discussed under the heading of sacred landscapes in the anthropological and religious study literature on India (cf. Eck 1981, 1998b; Gutschow et al. 2003). In the following, I prefer the term powerful or holy, since sacred, at least since Durkheim, has borne the notion of being opposed to something profane and thus as being set apart from the realm of everyday life. The usage of the terms powerful and holy instead of sacred is also an answer to Descola because it points to a concept of human–nonhuman relations that differs from Western cosmology (see chapter 1). Social relations, as the previous chapter has shown, are not exclusively relations between humans, but also relations between humans and deities. Moreover, powerful places are not set apart from the environment of everyday life. Although they might correspond to rather remote places in the physical environment, they do not make up a separate sphere. Religious aspects are intertwined with social, economic, historic, and physical aspects of places; the landscape that people worship in is the landscape of everyday activities. As Sax notes in his ethnography of Garhwal, "Local shrines are also important because they are part of a landscape to which people are deeply and substantially related" (Sax 2009: 54).

The aim of this chapter is, first, to explore religious meanings of the mountains in addition to and apart from the Shiva mythology—which is as a rule mentioned first in the context of the Gaddi and the Dhauladhar region. Second, the aim of this chapter is to analyze two types of religious activities that lead people to physically move into the mountains. The first practice of *jāgrā* and *jātar* was already referred to in chapter 4 as a means of relating to family deities and maintaining links to ancestral villages. In this context, I look at *jāgrā* and *jātar* as occasions for moving into mountains to visit temples in villages or in more remote dwelling places of deities. The second practice, *nhauṇ* (a bath), is directly linked to high-altitude places and water sources in the mountains.

I have chosen to structure this chapter on deities and the mountains around these practices. On the one hand, I have done so for theoretical reasons because of my aim to follow an activity-centered approach to environment as advocated by Ingold. On the other hand, I have done so because of my fieldwork data. The focus on these movements that are kin- or small-group-organized activities is ethnographically founded. The movements, especially as part of *jāgrā* and *jātar*, are a way of relating to deities that was very prominent in the Dharamshala area where I did my fieldwork. Fieldwork based in Bharmaur might have resulted in more attention to the notion of village deities, albeit the activities described in the following are equally part of religious practices in Bharmaur. In contrast to Dharamshala, every village I visited in Bharmaur had a presiding village deity. The activities at the village deities' temples have a collective character during yearly festivals, also called *jātar* in Bharmaur, which in many cases not only involve the inhabitants of one village, but also link several villages.[1] In my fieldwork area in Kangra, on the contrary, the activities described in the following are conspicuous among religious practices among the Gaddi. I start out, however, with an introduction to Gaddi deities.

Gaddi Deities

In the preceding chapters, I have now and then referred to Gaddi deities without qualifying this term. The expression Gaddi deity is not my analytical category but is taken from local language. Gaddi people usually refer to their deities as Gaddi deities, either in a collective sense when talking about *hamārā devī-devtā* (our deities) or as a qualification to the identity of a certain deity, for example, describing a goddess as being a Gaddi goddess. What makes those deities Gaddi deities?[2]

First, Gaddi deities are differentiated from other people's deities, in other words from those associated with the Pahari speakers in Kangra and wider Himachal, or with the people from Punjab. As one informant, who was about to move with his sheep and goats to the winter grazing areas, put it, "The deities in Punjab [i.e., the north Indian plains] and in the mountains are *alag* (different) from each other." Before saying that, and much to my surprise, he had even denied that there were deities in Punjab. He then qualified his statement confirming that there are of course deities in Punjab but not "ours." He continued to relate that people in the plains have their own temples and deities who are different from the temples and deities in the mountains. When shepherding in Punjab, he explained, they do visit the temples, but only in order to *mātā dekhnā* (see the deity), not for other reasons. I will comment on the last statement below. Here I want to point to the emphasis my interview partner put on the fact that their own temples are in the mountains. Gaddi people, he said, do not build temples in Punjab, whereas in the mountains everybody can build a temple *apnī khuśī ke liye* (as he or she wishes).

The notion of "our deities" as opposed to the "others' deities" is shared by Pahari people. In conversations with non-Gaddi neighbors in my fieldwork villages, Pahari speakers also pointed out differences between their deities and the deities of the Gaddi people. One young woman explained, "Ours are the *mātās* [goddesses]. Our deities are in Kangra [in the valley], not in the mountains. Kangrā Mātā, Chāmuṇḍā Mātā, Jvālāmukhī-ji [names of three deities]. We also go to Bhagsu Nag, sometimes. But Lord Shiva and Mani Mahesh is the Gaddi's [thing]." Her brother's wife added, "We don't give goats to the *mātā* [whereas the Gaddi sacrifice goats]."[3]

The goddesses of Kangra that the women mentioned as their goddesses are the deities of the goddess temples of Kangra and adjoining regions (cf. Erndl 1993). In her analysis of the Hindu goddess of Northwest India, Erndl worked on seven goddess temples also known as the seven sisters: Vaisno Devī in Jammu and Kashmir; Jvālāmukhī, Chāmuṇḍā Devī and Kangrevali Devi (also known as Bajreshwari Devī or Kangrā Mātā) in District Kangra; Chintpurnī Devī in District Una (Himachal Pradesh); Nainā Devī in District Bilaspur (Himachal Pradesh); and Mansa Devī close to Chandigarh in Haryana.[4] According to Erndl, these goddesses are referred to as the seven sisters because this is a common way "of speaking of collectivities of goddesses" (ibid.: 37). I will give an example of a local variation of this list of goddesses—specified by Gaddi women—below. One way in which the seven goddess temples listed above are connected is as *śakti pīṭhā* (seats of power). A (greatly abbreviated) story on the origin of the *śakti pīṭhā* I was told in Kangra is as follows:

Satī, the wife of Shiva, got so upset when her father invited her without her husband Shiva to a grand sacrifice to which all other gods were invited, that she killed herself by throwing herself into her father's sacrificial fire. Shiva in grief started to dance furiously over the earth with the dead body of his wife in his arms. His dance became so violent that *Satī*'s body was torn apart without him noticing. Shiva distributed her body parts over the earth. The *śakti pīṭhā* are the places where the parts of *Satī*'s body fell. *Jvālāmukhī*, e.g., is said to be the place where her tongue fell, and *Kangrevalī Mātā* the place where her chest touched the earth. (From interview notes, translated by author)[5]

The *śakti pīṭhā* are an example of the "process of duplication and multiplication" that, following Eck, is characteristic for the "pluralistic and widespread Hindu imagined landscape" (Eck 1998b: 167). Goddess temples connected to a *śakti pīṭhā* are found throughout the Indian subcontinent and are linked at local as well as at pan-Indian levels. Concerning the *śakti pīṭhā*, Eck stated, "Just which *pīṭhas* are part of the group is far less significant than the fact that there is a grouping in which, ultimately, every *devī* may be said to participate" (Eck 1998b: 175; emphasis in orginal).

The regionally famous goddesses' temples of Himachal Pradesh and adjacent districts described by Erndl belong to the deities from the plains with which the Gaddi deities are contrasted in local understanding. By opposing Gaddi deities with Pahari and Punjabi gods and goddesses, or deities from the plains in general, it is not implied that Gaddi people do not visit the other temples, as clarified by the statement quoted above. On the contrary, all the larger temples, and certainly the goddess temples of the Kangra Valley, foremost Chāmuṇḍā Mātā and Kangrā Mātā, are well known by everyone living in the area. Visits there are sometimes combined with trips to the market, or conducted if the temple is passed on the way to the house of a relative. Even Vaisno Mātā in Jammu is visited by some, for instance, on trips organized by regional colleges that take student groups there (as the Panjab University in Chandigarh does). The pilgrimage to a goddess temple, including Vaisno Mātā, is moreover popular among young married couples. Groups of young women or young men, respectively, also get together on day trips to travel to the famous temples in the region.[6]

The difference expressed in ideas about "our" and "other people's" temples becomes most clear when one looks at practices of worship connected with the deities. As stated in the interview quoted above, Gaddi people go to temples in Punjab for *mātā dekhnā* (to see the mother) but not for other reasons—which means they generally do not carry out specific ritual activities at those temples that establish ongoing relationships with the deities and are linked to one's personal concerns. As Eck states, the "central act of Hindu worship, from the point of view of the lay person" is *darśan* (seeing); this means "to stand in the presence of the deity and to behold the image with one's own eyes, to see and be seen by the deity" (Eck 1998a: 3). While *darśan* is a central act of worshipping deities for Hindus in general, it does not express any special relationship with a deity among the Gaddi. One can, in short, go to a temple to *mātā dekhnā* (see the mother) or because one has some *kām* (work) to do. Specifically aimed ritualized activities, commonly referred to as work, are carried out for Gaddi deities, whereas *darśan* or *mātā dekhnā* is practiced with all deities. With *jāgrā* and *jātar,* this chapter shall describe two examples of activities that are an expression of this special relationship to Gaddi deities.

To sum up, the expression "Gaddi deities" denotes deities conceptualized as Gaddi in opposition to Pahari or Punjabi. What makes them Gaddi is not only that Gaddi people worship them, but also that the practices connected to their worship as well as their dwelling places are located in the mountains. Chapter 4 established that the Dhauladhar range usually referred to as the mountains is seen as Gaddi area. In its widest meaning, the mountains are considered an inside space on the level of Gaddi versus Pahari people. But mountains and plains are opposed not only in terms of human dwelling—by where Gaddi people live—but also by where their deities live. Defined through dwelling places of deities, the Dhauladhar again becomes "ours," and here the border appears even more rigid than that associated with human settlement patterns. Whereas Gaddi people are acknowledged to live in many parts of India apart from Himachal Pradesh, especially in Chandigarh or Delhi, the acknowledged realm of Gaddi deities remains the mountains.

Before starting with the description of Gaddi deities and related activities, a further important concept concerning deities has to be introduced to clarify associations with the term deity: the distinction between *devtā* (deity) and *bhagvān* (god). In chapter 3, I described the importance of the god Shiva for the Gaddi. Shiv-jī is said by Gaddi people to be "our god." Shiva, however, is not classed as a Gaddi deity. The deities I am concerned with in this chapter, accordingly, are the smaller deities apart from Shiva that the Gaddi people worship. Most of the Gaddi deities are either a *mātā* (local goddess) or a *nāg devtā* (serpent deity). Furthermore, certain *bābā* (the colloquial expression for *sādhu,* meaning holy man or ascetic world renouncer), are revered and worshipped as deities after their death.[7] In Bharmaur there are, moreover, *satī mātā* temples in several villages—this means that the goddess is said to be a woman who died on her husband's funeral pyre and subsequently became revered as a deity. Two important deities that appear to fit into neither of these categories are Kelang (see below) and Buārī; both are inter alia Gaddi family deities.[8]

The distinction between *bhagvān* and *devtā* appears to be obvious for the people in everyday interactions, so much that it goes without saying for them. It becomes particularly visible in ritual practices, if one looks at how worship is performed, by whom, through whom and on what occasion.

The difference in the worship of Gaddi deities becomes evident in the contrast to two rituals popularly referred to as *kathā* (short for *viṣṇu narayān kā kathā*, a ritual addressed to the god Vishnu), and *shānti havan* (a ritual performed for the peace within one's house and family that is centered around the sacrifice of vegetable offerings into a fire). Both the *kathā* and the *shānti havan* are popular and frequently performed by Gaddi families, but are not specific to the Gaddi, nor are they seen as such. Both are addressed to gods from the larger Hindu pantheon including Ganesh, Vishnu, and Agni, which are worshipped through the mediation of the presiding Brahman priest who is usually the family *purohit* and a Gaddi Brahman. The term *havan*, as in *shānti havan*, denotes a fire offering (also known as *homā*), which is a form of *pūjā* that is often an element of larger rituals. It always requires a Brahman priest. The worship of the deities I am concerned with in this chapter, on the other hand, is in general not mediated by a priest, but rather is performed directly by the devotees.[9]

Deities, in comparison to gods, can be seen as more accessible to their devotees. Accessibility is manifest in two ways. First, with deities a direct communication through their possessed oracles is possible. Second, deities are accessible because they can be addressed for very practical and concrete troubles of their devotees. They are approached in case of illness, childlessness, problems in school, and so on. As Fuller writes, "Vishnu and Shiva, as great gods with general powers over the cosmos, are normally thought to distance themselves from mundane problems affecting ordinary people. For this reason, Hindu rarely ask them for help either with collective afflictions, such as epidemics or drought, or with personal troubles, such as illness or childlessness" (Fuller 1992: 36).

The distinction between *devtā* and *bhagvān* on the level of language is not consistently kept in practice—and it would at times be hard to do so. The god Shiva—who despite the Hindu conceptualization as a great god, the Gaddi in many respects worship as an accessible deity —is intimately connected to and at times identified with serpent deities.

Another case that shows that the *devtā-bhagvān* distinction is not a clearcut distinction is the case of the goddess who can take both the identity of a local deity and that of the great goddess. This blurring of the distinction can be related to the fact that what Fuller summarized as a general Hindu idea holds true for Gaddi deities as well: There is "no sharp opposition between distinct deities or forms of them, on the one hand, and variant names for the same deity or form, on the other. Thus a single deity with different names may be seen, in another context or from another perspective, as a set of deities" (Fuller 1992: 30). It is important, however, to keep the *devtā-bhagvān* distinction in mind since it is crucial for an understanding of ritual practices—that is, for the understanding of which deity is worshipped how, through whom, and when. The focus of this chapter is on how the Gaddi conceptualize deities as deities belonging to a particular place.

Many Gaddi deities derive their name from their place of dwelling. Often this is a place name—for example, Gūne Mātā and Bannī Mātā (see below), but there are also the *jhot ki mātā* (the goddess of the pass) or goddesses such as *galu mātā* (*galā* meaning a neck-shaped ridge or pass) whose names describe the physical location of their abode. The stories connected with the deities are usually local stories that tell about what happened at a certain place at a certain time. They are not primarily connected to a larger mythology such as that of the *śakti pīṭhā*.[10] This was also noted by Vogel whose accounts of the deities of the region (here the serpent deities) have been authoritative for the colonial gazetteers: "The Nāgs, who are nowadays worshipped in the Alpine Panjāb, have each a personal name, the origin and meaning of which are in most cases obscure. Sometimes they are named after the village to which their temple belongs. It but seldom happens that one meets with a name which is familiar from ancient literature" (Vogel 1972: 250).

Gaddi deities, on the one hand, generally are characterized as living in the mountains. On the other hand, they can be differentiated into deities whose temples are in the village and who dwell in the forest. Distinctions between deities of the village and deities of the forest are neither clear-cut nor strongly elaborated, as the examples below will illustrate. However, some goddesses are known as *ban khandī* (forest dwellers), and some are considered to be a manifestation of the goddess Kali, without any strict coherence between both categories in everyday discourse. Forest dwellers and Kali are both—rather loosely—connected to the notion of living in remote places and of being especially powerful. Since these dwelling places in general have been a topic of scholarly discussion, I will briefly comment on the debate on the association of forest, and especially forest-dwelling goddesses, with fierce deities.

Concerning dwelling places of deities, in the literature on South Asia two classical oppositions have been described and juxtaposed. These are the opposition of village and forest that is described, for example, by Malamoud (1996) for Vedic texts and by Zimmermann in his analysis of ecological concepts in ayurvedic medicine (1987) and the opposition of benevolent and fierce deities (Babb 1975; Erndl 1993; Michaels et al. 1996a; Sax 1996). Fierce deities are commonly connected to the forest and remote dwelling places, whereas benevolent deities reside (have their temples) in the village. The dichotomy contrasting the benevolent and malevolent qualities of gods was coined by Lawrence Babb. Babb further postulated that the qualities benevolent and malevolent are associated with male and female deities, respectively (1975: 216f). Within the group of female deities, this distinction appears again: marriage is juxtaposed with benevolence and unmarried status with malevolence (ibid.: 222). The latter category is thereby often linked to blood sacrifice and exemplified by the goddess in her form of Kali.

While the opposing of qualities has remained an analytical tool in the study of Hindu deities and especially goddesses (Erndl 1993; Michaels et al. 1996b), Babb's dichotomies have been subjected to profound criticism (Erndl; Michaels et al.; Sax 2002): "The problem with the debate over split goddesses is that it is all-too-often represented as a choice between competing essentialisms. A contradiction arises when it is claimed that the essence of the goddess (and, by extension, women) is at the same time *ugra* (fierce) and *śānta* (peaceful)" (Sax 2002: 156).

Michaels, Vogelsanger, and Wilke also assert that a dichotomous classification of goddesses according to their character is not accurate but rather that every goddess unites wild and gentle features (1996b). The authors argue that identities of goddesses are not ambiguous or contradictory, but positively stress the goddesses' polyvalence (ibid.: 21). As Michaels, Vogelsanger, and Wilke state, qualities associated with deities are perceived as a continuum on which every deity can move (ibid.: 22). However, rather than conceiving of a deity depending on the perspective taken, a further step to overcome the dichotomous view is to look at actions performed by deities and worshippers rather than to start from qualities of deities. I here endorse Mol's advocacy for looking at what is done—to study the enactment of reality—rather than to look at objects (or deities) from the focus of different perspectives (Mol 2002: ix).

Specific to Gaddi deities is that animal sacrifice is not significant for the classification of a deity since principally all Gaddi deities eat meat. It has often been argued that fierce deities or fierce manifestations of deities, such as Kali, are appeased with blood sacrifice. Since there are no vegetarian Gaddi deities, and again Shiva is no exception here, animal sacrifice, in my understanding, is no criterion for distinction within the Gaddi pantheon. From the way that *bali* (animal sacrifice) is performed and talked about—rather than demanding sacrifices the deities *lenā* (take) sheep or goats as offerings—instead of being linked to fierceness it is perceived as pointing to the Gaddi-ness of a deity. The practice of animal sacrifice thus does not make a distinction between Gaddi deities, but rather distinguishes Gaddi from mainstream Hindu practices.

To Go With a Goat: *Jāgrā* and *Jātar*

Throughout the preceding chapters, I have referred to religious practices that are linked to temples, especially temples in the mountain, called *jāgrā* and *jātar*. Since they have many features in common, I will treat them together and point out differences where necessary. Typically, both activities are also talked about as *bakrī leke jānā* (to go with a goat), because what one does is to go to a temple and give a goat (or sheep) to the deity. There is, however, an important difference between both: *Jāgrā*, related to the verb *jāganā* (to be awake, vigilant) involves traveling to a temple and holding a night vigil there.[11] *Jātar*, linked to the Hindi word *yātrā* (journey), is performed during the day and does not include a night's stay at the temple.[12] *Jāgrā* and *jātar* can be analyzed in several respects. Here I look at them as practices of place-making in terms of very concrete and physical ways of engaging with the environment.

Jāgrā and *jātar* are considered to be specifically Gaddi religious activities and are as such usually mentioned together with the *nuālā* by Gaddi people. Both are performed when one's wishes are believed to have been granted by a deity. Thus, like the *nuālā*, they are rituals of thanksgiving. Whereas the *nuālā* is performed for Shiva, *jāgrā* and *jātar* are performed for Gaddi deities. All three are social events and bring prestige to the patron. The *nuālā*, as the Gaddi ritual par excellence, is somewhat more elaborate than the *jāgrā* and *jātar* rituals. Among other things, this becomes visible by the requirement of specialists for the *nuālā* ritual.

Concerning place-making, the creation of a temporary ritual space for the *nuālā* is a central difference to the *jāgrā* and *jātar* rituals (generally, one of the central aspects is, of course, the deity for whom the ritual is performed). The ritual space for worship in a *jāgrā* or *jātar* is a permanent ritual space: a temple either within the village, house, or in the mountains. For the *nuālā* ritual, a temporary ritual space is constructed at the patron's home. Thus, while during the *nuālā* Shiva is invited into one's home, *jāgrā* and *jātar* require a visit to the deity. *Jāgrā* and *jātar*, thereby, do not necessarily involve a physical journey of the devotees. They can be held at a temple erected for the deity at one's house. However, they are always framed as the devotees visiting the deity, and not the other way around; thus, their performance implies the idea of a journey. In the *jāgrā* and *jātar* rituals, it is the people who move (even if only to the room of the house in which the temple is situated), while the deity remains static.

As rituals performed to repay a deity for a received favor, *jāgrā* and *jātar* are follow-up activities. They follow a prior visit to the temple when a wish was voiced and a retribution has been promised. To my knowledge, there is no difference between a *jāgrā* and a *jātar* concerning the deity it is performed for. The same deity may receive both. Rather, what is promised to the deity when asking a favor is decisive for the kind of ritual performed later.[13] On the one hand, each *jāgrā* or *jātar* is held on a specific occasion with a concrete purpose. On the other hand, these activities express gratitude for the well-being within one's family, and from this perspective, they are not singular events but rather are one of many related acts ensuring the continuous protection and goodwill of a family deity. What is included in this well-being can be deduced from the favors asked—fertility and children, especially a son; successful education of one's children; finding a job; but also health, recovery from illness, and protection from affliction.

It is a family's *kul* deities that are continuously involved (and invoked) in the process of attaining well-being by members of the respective families. However, both a couple's family deities and a woman's natal family deities are approached. The latter is often asked for fertility—the birth of children—and the first haircut of a child is often (not always) performed at the temple of the mother's natal family's *kul* deity. A man I interviewed who had staged a *nuālā*, a *jāgrā*, and a *jātar* on the occasion of his retirement as a government employee made it quite clear that several occasions for approaching a deity over the course of time are seen as a process of receiving continuous protection from the deity. He explained,

> We always went [to the deities]. When the boys were small, we kept going there. Now, it is all fine. I have retired. My sons both got their [university] degrees. One now has a job in Delhi. So we are giving a *nuālā* to Shiva now. And we will be going to the *mātā*, too. We are doing this now, [because] we are *khuś* [happy]. She has always helped us. So we are going to the *mātā*. (From interview notes and transcript, translated by author)

The deities involved on this occasion were the god Shiva for a *nuālā*; Gūne Mātā—the family deity of his wife's natal family—for the *jāgrā*; and a further *mātā*, one of his family deities, for the *jātar*.

What happens when the promise to a deity is not fulfilled? As noted above concerning the debate on fierce deities, a protecting deity can turn into an afflicting deity. Promises to a deity are binding. A common reason explaining affliction by a deity is that someone forgot to fulfill a promise given to the deity. A couple might have promised to hold a *jāgrā* if their wish comes true, but later forgot that they had promised to return to the temple and sacrifice a goat there. This forgetfulness is a common diagnosis for the reason for someone in the family, most probably the couple themselves or their children, falling sick, suddenly performing badly in school, or any other persistent form of disturbance of the family's well-being. It is said that the upset deity grabs a person and causes them to fall ill.

Several activities make up a *jāgrā* or *jātar*: First, all *khās riśtedār* (special relatives) are invited. The patrons of the ritual and their invitees set off from the house of the patron to the deity's temple on foot if close or by car if more distant. The journey is marked as a *jāgrā* or *jātar* by carrying a red flag (*jhaṇḍā*) and a trident (*triśūl*). Furthermore, a basket with *prasād* is taken along, that contains a dish from pulses and fried leavened bread called *boberū* (Hindi: *pūrī*). The way from the house to the temple, or at least the part that is walked on foot, is marked by the patron's wife who usually paints two symbols at regular distances on the ground: a white circle (painted with a liquid mixture containing yogurt and water) with a red dot (vermillion) in its middle and a trident in white color with a red dot (see figure 6.1). These symbols are drawn to purify the way to the temple and to ward off evil influences through spirits. Along the way, the women pause to sing devotional songs. Arriving at the temple, the participants wash their hands, feet, and face, then go to see the deity (*mātā dekhnā*) in the temple. The red flag and the trident are placed at the temple in a stack of flags and tridents brought by previous *jāgrā* and *jātar*.

The offering of the sheep or goat, *bali*, is the actual beginning of the worship in the temple. It is usually performed soon after the arrival of the group. In general, male goats are sacrificed to female deities and rams to male deities. There are some *nāg* deities, however, who are known to take both. The offering itself involves the same steps as described for the *nuālā* in chapter 3. After the offering has been accepted by the deity, the animal

Figure 6.1 Markings drawn along the path of a *jātar*. Photo by A. Wagner (2007).

is beheaded and skinned. Participants then start to prepare the meal. Usually male relatives from the family of the patrons prepare the food. In the meantime, people sing devotional songs, and the *prasād* that was brought along is offered to the deity and then distributed among the participants. A further *prasād* handed to the participants are parts of the internal organs of the sacrificed animal; for a goat sacrificed to a *mātā*, this is usually a portion of fried liver. The meal is served when ready to all invitees. The meal itself is also *prasād*. It is *bhog* (food offered to the gods). After the patron of the ritual offers the food—one plate of the dishes—at the temple, its remainders become leftovers of the deity. The meal is eaten on plates made out of leaves. People eat sitting down in lines. Everybody served together sits down and gets up at the same time. If a *jātar* is held, the participants return home after eating. In a *jāgrā* singing and dancing continues all night. The actual night vigil applies to the patron of the ritual, or the oldest male member of the family that stages the *jāgrā*. For the *jāgrā* to be successful, he has to stay awake all night while the others may go to sleep. While the way to the temple is a collective journey of all invitees, the departing invitees may leave in individual groups.

Possession also occurs frequently during the dancing as well as in the process of offering the animal. The deity and, often, other deities apart from the presiding deity of the temple sometimes "come over" someone. This is considered a good sign: first, because of the presence of the deity, and second, because people can interact with the deity. Deities communicate through their oracles, if they are happy and pleased with the ritual, the motivation of the patron, the received offerings, and the kind and number of participants. I witnessed, for example, one *jātar* where the deity's oracle communicated that the goddess was unhappy with the fact that, while the patron's maternal relatives had come, many of his paternal relatives had not come. Deities also might not be satisfied with the kind or quality of their offering and demand more. The interaction with the deity's oracle also provides an opportunity for those with preoccupations to address the deity and ask questions concerning the reasons for and resolutions of their problems.

Having pointed out the distinction that is made in Kangra between Gaddi and Pahari deities, it is important to note that the songs sung at a *jāgrā* are often so-called *bhajan*. *Bhajan* are devotional songs, usually addressed to the goddess; there are *bhajan* to Shiva and other deities as well. In Kangra, these songs are sung in the Pahari dialect of Kangra (there are *bhajan* in Punjabi and Hindi, too). There are also songs in the Gaddi dialect dedicated to goddesses, but Pahari *bhajan* are today more popular. Moreover, often only the old women still know the full texts of the songs in Gaddi by heart. Most of the songs I heard, at the *jāgrā* and *jātar* I attended during my fieldwork, for example, at Bannī Mātā, Gūne Mātā, and a couple of smaller temples, were Pahari *bhajan*.

The texts praise the goddess and her power, and tell what makes up this power by listing who comes to the temple with which request on his or her mind. Parallel to wishes expressed in *nuālā* songs, the goddess' power following the texts lies in granting fertility (children) and curing (lameness, leprosy, blindness). Pressing daily concerns for which devotees come to temples, such as education and employment, as such, so far, are not expressed in the songs. The songs also address deities by name—for example, Nainā Devī, one of the seven sisters in Himachal. Thus these *bhajan*, as the listing of sister relations between the goddesses, link Gaddi deities to the larger goddess temples in the region. Furthermore, the identity of the deity seems of little importance; the emphasis lies rather on the songs being devotional and thus appropriate to the occasion. In this, singing at a *jāgrā* contrasts with the singing at a *nuālā*. At the latter, the participants are rather particular that songs in Gaddi dialect should be performed. Concerning the *jāgrā*, the same songs are sung during night vigils at *nāg devtā* temples and at *mātā* temples, and *bhajan* dedicated to Shiva are sung on both occasions as well. Two examples of popular *bhajan* that I recorded during a *jāgrā* to the Bannī Mātā temple in Bharmaur are given in the appendix.

In chapter 4, I described how through rituals, such as *jāgrā* and *jātar*, the link between a family living in Dharamshala and their ancestral village in Bharmaur is kept up. I now extend this idea, suggesting that these rituals link people to places in the physical environment, importantly not only to villages, but also to places in the mountains. By thus traveling through the landscape, people enact environment. Before I further develop this thought, I will introduce two temples in the mountains to which *jāgrā* and *jātar* are frequently led to convey an idea about the nature of the places and deities involved.

Gūne Mātā and Bannī Mātā

The temple of Gūne Mātā in the district of Kangra and the temple of Bannī Mātā in the district of Chamba are two locally quite famous goddess temples. Both goddesses are family deities of Gaddi families and are among the relatively larger and well-known temples in the area. The temples are situated at relatively high altitudes and thus exemplify places for *jāgrā* and *jātar* activities that lead people to move into the mountains.

The temple of Gūne Mātā is located on the southern slopes of the Dhauladhar. Gūne Mātā is a local goddess belonging to the Kangra side

Visiting the Deities, Enacting the Mountains • 113

of the Dhauladhar. She has not been brought from Bharmaur. The Gūne Mātā temple lies on a ridge that steeply falls off to riverbeds on each side. The temple is situated at an altitude of approximately 2,300 meters and above the villages on the same mountain ridge. Gūne Mātā is an example of a *ban khandī* (forest dwelling deity). The temple's location itself is quite level with an open view of the Dhauladhar Mountains as well as over the Kangra Valley (see figure 6.2).

Gūne Mātā is a locally well-known temple. Furthermore, its location within walking distance of Nadi village, itself part of the Dharamshala tourist circle, has started to draw tourists to the temple, so far mostly Indians, including youth trekking groups. However, such visitors usually visit the temple only once. The large majority of the goddess' devotees are Gaddi families. The temple is surrounded by rooms for pilgrims and facilities for cooking, as well as several small shops selling refreshments and materials for the *pūjā* in the temple. I have been told that the road currently under construction from Nadi onwards was planned to go up to the temple of Gūne Mātā, but the goddess opposed this idea through an oracle and decreed that whoever wants to visit her will have to walk on foot from the last village on the way.[14]

Gūne Mātā is named after Gūnā, the place where the goddess' temple is located. Gūnā, however, is not the original place of the deity. Her first place is a couple of hundred meters in altitude above the present one. At

Figure 6.2 At Gūne Mātā with the temple on the right and the view over the Dhauladhar in the background. Photo by A. Wagner (2007).

her original place, she is called Cunje Mātā. *Cunje* means beak in Gaddi and refers to a large beak-shaped rock beneath which the dwelling place of Cunje Mātā is situated. Thus, in spite of being strongly linked to a place, the goddess may multiply her places; in the process, the name she is known by also changes. The deity's dwelling place at Gunā and the area surrounding the Cunje rock are part of the land belonging to the people of a village situated on the same mountain slope at a lower altitude. The village's inhabitants still go up to these lands to graze their cows in the summer and to cut grass for fodder storage for the winter months. They also run the shops and build the facilities for pilgrims at the temple. The following story about the goddess of Gūne Mātā was related to me by a man whose family worships Gūne Mātā as their *kul* deity:

> A man from our *śarik* [descent group] used to go up to Gunā to graze his cows. He stayed up there alone in the forest. The goddess dwelling in the area did not approve of his presence, since humans cause a lot of dirt by defecating and urinating and creating all the human waste that is present wherever humans live. She tried to scare the man away by creating a lot of noise, because deities do not appear directly in front of humans. But he was a very strong man who was not afraid of bears and tigers [bears and leopards are both still encountered in the area today]. And all he did was to set out to see where the disturbing noise was coming from. The goddess realized that this man was strong and potentially dangerous. She appeared to him in his sleep. She showed him her place beneath the rock and told him that that was her place and that she wanted to stay there. He subsequently built a temple for the goddess beneath the Cunje rock. The *pūjarī* of Gūne Mātā are chosen in the line of his descendants. The goddess was brought down to Gunā one or two generations ago where a bigger and more easily accessible temple was built for her. She came to be called Gūne Mātā at the new place. (From interview notes, translated by author)

The story of Gūne Mātā shows that the temple is established at a place in the mountains that is important for economic activities. The deity, albeit a forest-dwelling goddess from high altitudes, is not primarily linked to transhumance. The story points to grazing cows and thus shows that places in the mountains are not necessarily connected only to shepherding, but also to subsistence activities carried out from the village. This does not mean that the temple is unrelated to transhumance activities: several flocks on their way to the higher pastures also pass it. Although humans frequent the area of Gūne Mātā, the story about how the deity revealed herself establishes that the place is the domain of the deity who was disturbed by human presence. The notion that humans need to respect a deity's dwelling place, as the man in the story does by building a temple for the goddess, is common in connection to high-altitude places.

Gūne Mātā is explicitly considered a good place and a pleasant location for participating in a *jāgrā* with dancing and singing all night. As a tranquil, high-altitude location in the mountains on a small plateau enlarged by a terrace that allows a scenic view of the mountains and the valley, and known for a cooling wind during the hot season, it unites basic aesthetically valued qualities of places (see chapter 8). The plateau and temple's terrace make the place available for cooking, dancing, and sleeping relatively spacious. Due to its proximity to Dharamshala and Nadi, the temple is comparatively easily accessible, which enables many people to participate in *jāgrā* to Gūne Mātā. The way up to the temple, although about a three-hour walk from Nadi, is not very steep or otherwise difficult to walk, so that many small children take part in activities at the temple, too. Gūne Mātā is not only the family deity for the descent group who owns the land around the temple, but also is the deity for many other Gaddi families who have taken to worshipping the deity. Being virtually known by every child, the relation between people and the place is characterized by a certain intimate knowledge in that many people from around Dharamshala know the place well through repeated visits.

The temple of Gūne Mātā is mostly visited in months of Barsākh (April–May), Jheṭ (May–June), and Hāṛh (June–July), that means during the *tūndī* season (heat or summer, Hindi: *garmī*) and early *barsālā* (monsoon, Hindi: *barsāt*). During the monsoon, Gūne Mātā becomes less frequented. Monsoon is the time for going to Bharmaur—that is, to cross the Dhauladhar. One of the temples that is visited there is the temple of Bannī Mātā. A

Figure 6.3 View of Bannī village—the cluster of houses on the ridge in the center. Photo by A. Wagner (2008).

comparison of the timings of visits to Gūne Mātā and Bannī Mātā shows how places are visited following a seasonal cycle. Appropriations of place thus occur according to time.

Bannī Mātā is visited during the monsoon, the *barsālā* season, especially in months Sauṇ (July–August) and Bhaḍom (August–September). The time to go to Bannī Mātā also falls together with the season of village festivals in Bharmaur (in August) and the period for the Mani Mahesh Pilgrimage.[15]

The temple of Bannī Mātā is situated in the center of the village of Bannī, after which the goddess is named (see figure 6.3). Bannī Mātā translates as the goddess of Bannī. Bannī is a small village in the Bharmaur subdistrict of Chamba, to the north of the Ravi River, geographically situated within the Pir Panjal range at an estimated altitude of about 3,200 meters. Bannī Mātā is a famous regional deity. Her devotees are mainly Gaddi people who come to visit her temple from the district of Chamba as well as from that of Kangra. She is a *kul devī* (family deity) of Gaddi families, but she also is visited by other people from the region, for example, from Chamba town.[16] In 2008, the village could only be reached on foot. The first part of the way, however, has become a motorable road. The government of Himachal Pradesh has set up a small government rest house below the village, which is the only available room facility. Pilgrims usually sleep on the temple's veranda. Several goddesses' statues are placed inside the temple at Bannī. One of them depicts the deity as Kali (as a black goddess) and another one as an eight-armed Durga riding on a lion (see figure 6.4). Bannī Mātā is further explicitly said to be the goddess Kali. This shows that the goddess is conceived as both a local deity and an appearance of the great Hindu goddess.

As in the case of Gūne Mātā, Bannī is not the original place of the goddess. Bannī Mātā is also known by the name Charolevālī Mātā. *Charolā* means gate in Gaddi. Charolā is a place on the shepherds' route to Lahul that is passed by the flocks that cross the Kalicho Pass. The local people describe the place as a natural gate leading to the pass. Charolā is the old place of the goddess, where she is said to have first manifested herself through the splitting of a rock from which three tridents emerged. As her present *celā* recounts, a first temple was built to the goddess a little beneath the split rock at Charolā. A second temple to the goddess was erected in the village of Liyūṇḍī, which is situated on the way from Bannī to the pass. The family from which the line of oracles of the goddess originates is from Liyūṇḍī. A few generations ago, as the *celā* told me, the goddess was taken down to Bannī, which is also the place of residence of the present *celā*. The goddess, as her temples multiplied, moved down from the place where she guards the pass toward more-accessible and lower-

Figure 6.4 Bannī Mātā statue(s) decorated with cloths donated by devotees in the temple at Bannī. Ribbons tied on the wooden frame at the time devotees made a wish can be seen. Photo by A. Wagner (2008).

lying villages. Thus, Bannī Mātā is a forest-dwelling deity at Charolā who has been brought into the village at Bannī. However, as stated above, a transgression of the forest-village divide is of little concern for the conceptualization of the goddess. This again shows that there is no essentialism in the opposition of forest and village as dwelling places of deities.

Shepherds who take the route over the Kalicho pass—that is, via Charolā—to their summer pastures in Lahul sacrifice a goat to Bannī Mātā before crossing the pass. Axelby, who has done fieldwork among a group of shepherds crossing the Kalicho pass, reports on the shepherds' worship of the goddess:

> Before crossing the Pir Panjal range, the shepherds must appease the deities of each pass. During the second half of Asarh [Gaddi: Hāṛh] (early July) they undertake a series of religious ceremonies culminating with the ritual slaughter of a number of animals. On the third Tuesday of Ashar [sic] a series of sacrifices are made at Banni village and permission to make the pass crossing is requested from the Goddess.... Once permission has been received from Banniwali Bhagwati the presiding deity of the pass, the shepherds are free to cross Kalichho during the last four days of Asarh. (Axelby 2005: 230–231)

But since Bannī Mātā is a *kul devī* of Gaddi families, her worship is importantly not only centered on transhumance (on predominantly male activities), but also on the concerns of women, children, couples, or even several generations as a unit.

Bannī Mātā is believed to be an especially powerful deity. It is said that whoever asks something from her truthfully from his heart will have his wish fulfilled. She will give children to those who are childless, a job to those without employment, food to those without food. At the time of asking a favor from Bannī Mātā, the wisher ties a ribbon around a pole at the temple. When his or her wish is believed to have been granted by the goddess, the wisher visits the temple again to repay the goddess with what had been promised to be given in return. For Bannī Mātā, as for female deities in general, predominantly goats are given in sacrifice. The devotees will lead a *jāgrā* or *jātar* to the temple, untie their ribbon, sacrifice a goat, and give what else they promised to give in return. These are commonly brass bells. The bells are put up on the temple grounds, often with the name of the donor engraved on it. The number of bells at the temple further testifies to the power of the goddess in assisting people with their problems.[17] One does not accompany someone else's *jāgrā* to the temple before repaying one's debt to the goddess.

The power, *śakti*, of the deity is also experienced through her *celā*, or oracle. Only one person at a time is the *celā* of Bannī Mātā. The succession to the role of *celā*, who is at the same time the temple *pūjārī* (person taking care of a temple), runs in the *celā*'s paternal family. The goddess is said to choose her next *celā* after the death of the previous one by coming over the chosen person and making him "play." When the *celā* of Bannī Mātā, presently an old man around eighty years of age, plays—becomes possessed by the deity—he drinks the blood of the sacrificed goats and substantial amounts of liquor. Bannī Mātā is widely known for her blood-drinking *celā*. The drinking of the blood of the sacrificed animals is considered a sign of *śakti* (power) of the deity. The amount of blood swallowed is said to be not consumable by a human being and the drinking of the blood is interpreted as a sign of the involvement of the deity who is understood to consume the blood, not her human oracle. The drinking of the blood by the *celā* is a further manifestation of the goddess' power and its performance enhances Bannī Mata's reputation as a powerful goddess.

I visited the temple of Bannī Mātā in August 2008, on invitation of a family from Dharamshala. We were not the only group taking a *jāgrā* to Bannī Mātā. As it was the season for going to Bharmaur, the temple was rather busy. During our four-day stay in Bannī, we met five other groups who visited the temple, two of whom had come from Kangra as well. Two of the other *jāgrā* were held in the same night as the one I accompanied. While the offering of the goat to the deity generally occurs at *jāgrā*, the institution of the goddess' oracle distinguishes the temple of Bannī Mātā.

The *celā* usually plays twice a day, at about 9:00 a.m. and 9:00 p.m. We had arrived at the temple in the evening and the people I accompanied had wanted to offer their animal at the temple during the time the oracle played the following morning. But this morning the goddess did not appear in (literally come over) her oracle. So the offering was performed afterwards, without the mediation of the *celā*. After it was accepted, the animal was butchered and prepared for the communal meal. In the evening, however, the *celā* played. The old man went into a trance inhaling the smoke of burning coals accompanied by musicians playing the *nagārā* (bowled drum) and a flute. He first distributed *ṭīkā* (marks of blessing) by applying a dot of red powder to the forehead of the devotees, and then threw the remaining powder toward the ceiling. Then two goats of the other groups that had been offered and accepted before were, one by one, brought onto the temple's veranda and decapitated. The *celā* immediately lifted up the carcass and sucked the blood shooting out from the animal's body. A participant from another group reported having witnessed the *celā* drink the blood of as many as seven goats in a row. Following the drinking of the blood, the *celā* demanded liquor; participants handed several bottles to him successively of which he swallowed several mouthfuls each. Afterwards he handed out blessings by sprinkling water over the crowd, distributing sips of water to the bystanding devotees, and hitting them on the back with his *sangal* (iron chain). He also started to speak and the devotees entered into a discussion with the goddess inquiring about her satisfaction with the performance of the *jāgrā* and about the problems they had come for. When the *celā* stopped playing, the night vigil started. A communal meal for all groups together was served with the meat of the sacrificed animals. While some devotees then went to sleep, seeking shelter from the chill at night in the mountains under wool blankets, others worshipped the goddess by singing and dancing until dawn.

The way both goddesses are conceived and the activities connected to their worship show an interrelationship of religious, social, ecological, and economic aspects that make up the power ascribed to the deities. When worshipped as family deities, both goddesses are part of the network of social links a family maintains. In this respect, visits to Bannī Mātā are an example of how families settled in Kangra keep an ongoing link to Bharmaur. But both goddesses also show connections to economic activities as well as to the mountains and high-altitude places.

In spite of the fact that in this section both goddesses have been viewed as deities related to a certain place, it should be noted that local people situate both goddesses not only in relation to their dwelling places, but also in relation to the goddess temples of the region. Some of the people I questioned about the two deities described above mentioned that Gūne

Mātā and Bannī Mātā are sisters; in one case they are the same goddess. One woman put an end to my questioning by stating, "Some say they are sisters, some say they are the same *mātā*, but after all who can know for sure about the relations of deities? They are deities [and not humans] after all." Still there is another set of relationships that either Bannī Mātā alone or both goddesses are linked to: the nine sisters. The nine—or as mentioned above seven—sisters are the goddesses of the larger goddess temples in the region. As pointed out above, their exact number and identification vary. In this context, Bannī Mātā, or Bannī Mātā and Gūne Mātā, are included in the wider network of goddesses' temples and thus not set apart as Gaddi deities but integrated into the network of goddesses' temples of Himachal Pradesh and beyond.

Enacting Environment through Movements

The temples of Gūne Mātā and Bannī Mātā are only two examples of temples in the mountains to which *jāgrā* are led and performed. There are countless small temples in the mountains, as in villages, whose deities are visited in *jāgrā* and *jātar* rituals. What guides people through this network of temples in the villages and mountains of the Dhauladhar are first of all kinship relations. The temples are generally visited either because they belong to one's family deities or the family deities of one's relatives who called on their relations to join them on their *jāgrā* or *jātar*.

Erndl has stated that pilgrimage as a passage through space moves from the familiar environment of the home to the unfamiliar environment of the temple and back to the familiar environment of the home (Erndl 1993). This stands in striking contrast to conceptions of place in a *jāgrā* or a *jātar*, although both instances like pilgrimages involve the undertaking of a journey. Regarding *jāgrā* and *jātar*, people maintain intimate and personal relations with the deities they visit as well as with the places these deities live in. In these respects, the visits to these places are not seen as singular events. "Oh, we keep going there. It's our family deity!", was a common response I received when asking people about their relation to a temple or a deity's dwelling place in the mountains.

Going to family deities' temples in the mountains are rather habitual journeys for the family members concerned. These movements in space are not about going from the familiar to the unfamiliar, but about moving between places perceived as inside space. People move from the familiar of the home through the intervening mountains or jungle to the familiar of the deity's temple. From this perspective, visiting deities is very similar to visiting kin.

What is more, just as humans travel to visit their deities, the deities are also apt to travel and visit their devotees. The idea of a passage through space with the purpose of visiting hints at the structural counterpart to a *jāgrā* or a *jātar*. Erndl writes on the Serānvāli goddess worship and associated *jagrātā* performances (night vigils at a devotee's home): "Structurally, the performance of a jagrátá is the counterpart to pilgrimage" (Erndl 1993: 85). Gaddi people do not perform *jagrātā* nor a worship for Gaddi deities at home that could be counterposed to movements to the temple. Here the contrast between pilgrimage to a temple and worship at home is not convincing. The counterpart of visiting a deity is the occasion when a deity is invited to be a guest at a celebration at one's home.

Family deities are sometimes invited to marriages or other celebrations to the family's home. This is not a general requirement but depends on family traditions. To invite the deity, someone goes to the temple, formally invites the deity, and takes the deity back to the house in form of her or his symbol. Unlike other parts of the Western Himalaya, where the traveling of deities as *mohrā* (statues) or masks in palanquins is prevalent (see Sax 1991 for Garhwal; Diserens 1995–1996, Luchesi 2002, and Berti 2001 for Kullu; Sutherland 1998 for southeastern Himachal Pradesh), Gaddi deities travel—rather simply—with the symbols that represent them. Most often for *mātā* as well as for *nāg* deities this is a *triśūl* (trident). The trident in which the deity is taken to the house is one of the tridents that are brought to the temple when leading a *jāgrā* or *jātar* there. After the marriage or event for which the deity was invited, she or he is taken back to the temple in the trident. In sum, both humans and deities undertake concrete, physical movements in the landscape to visit each other at their place of dwelling.

These movements in the mountains, which are primarily religious activities, are also a way through which people get to know and become familiar with places in their environment. I classify them as movements that are carried out from the village and lead different categories of people— women, children, and men, and not only shepherds—into the mountains. The temples visited belong to family deities, and thus can be seen as an extension of the notion of a social inside space. Furthermore, they also are places to which a special power is attributed.

High-Altitude Lakes, *Nāg* Deities, and the Practice of *Nhaun*

A further practice that involves physical movements into high altitudes is *nhaun* (Gaddi for bath). *Nhaun* is the day of the year on which one bathes in lakes and springs connected to Shiva and *nāg* deities. The term *nhaun* means both the practice of bathing in the holy lakes or springs referred to as *nhauṇ karnā* (to do the bathing), and the date on which the bathing is performed.[18] In practice, visits also occur before and after this date, as with the Mani Mahesh Yatra, but *nhauṇ* is the most auspicious day for the bathing.

Nhauṇ, also known as Radhashtmi (Radha's birthday), is the eighth day of the bright half of the month Bhaḍom (August–September), fifteen days after Janmashtmi. In 2008, it fell on September 7. *Nhauṇ* is the last day of the Mani Mahesh Yatra and (as Janmashtmi) contrasted with the festival of Shivratri in the month of Phāgūṇ (February–March) (chapter 3). It is also said to be the day when Shiv-jī collects all snakes and insects and departs from Mount Kailash. While Shivratri, the date when Shiva returns to Kailash Parvat, is connected to fasting, his depart from Kailash is connected to bathing.

These dates are widely mentioned in the literature for bathing in the Mani Mahesh Lake. However, *nhauṇ* is not specific to the Mani Mahesh Pilgrimage. Mani Mahesh is not singular in this respect. Not being exclusive to Gaddi people, the date of *nhauṇ* (or nahon) is celebrated throughout the district Chamba and in Chamba town where people bathe in additional local water bodies connected to Shiva (K.P. Sharma 2001: 108–109). Around Dharamshala, *nhauṇ* is an auspicious date for bathing in all holy lakes and springs connected to Shiva and *nāg* deities.

Holy lakes or *ḍal* are high-altitude lakes in the Himalayan ranges. More exactly, *ḍal* is the term by which these holy lakes are known in western Himachal Pradesh.[19] Most but not all of the holy lakes in the Dharamshala area are situated behind the pass, to the north of the Dhauladhar range. Each *ḍal* is connected to a deity. The most famous lake is the Mani Mahesh Lake beneath Mount Kailash, which is a *ḍal* of Shiva. On the pilgrimage route to Mani Mahesh, lies Gauri Kund, a holy lake of Shiva's wife Gaura (Parvati). Several small lakes are situated north of the Indrahar and the Gasutri Pass: Nāg Ḍal, the abode of a *nāg* deity, Lamb Ḍal, a lake connected to Shiva, and a third lake of the goddess Kali. The *ḍal* of Kali is the only one among these holy lakes that is not visited. It is said it cannot be approached by humans and whoever attempts to go there does not return. A few lakes such as Ḍal Lake below Nadi, close to McLeod Ganj, and Kareri Ḍal above the village Kareri, are situated to the south of the Dhauladhar.

These *ḍal* lakes of the Dhauladhar are interconnected through their stories and legends, as well as through practices. There is an old story I was told by one of my hosts about a man who lost one of his golden earrings during the Mani Mahesh pilgrimage in Bharmaur while bathing in the Mani Mahesh Lake. In anger he threw his second earring into the water, too. About six months later, when he was washing his face in the Ḍal Lake

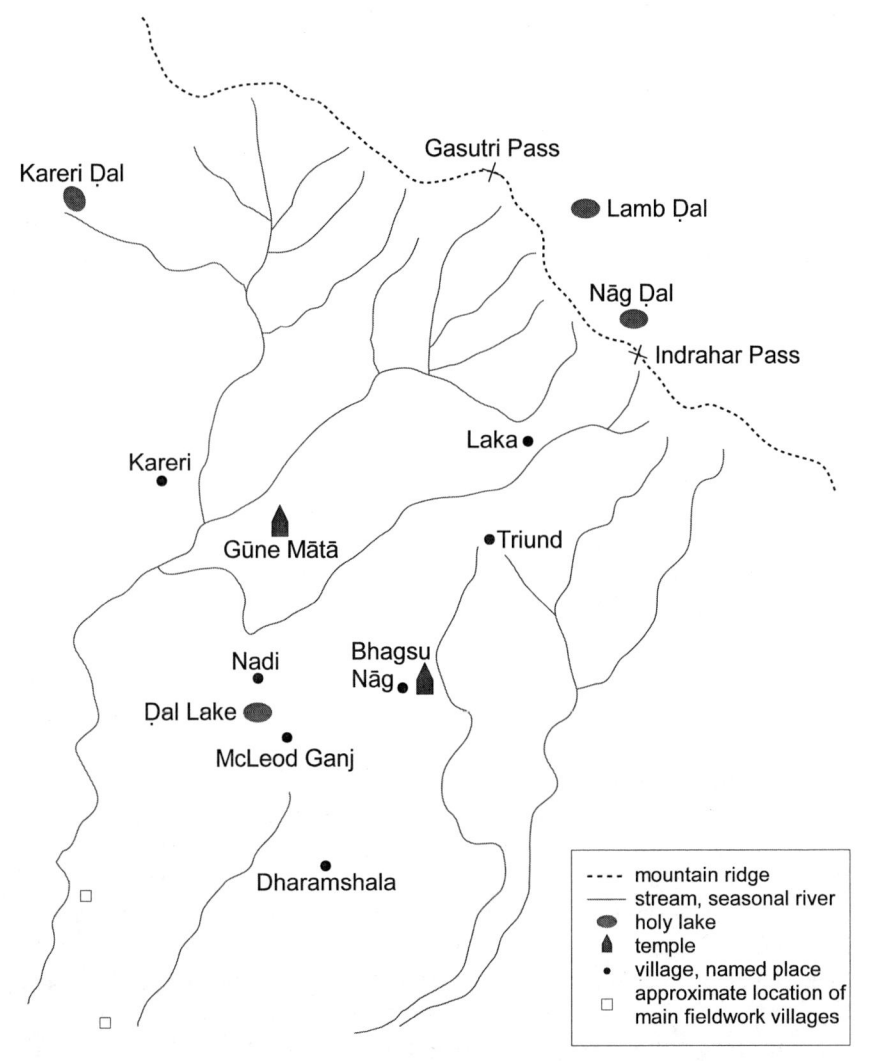

Visiting the Deities, Enacting the Mountains • 123

Map 6.1 Map of important places on the southern slope of the Dhauladhar around Dharamshala. Map not to scale. (Based on a public domain map, University of Texas Libraries, scale of original 1:250,000.)

at Nadi, he was suddenly holding his pair of earrings in his hands. The earrings disappeared and reappeared due to divine agency. The reappearance of the lost earrings at Ḍal Lake, moreover, shows an interconnection of the holy lakes with each other.

A further famous story is told about the Mani Mahesh Lake. This is the story of Trilochan, a Gaddi shepherd or low-caste (Sipi) *celā* from Sachuin near Bharmaur—depending on the version—who disappeared at Mani Mahesh, crossing over to Shiva's abode on Mount Kailash through the lake.[20] Trilochan serves Shiva at Mount Kailash, tailoring the Gaddi men's cloth *colā*, and is sent home six months later paid in gold (which he does not realize at first) and put under the obligation not to tell anyone where he had spent the six months. He eventually tells his wife and has to leave his home—in one version he falls off a cliff at Kharamukh (the confluence of the Budhil and Ravi rivers in Bharmaur). In another version, he wanders off into the mountains as an ascetic renouncer.

In these narrations, the aspect of *ḍal* as crossing places to the divine comes to the fore. The *ḍal* are *tīrthā* ("ford, as well as any watering or bathing place" [Eck 1981: 325]). Both the Mani Mahesh Lake and Ḍal Lake are crossing places where contact with the divine or divine interference, as retold in the happenings with the golden earrings, are thought possible. In both narrations, of the golden earrings and of Trilochan, the time interval between disappearance and reappearance is six months. In the case of Trilochan, this is also a date of postmortem rituals that his family performs for him. In addition, six months is the time span for transhumance, seasonal migration, and rituals associated with the god Shiva's migration, namely Shivratri and *nhauṇ*.

However, high-altitude lakes are not only *tīrthā*, but also *dhām*. The term *dhām* means dwelling or abode. Here the implication is not that of a crossover to another realm but the notion that the divine being dwells and is present in that place (Eck 1998b: 180).

The aspect of a high-altitude lake being the dwelling place of a deity is exemplified by the lake known as Nāg Ḍal situated north of the Indrahar Pass. The *nāg* deity of Nāg Ḍal, is, on the one hand, a family deity of Gaddi families who worship the deity and visit the lakes because it is their *kul* deity. On the other hand, as a high-altitude lake connected to a serpent deity, Nāg Ḍal is visited by people who come to bathe in the lake during a certain period of the year. Before I describe the practice of visiting these high-altitude lakes and the rules of behavior applying in high-altitude places, I will give some background information on the *nāg* or serpent deities.

Nāg deities are closely associated with water sources, springs as well as high-altitude lakes. The worship of *nāg* deities is quite common in the Western Himalaya. While serpent deities are worshipped in several parts of India, it takes a special form in the Western Himalaya region (Vogel 1972): "[T]he Naga cult in the Western Himalaya is much more powerful than in the plains. While in the plains, the Naga is only a fearful earth-deity identified with the venomous reptiles, in the Western Himalayan region, he is not only the custodian god of the subterranean entities (lakes, rivers and fountains), but also of the weather, rain and cloud." (Handa 2004: 71).

Within Himachal Pradesh, there are several named *nāg* deities whose temples are connected to a specific region (see Berti 2009; Sutherland 1998). In Bharmaur subdistrict, there is a deity called Kelang with its main temple at the village of Kugti, located East of Bharmaur town. Kelang is on the one hand a male *nāg* deity, and called Kelang Nāg. One legend tells that the deity came from Lahul and traveled over the Kugti Pass to Bharmaur clinging in form of a serpent to a ram's horns (*Gazetteer of the Chamba State 1904* 1996: 188–189; Noble 1987: 99–100; Raṇapatiyā 2001: 49). On the other hand, the Kelang *devtā* from Kugti is identified as Shiva's son Karttik who, as several people in Bharmaur pointed out to me, is called Kelang in Gaddi dialect and is the deity of the Kelang temple in Kugti (see also Raṇapatiyā ibid.). Kelang is also worshipped as a Gaddi family deity and is one of the widespread *kul* deities that are worshipped by many families.[21]

Another *nāg devtā* referred to as Indru Nāg is found in temples in the region to both sides of the Dhauladhar in Kangra, more exactly around the Indrahar Pass. Raṇapatiyā mentions that the *nāg devtā* temples in the Bharmaur villages of Kuarsi, Sāmrā and Chanota are all dedicated to Indru Nāg, the deity of the Chanota temple being identified as Bāsukī Nāg as well (Raṇapatiyā 2001: 52). Indru Nāg is also identified as the deity dwelling in the high-altitude lake Nāg Ḍal. And there is further a well-known Indru Nāg temple close to Kanyara, east of Dharamshala, in the district of Kangra.

More generally in Himachal, *nāg* deities are said to have power over rain (Khapatiyā 1981: 59; Raṇapatiyā 2001: 51; Vogel 1972: 247) and are often associated with springs or lakes (Vogel: 248; Smadja 2009b: 213; Sutherland 1998: 215–216). They are further protectors for animals grazing in their domain (Raṇapatiyā 2001: 51). From my fieldwork, too, there is an important association of *nāg* deities with water—springs and *ḍal* as well as rain. These *nāg* deities are not necessarily named or related to the name of a well-known *nāg* but rather simply referred to as a *nāg devtā* or connected to a place or village name. It is common to find a small temple or simply a *nāg* image next to a spring, most often if the spring belongs to a village, thus reinforcing the link between serpent deities and springs. In addition to the link between water and divine presence, there is a connection between springs and deities through divine intervention. Below I exemplify this aspect through the story of the springs at Bhagsu Nag.

Nāg deities usually appear as serpents, but also appear in human form.[22] Or as my informants said, *nāg* deities can take on any form. The old stone slabs I have seen in temples in Bharmaur (these slabs are less frequent in

Kangra) show human alongside serpent images of the deity. Furthermore, there are male and female serpent deities, called *nāg* and *nāgin,* respectively.

There is a strong link between *nāg* deities and Shiva (see also Handa 2004: 11). The connection between *nāg* deities and Shiva is well known and usually explicitly recognized by local people. It is sometimes explained by reference to the iconographic depiction of Shiva wearing a snake around his head. Furthermore, it materially exists in the temples themselves. It is common to find a Shiva *liṅg* inside a *nāg* temple; conversely, a serpent commonly guards the *liṅg* in Shiva temples. One example of a temple that explicitly is held to be both a Shiva and a *nāg* temple is the temple of Bhagsu Nag.

The temple of Bhagsu Nag is in the center of the old village of Bhagsu Nag and has been erected around the village's springs (figure 6.5). Bhagsu Nag is a village in Kangra, close to the tourist center and seat of the Tibetan government in exile in McLeod Ganj. The village is situated at an altitude of approximately two thousand meters; from the village there is a path leading to the Indrahar Pass. Bhagsu Nag is also known as Bhagsu Nath, especially in some of the tourist maps of Himachal Pradesh (*nāth* is translated as lord, and also refers to followers of a Shivaite sect). Handa states that the village is referred to as Bhagsu Nath by non-Gaddi people, whereas Gaddi people call it Bhagsu Nag. According to Handa, one expla-

Figure 6.5 Water sources inside Bhagsu Nag temple. Photo by A. Wagner (2008).

nation for the discrepancy in the names is that the former Bhagsu Nag that referred to a *nāg* deity was changed into Bhagsu Nath under Brahmanic influence (Handa 2004: 133). The place name has not changed for the local population in my experience, nor, for example, in its Hindi spelling on the road signs. I do not follow the historic developments of the temple and its perception by different groups of people in this section. It is the perception of the temple today, and its related activities in which I am interested in the following.

The economy of Bhagsu Nag has undergone drastic changes in recent years. While local people from Bhagsu Nag as well as from surrounding villages report that Bhagsu Nag used to be one of the very poor villages in the area in former times, today it is one of the main tourist spots. In addition to foreign tourists, who started to contribute substantially to the village's economy from the 1990s, it has recently become increasingly popular among Indian tourists who mainly come to visit the temple and the waterfall of Bhagsu Nag and maybe trek to the snow line below the Indrahar Pass. It cannot really be said to be a village anymore, with restaurants, shops, and tourist hostels that keep growing one story taller after each tourist season.

The temple of Bhagsu Nag—in spite of its name—is today widely known as a Shiva temple to the tourists who come to the village. For the Gaddi people, however, Bhagsu Nag is both a temple of Shiva and—as the village's name suggests—of a *nāg* deity. The temple management has been taken over by the government who installs the priest, currently a Pahari-speaking Brahman from the Kangra Valley. But I was told that in former times the *pūjārī* used to be from a Gaddi (non-Brahman) family of Bhagsu Nag. The temple area itself includes several small temples, the main one holding a Shiva *liṅg,* which is said to be situated on top of Bhagsu Nag's springs, and the springs and water outlets of the springs, which are channeled into a large swimming pool. There is also a separate, secluded bathing spot for women and a shelter for pilgrims. The springs are central to the temple. I collected the following story about their origin from a resident of Bhagsu Nag:

> Long time ago, there was a severe drought in Rajasthan. There was a *rājā* [king] named Bhagsu from Rajasthan who came to Himachal in search of water. He went into the mountains and came upon Nag Ḍal [the holy lake north of the Indrahar Pass]. The *nāg* of Nag Ḍal was sleeping and the *rājā* stole a pitcher of water from the lake. The *nāg* woke up, noticed the theft and pursued him. He caught up with him at the place of the temple of Bhagsu Nag and slew him. The *nāg* asked the dying *rājā* why he was stealing his water. The *rājā* then told him about the drought in his country. The *nāg* told him that this being the reason he could have asked for water and he granted the *rājā* a last wish. The *rājā* asked for water in his country and he asked for

his name to remain at the place where he died. His name was attached to the name of the *nāg*. Therefore the place is called Bhagsu Nag. When the *rājā* was hit by the *nāg* his pitcher of water fell down and spilled over. Where the pitcher spilled, water starting flowing continuously. There is said to be an identical temple that also has springs in Rajasthan. (From interview notes, translated by author)

A slightly more elaborated version has been published by Dhobal, an author from Bhagsu Nag, in a leaflet that is sold at the temple (Dhobal n.d.). In this version, the *rājā* is not a common king but a demon king from Rajasthan. The leaflet moreover establishes a connection between Shiva and the *nāg* deity. It reads, "Bhagsunag [sic] is an extremely old *sthān* (place) of Lord Shiva" (ibid.: 17, my translation). Dhobal mentions that it is held that by bathing in the pure water of the springs below the temple all kinds of illness will "go away." He further adds the information that before the arrival of the Dalai Lama and subsequently the tourists, the temple was exclusively visited by local Gaddi families. Bhagsu Nag then was—and still is—a *kul* deity for Gaddi families.[23]

The story about the springs of Bhagsu Nag establishes a connection between the water sources of Bhagsu Nag and the high-altitude lake behind the Indrahar Pass. As the story of the origin of the springs at Bhagsu Nag shows, the *nāg devtā* of Nāg Ḍal is the same as the one of the temple in Bhagsu Nag. This link between the two places, as well as the connection between *nāg* deities and Shiva, is acted out in the practice of *nhauṇ*.

Many people from the Dharamshala area trek to Nāg Ḍal or Lamb Ḍal, but also to Bhagsu Nag and Ḍal Lake on *nhauṇ*. A shopkeeper from Bhagsu Nag told me that he started organizing a *laṅgar* (meal for devotees) at Lamb Ḍal a couple of years ago. While he estimated that the number of visiting devotees had been around 100 to 150 in previous years, he said they were catering to almost 1,000 people in 2008. He could not tell why the popularity had increased so much, but attributed part of the increase to the fact that the word had spread that there was food catering and the comfort that goes with it. He stated that most of the people coming to Lamb Ḍal were local Gaddi people.

Participating in *nhauṇ* is not a collective activity that involves the whole family as much as rituals such as *nuālā, jāgrā,* and *jātar* do. People will certainly not go on their own; for example, the women of an extended family, girlfriends, a father with his children, or brothers and cousins might go together. However, it is not an activity that stresses relations among relatives and would require formal invitations.

In September 2008, I accompanied my hosts to Bhagsu Nag to see and do the *nhauṇ* with them. We stayed overnight with their relatives in Bhagsu Nag, who also run the hotel I usually retreated to. The best time for bathing is the early morning between 4:00 and 5:00 a.m. When we went down to the Bhagsu Nag temple shortly before 5:00 a.m., it seemed that half of Bhagsu—its local inhabitants, not the tourists one usually meets in the streets—was on its way to or from the temple. I had never seen so many people from Bhagsu at one time in the streets before while the village seemed empty of tourists. Since it had been raining the night before the temperature was quite chilly and at 5:00 a.m. it was still dark. The temple was busy. We first went down to the outflow of the springs and the pools. Having a severe cold, I was glad to realize that other people, too, had opted for washing their face, hands, and feet instead of taking a full body bath. Most people however, similar to the group of women I had come with, dived into the pool for men or shower for women, respectively. Moreover, people had brought bottles that they filled with water to take home to use for *pūjā* (during which water is often sprinkled) and to give to relatives and neighbors who had stayed at home. After bathing—performing the *nhauṇ*—we went to the temple's main shrine, which is situated above the springs for a *darśan* of the Shiva *liṅg*. Inside the shrine, the head-priest was giving out *prasād*. Having performed the *nhauṇ* at the springs of Bhagsu Nag, it is common to continue to Ḍal Lake to bathe there, too, and vice versa. Bathing takes place during the whole day, especially with people who bathe at both places. The most auspicious time for the *nhauṇ*, however, is before sunrise. After noon, most local people had completed their *nhauṇ* and the visitors to the temple were again mainly tourists.

Bathing in the holy lakes and springs connected to Shiva and *nāg* deities is considered to be auspicious and purifying. It is also said to protect from illnesses and cure the sick. As *tīrthā* (cross-over places) as well as dwelling places of deities, *ḍal* and springs bring humans into contact with the divine. Through the performance of *nhauṇ*—that is, the purification of the body at an auspicious time—the power and purity of the place is appropriated.

Power of Place: Performing Altitude

Gaddi people frequently point out that there are certain places in the mountains that have a special power. These are always at high altitude and dwelling places of deities. In those places, certain rules of behavior apply. A failure to follow those rules leads to a punishment by the deity. These rules and prohibitions are connected to concrete places associated with the presence of a certain deity—in other words, the rules are place specific and do not generally apply to the mountains, to high altitudes, or to temples. But, for instance, high-altitude lakes are often places where a special code of conduct applies.

The rules, independent of the concrete place, are usually the same. One may not urinate or defecate indiscriminately, but only in circumscribed areas. One may not spit or litter. The fire for cooking can be lit once in the morning and once in the evening, but not in between. When a visitor arrives at a *ḍerā*, the shepherds cannot cook food or tea for him if they have to light the fire again. At meal times, everyone has to serve him- or herself—which is contrary to the usual eating pattern where one person serves the others and is in turn served after they have finished. Leftovers of food may not be kept but are to be buried. One cannot commit any *galat bāt* (wrongdoing). Loud noise and fighting with others are forbidden.[24]

A failure to follow these rules by shepherds is believed to lead to the disappearance of sheep and goats from the flock. It is said that *"bheḍ bakrī gum ho jāte hai"* (the animals get lost). But the consequences of misbehavior are not suffered by shepherds and their flock alone. Related to a powerful place within the Dhauladhar range, a Gaddi Brahman woman from the Bharmaur area narrated the following event:

> This thing has happened to my mum and so we know about these things. Once she had gone . . . with her *māmā* [MB] with the sheep and goats. And there, above where *Śiv-ji's* Kailash is, behind there, the camp had been put up. She had gone for the first time. She did not know that one can't do *latrine* there. Now with women it is like this, that they are in front of *gents* a little bit . . . she went a little bit to one side. And they [her MB and the other shepherds] had not remembered that they should have told her that it is done like this [how it is done]. She sat down a little bit on the side to pee. And when she sat down, there was nothing below her. When she got up there was one snake sitting there like this, one like that, and one like that [indicating that snakes had come from three directions and joined their heads below her]. Three snakes were sitting there. So this [place] had become *chot* [impure]. . . . This is what happens. Well, this is something from our *bītī hui bāt* [past experiences]. Afterwards they told her that one can't do it like that—this means where we have put up our camp, within there you have to do *latrine* you may not go beyond [the space of the camp]. (From interview transcript, translated by author)

From this story nothing more happened than the appearance of snakes as a sign that the woman's misbehavior had spoiled the purity of the place, made it impure, in Gaddi *chot* (Hindi *chūt*). Nāg Ḍal is another place that has the special power of divine presence. Here people report having witnessed the water of the lake suddenly turn black and rise, which is understood to be the consequence of noncompliance with the rules of conduct.

The existence of certain rules concerning the behavior at places where deities dwell is not unique to the Himalayan region. For the Sundarbans in West Bengal, Gosh mentions prohibitions, quite similar to those described above, namely restrictions on urinating, defecating, and spitting (Gosh

2008). I am struck by the contrast of holy places where things humans usually leave behind are considered as dirt whereas they are normal in the village. But I do not agree with functionalist explanations of these rules: for instance, Gosh argues that the rules are a sign of an environmental consciousness embedded in cultural practices (ibid.).[25] Raṇapatiyā's interpretation in terms of purity of place from the vernacular literature offers a more convincing path. Following Raṇapatiyā, these codes of conduct apply in dwelling places of deities so that the purity and serenity of the place are respected (Raṇapatiyā 2001: 54). The idea that a deity's dwelling place needs to be respected and kept free of pollution is also expressed in the story of Gūne Mātā. Here the commentary of the story states that the goddess was opposed to human presence because of the dirt that invariably occurs where humans are. This interpretation also fits what people told me about places where a special code of conduct applies—that is, that by leaving waste products the place becomes *chot* (ritually contaminated or impure).[26]

These rules, however, are not exclusively concerned with impurity caused by pollution through human and other waste products. The purity of place further demands harmony and equality. The code of conduct in these powerful places in this respect requires an altered social practice. The prohibitions concerning the serving of food, for example, undo social hierarchy and thus stand in contrast to norms and behavior connected with the village and everyday life. The prohibitions on fighting and loud noise are another example. The mode of conduct in holy places at high altitudes makes those places stand out from the places of everyday life. Although visiting deities is similar to visiting kin, the dwelling places of deities, at least at high altitudes, as the special code of conduct shows, are places in which humans are only visitors who need to abide by the rules of the place, which is perceived to have a power and authority beyond that of human agency.

Some of these places are further said to have a special power over goats and sheep. Shepherds commonly report that on certain high-altitude pastures they can send off the flocks to graze by themselves in the morning and they will come back on their own in the evening. Not only will they graze on their own, but also they are protected from attacks by bears and leopards. Following the interpretation in these accounts, it is possible for shepherds to positively appropriate the power of high-altitude dwelling places of deities for the guidance of their flocks.

The stories around mountain dwelling goddesses, the *ḍal*, the practice of *nhauṇ,* and the mode of conducted at certain powerful places all bring an importance attached to altitude to the fore. Movements undertaken to visit holy lakes are thereby movements up. While I framed *jāgrā* and *jātar* as visits to the familiar (of a deity's dwelling place) that have a counterpart in inviting the deity into one's home, concerning *nhauṇ,* the movement is unidirectional. Directions of visits are not reversed, except in the water that is brought back home to the village. The holy lakes and springs draw their power from their connection with altitude. The environment unfolds in these movements as dwelling places of deities become meaningful as powerful places through being there, through the bodily presence that requires, for instance, a change in behavior. By observing the rules of behavior in powerful places—for example, by cooking only once, or by shepherds letting their flocks graze and return by themselves—people thus perform high altitudes. Making place in high altitudes is about an appropriation of place through the bodily presence and activities it involves. In the example of *nhauṇ,* it is the power and auspiciousness of the high-altitude lakes and springs that are appropriated by the devotees for gaining individual purity.

In closing this chapter, I want to come back to the idea of a processual understanding of environment. The perspective of environment as coming into being through practical engagements was already foreshadowed in chapter 5, in seeing the environment as something that is walked or enacted in movements. The movements inherent to the religious practice of *jāgrā* and *jātar* as well as *nhauṇ* exemplify the active making of environment. The notion of an inside space was extended in the analysis of *jāgrā* and *jātar* as journeys to visit family deities and thus places belonging to category of the familiar. Beyond the notion of an inside *jāgrā, jātar* and *nhauṇ* can be seen as actions of creating networks of places that make up the landscape of the Dhauladhar. These networks for different persons include different temples, high-altitude lakes, or paths through the mountains. The practices that lead people to undertake these journeys, however, are shared.

These practices enact an environment in which ecological, seasonal, social, spiritual, and economic aspects cannot be separated but are mutually involved with each other. This involvement does apply as discussed in chapter 1, on the one hand, in Descola's sense as a non-Western conceptualization of human–nonhuman relations that does not radically distinguish between physical, social, and spiritual spheres. On the other hand, it applies in Latour's sense of a reality that is constituted by these involvements and interrelationships.

An analysis of when temples and holy lakes are visited reveals a clear time-place framework. Before and during early monsoon is the season to go to visit temples on the southern slopes of the Dhauladhar, while the heavy rains are the time to cross the passes and go to Bharmaur, but also to visit high-altitude lakes. The day for *nhauṇ,* too, corresponds with the overall seasonal framework of visiting high altitudes and thus to notions about right places and times. But while climatic conditions seem dominant in this time-place structure of activities, a closer look reveals further correlations such as with the pastoral cycle—*jāgrā* or *jātar* are commonly held when the flocks have moved through the villages and people purchased animals to give in sacrifice from the owners, with agricultural periods, and, as in the case of seasonal migration, with institutional limitations such as school vacations.

Notes

1. Kaushal has published on the large village festivals in Bharmaur subdistrict (2004). The topic of village and territorial deities in the Western and Central Himalaya has further been discussed by Berti (2001, 2009), Sax (1991, 2002), and Sutherland (1998). In my fieldwork area in Kangra, many villages do not have presiding village deities comparable to those in Bharmaur. In some villages, a temple that is recognized as the village temple, at least by parts of its heterogeneous population in terms of dialect group and castes, is dedicated, for example, to Shiva rather than to a localized deity. Some Kangra villages have local village deities; a well-known example is the village of Bhagsu Nag. Phillimore (1982: 68) also reported village deities and corresponding village festivals linking several villages from his fieldwork village in western Kangra. But this is not the rule. Note also that one deity can be worshiped both as a family and as a village deity.
2. The common expression translated here as deities is *devī-devtā*. *Devī* is the female correlate to *devtā* and corresponds to local goddesses but also denotes the goddess (in her appearance as the great goddess). The term Gaddi deity does not cover all categories of powerful beings: In this chapter, I am not concerned with other powerful beings such as ghosts, demons, or spirits that are seen as dwelling in the mountains and might have qualities and characters that differ from those outlined here for Gaddi deities, notably regarding fierceness and afflicting potential.
3. The women told me that although they do not sacrifice animals to the goddess, they do occasionally, for example, on the occasion of weddings, sacrifice to Baba Balak Nath. Baba Balak Nath is a worshipped saint whose main temple is in Hamirpur district, Himachal Pradesh. Also, other non-Gaddi villagers bought animals when the Gaddi flocks were in the village to raise at home and later give to a deity, as they said. This is contrary to the common assumption that apart from the Gaddi other castes in the Kangra Valley would not sacrifice animals. It is noteworthy that the people who told me about the giving of animals to a deity do not belong to the lower strata of the caste hierarchy, but are at least part of the *vaiśyā* (agricultural castes).
4. For a description of the goddess temples of Himachal Pradesh and their locations, see also Mitra (2007).

5. For a discussion of the history of textual versions of their story including a history of their numbers and locations throughout India in the Puranas and tantric literature, I refer the reader to D.C. Sircar (1973); for an outline of the features of text-based versions, see also Eck (1998b). There are other stories besides the one of the *śakti pīṭhā* connected to each of the goddess temples in the region. Some of the versions are collected in K. Singh (2004–2005), Mitra (2007), and Erndl (1993).
6. For an overview on the more well-known temples in Kangra and Chamba, which includes, but goes beyond, the goddess temples, as well as the stories connected with them, see K. Singh (2004–2005).
7. Probably the most widely worshipped *bābā* are Jai Krishan Giri or Naga Baba, a highly respected *sādhu* from Bharmaur for whom a temple was erected in the Chaurasi temple complex in Bharmaur town, and Baba Balak Nath, a famous Himachali renouncer whose main temple is in Hamirpur District.
8. I have not collected any detailed information or stories on Buārī. I do know, however, that he is a family deity of many Gaddi families. According to some informants, Buārī is a *bābā*, but, according to others, he is a deity from Bharmaur who belongs to the entourage of the god Shiva.
9. More exactly, in *jāgrā* and *jātar* rituals no priests officiates unless they are combined with, for example, a *havan* for which a priest would then be called—the latter occurs, among other things, if a *jātar* is combined with a *muṇḍan* (a ceremony for the first haircut of a boy). Brahman priests further officiate at Gaddi life-cycle rituals and at the rituals for inaugurating a new home. A priest is also called for performing a birthday *pūjā* (chiefly directed at the god Ganesh). The latter is a rather recent "tradition," for which not necessarily the Gaddi Brahman family priest is called, but also other (i.e., Pahari-speaking) Brahmans.
10. Although these larger regional connections are not prominent, some deities are inter alia connected to the local Shiva mythology, for instance the well-known Brahmanī Mātā temple above Bharmaur town.
11. Keeping awake throughout the night is an aspect of religious observance in several Hindu religious practices or rituals.
12. As noted above, the word *jātar* has two meanings. It is also a term for *melā* (village festival) in Bharmaur and in the wider Chamba district.
13. Further, more pragmatic choices in regard to the temple probably influence the decision: availability of space to stay overnight, distance from the house, and so on.
14. This happening is not unique among deities in Himachal Pradesh. Luchesi (2006) has described an example from Kullu where deities act as authorities and enforce their will in land and building disputes.
15. In accord with the timings of the festival season in Bharmaur, an annual festival is also held at the goddess' temple in Bannī on the third Tuesday of Bhadom (Raṇapatiyā 2001; K. Sharma n.d.).
16. That Bannī Mātā is not exclusively worshipped by the Gaddi community, is, for example, evident from the VCD production *Jai Banni Mata* from Chamba that is addressed to and features a Chambiali audience (K. Sharma n.d.), and

was supported by conversations I had with people in Chamba town. Her main devotees, however, are Gaddi families, as her present *celā* confirmed.
17. Furthermore, the current temple structure is built of wood imported from the plains, rarely used in the area, which was also sponsored by a devotee.
18. Note that bathing in everyday usage is referred to by the verb *nhauhaṇā* (to bathe).
19. The probably most famous *ḍal* in Northwest India is the Dal Lake in Kashmir. In Himachal Pradesh, the lake at Khajjiar, a tourist spot in the district of Chamba known as Little Switzerland, is also a holy lake and dwelling place of a *nāg* deity.
20. The story is told in several versions; cf. Kaushal (2001b), Noble (1987), K.P. Sharma (2001) are three of them. Since I am chiefly interested in the aspect of *ḍal* as a crossover here, I content myself with roughly outlining the main aspects from versions in the literature and my field notes.
21. In this respect, he has a goddess as a sister, and if taken down to Kangra by a family, his sister has to be taken down as well. Here, as a man who had traveled to Kugti to bring the deity down to his house in Kangra showed me, Kelang is taken down in his symbol, which is an iron chain (*sangal*) and the goddess in a trident.
22. Khapatiyā in his section on deities in Himachal explicitly lists *nāg* under the category of "deities in human form" (Khapatiyā 1981: 59).
23. Handa reports two stories about the temple of Bhagsu Nag. One is a slightly altered and shortened version of the above, the other one does not refer to the local *nāg* deity behind the Indrahar Pass but to the larger Shiva mythology: "Vasuki, the king of serpents, robbed Shiva of the bowl that contained the water of immortality. Shiva held him guilty of theft. Scared by the punishment for the crime, he fled away, unwittingly holding the bowl upside down. Thus, the precious water spilled out all over. That incident happened at the place, which now is known as Bhagsu, that is, the place from where Vasuki escaped, i.e., *bhag*" (2004: 133). I add this story from Handa, to show that there are several legends around the spring's origin. Handa himself repeatedly notes that there are, on the one hand, local narratives about *nāg* deities and, on the other hand, Brahmanic influences connecting serpent deities to Shiva and Parvati (ibid.: 11), or as in the story above to textual traditions. In contrast to the version I collected among Gaddi people, this story establishes a direct connection between Bhagsu Nag and Shiva but in this does not stand in conflict to Gaddi perceptions of the temple.
24. These rules are also widely reported in the literature, which is remarkably unambiguous on this topic and matches my own findings (Axelby 2005; *Gazetteer of the Chamba State 1904* 1996; Kaushal 1998; Raṇapatiyā 2001).
25. As Gosh states, the prohibitions amount to the rule not to leave traces of human presence behind when moving into the wild, or not domesticated, parts of the forest. He interprets these rules in ecological terms as indicators for the existence of a local sense of nature conservation and ecological equilibrium as well as cautioning against an overexploitation of the environment (Gosh 2008). I do not agree with Gosh that these prohibitions can be satisfactorily

understood in ecological terms. Ecologically speaking, waste products in the village where they occur daily and in high density should be much more crucial for conservation than an occasional waste product in high-altitude places, if an environmental awareness underlies such rules. Furthermore, Gosh's interpretation presumes that the inhabitants of the Sundarbans would subscribe to an ecological consciousness based on the idea of a nature as a wilderness, separate from human influence (cf. for example, Cronon 1996), and thus superimposes the Western concept of nature on local ideas.

26. That deities punish humans for a ritual contamination of their place is not unique to high altitudes. Also, in temples devotees may attract the anger of a deity by approaching the deity in an impure state or by spoiling the purity of the temple environment (Fuller 1992: 16).

7

Environment and the Body
Understanding Water Change

The problem I am concerned with in this chapter can be summarized as follows: For someone traveling between different places, (some) illness or health-related problems are attributed to the water consumed at the new place. Water is emphasized in local discourse as the vehicle through which the change in place is experienced. It is more or less axiomatic that the change in the local water invariably experienced by the traveler can have adverse effects on his or her health. The phenomenon is that of "water change," as the young woman assisting me during the initial stage of my fieldwork said in English. Following my assistant, I use the term water change as an English translation of Hindi expressions such as *pānī badaltā hai* (the water changes). The notion of water change is not particular to the Gaddi, but rather is more widespread through Himachal Pradesh and North India. However, the way the Gaddi refer to a change in water might be particularly illustrating, since their lifestyle makes them sensitive to the perception of place-related phenomena such as water change.

The Phenomenon of Water Change

I first came across the phenomenon of water change when I fell sick during my fieldwork, and my hosts commented that this must be due to the water. We did agree on this point. I was taking my careless drinking of pipe water as the reason for an infection with some kind of waterborne bacteria. I discovered that my hosts were referring to something different, however. My traveling to and from my fieldwork villages, which implied frequent changes in place, was held to be the cause of my health condition; their explanation was that the local water had not suited me. In a different instance, I was advised to eat one time a lot instead of many times a little since this was the right way to eat given the local water and that therefore would solve my digestive problems. What is more, my partner who visited me in India and spent some time with me in village and mountains had a rather bad strain of stomach problems, sore throat, cold and cough, and minor accidents—all of which my Gaddi acquaintances commented on with the remark that the local water was not suitable for him.

Hindi phrases commonly used in North India to express that someone is affected by the local water are, for example, *pānī badaltā hai* (the water changes) or *hamārā pānī usko thīk nahīn lagā* (our water did not become her or him well). In case someone falls sick when traveling to a foreign place, people frequently commented *usko udhar kā pānī suit nahīn kiyā* (the water there did not suit him or her). A further common reaction to hearing about someone falling ill who has traveled is to simply remark, *pānī kī vajah se* (because of the water).

In everyday communication, a reference to water change does not need much clarification, since its meanings are well understood. To give an example, I was sitting in a courtyard in a village one afternoon drinking tea with two women and three girls from the neighborhood. The *māmā* (MB) of one girl had visited the village a few days before on his way to Manali, a (tourist) town in the neighboring district of Kullu. One woman inquired if the girl's family had received news from him, whether he had returned, and how he had liked Manali. The girl answered saying that he had called reporting that he had fallen ill on his trip and returned quickly, but was better now. The second woman present simply remarked, "Ah, because of the water," to which everybody (but me), nodded and the conversation changed to a different topic.

The topic of water change is omnipresent in colloquial language and part of everyday discourse. The change in water does thereby not only affect the digestive system, but also is part of an explanatory model (to use Kleinman's term) for a disturbance of one's well-being. A related observance on water as an explanatory model for illnesses has been made by Lyla Mehta and Anand Punja (2007). The authors studied a resettlement community in Gujarat where people, who had been resettled due to a dam project, fight water shortages and changing water supplies at the new place. "Resettlers say that with the different types of water they consume, their bodies cannot get used to one type of water and thus fails to build up a strong immune system" (ibid.: 199).

In my experience, among the Gaddi illness is attributed to a change in water only if a change in place is involved. Ill-being—for example, headaches, colds, or fatigue—experienced when static in one place, is often related to a change in climate or season but not to the local water. Thus, water change is a phenomenon that is related to a change in environment or movement between places. My following analysis of the phenomenon of water change is led by two interests that I will treat successively. First, I investigate how a change of one's environment is understood to affect one's health, and second I contextualize the role of water as the vehicle by which this change is expressed.

On the Connection between Person and Place in India

How are places thought to influence persons? Drawing on Marriott's transactional model and his theory of the *dividual* person in India (Marriott 1976), several authors have commented on how relations are substantialized in India. According to Marriott, in Hindu transactions actors as well as what they transact are considered to embody coded substances that are exchanged through interactions. Actors are therefore not separable from their actions since both share in the mixing and separation of substances that take place between dividual persons (ibid.). This applies not only to exchanges between human actors, but also to the relations between people and deities (e.g., Moreno and Marriott 1989), or to the relations between people and land (Daniel 1984; Sax 1991, 2009). Ramanujan states that Indians, despite the common perception that they are spiritually oriented, are in fact materialists in that all interactions between humans as well as between humans and nonhumans are thought to consist of an exchange of substances (Ramanujan 1989: 52). As persons, material and nonmaterial things, plants, or places are involved in a constant exchange of their substances, the recipients of substance experience biomoral losses or gains depending on the way the received substance is coded (Marriott 1976: 112).

In respect to the exchanges between person and place, the most detailed study applying Marriott's model remains Valentine Daniel's ethnography from Tamil Nadu, *Fluid Signs: Being a Person the Tamil Way* (1984). Daniel observes, "One of the most important relationships to a Tamil is that which exists between a person and the soil of his ūr" (ibid.: 63). The term *ūr* denotes a home, village, or place of belonging. The *ūr* is a person-centric category. The relationship between persons and an *ūr* or place is seen as that of an exchange of substances. On the one hand, a person absorbs the nature of the soil of a place by eating food grown on it or by drinking water from its springs or simply through residence. On the other hand, persons on their part affect the substance of a place through their food and water leavings, their cremated or buried bodies, and so on, which all mix with the soil of the *ūr* (ibid.).

A place and a person are seen as more or less compatible. Compatibility depends not only on an individual person, but also on his caste. The transformative relationship between *ūr* and person as described by Daniel is characterized by two kinds of substances. One is an inherent disposition or quality, while the other, which translates as intellect, is influenced by and adapts to the inherent disposition of other people or places (ibid.: 92). Daniel gives two examples of instances where the inherent dispositions of a person and a place come to the fore. First, according to Daniel, people who live in a village not considered to be an original village of their caste even after several generations comment that the soil of the place is not seen as perfectly compatible with people from their caste. People who have to live in a place not compatible with their inherent substance can adapt to the place when the place's inherent substance influences and changes their "intellect." However, they will never be as compatible as people who share both intellect and the inherent quality of a place. Moreover, the notion of compatibility between people and the soil of a place, or better between the respective inherent substances, not only applies to the context of the village, but also to the city. Following Daniel, people who want to leave for an unknown city to work there will look for relatives or at least people from the same caste who are living there. This is not done in order to establish contact with them, but to know whether one of one's kind can succeed in that place (ibid.: 81). Succeeding is here attributed to the compatibility of the inherent substances.

The notion of exchanges of substance between people and place is not restricted to South India. It has also been reported from North India (Lamb 2000; Polit 2006; Sax 1991, 2009). Mark Baker (2005) remarks that people in the Kangra Valley place a high importance on home grown crops—in other words on crops grown on their fields as opposed to grains purchased from a shop. This observation, on which Baker does not comment further, is clarified in the light of what, for example, Karin Polit observed for Garhwal. Similar to Daniel's findings from Tamil Nadu, Polit has argued for Garhwali people that "a person's 'nature' is strongly affected by the place he or she lives. The food from the fields, prepared by a certain person, and the water from the village well have a substantial influence on a person's character, appearance and health" (Polit 2006: 62). Sax writes on the notion of shared substances between people and their place of living in Garhwal:

> The air one breathes, the water one drinks, the soil in which one grows one's food—all of these affect one's body and mind, and the village environment

is in turn affected by the people who work on its soil, care for it, perform rituals on it, and return their waste products to it. This is not an abstract or sentimental connection, but rather a matter of shared mutual substance. You are not only "what you eat" but also "where you live," so that in a very real sense the substantial and moral natures of the villagers of Chamoli are partly determined by their constant transactions with the houses, villages, fields, and forests that make up their environment. (Sax 2009: 54)

Thereby, as Polit points out, the relationship between person and place differs according to gender and age, "because people of different age and gender are thought of as having different qualities" (Polit 2006: 35; see also Lamb 2000).

A slightly different perspective on the connection between person and place offers the concept of local biology. Local biology as an analytical concept was developed in the field of medical anthropology and has been adapted by sensorial anthropology. The concept of local biologies was first introduced in medical anthropology by Margaret Lock. Lock coined the term local biologies in her study on menopausal women in Japan. In their cross-cultural study of menopause-related symptoms, Lock and Kaufert (2001) argue for the recognition of the interconnectedness of biology and culture. Biology is local rather than universal, because human biology and culture stand in a feedback relationship mutually influencing each other. Local biologies here point to the way culture shapes the biological body through influences on lifestyle, food, health-related behavior, and so on (Lock and Kaufert).

The concept of local biologies has been taken up by Mark Nichter (2008). Nichter modifies the idea of local biologies as a description of the cultural influences on the biological body to include bodily experience. With the shift to sensorial experiences of the body and bodily processes, the concept of local biology becomes adapted to sensorial anthropology, which with Nichter "explores how sensations are experienced phenomenologically, interpreted culturally, and responded to socially" (ibid.: 166). Nichter's concept of local biology, which I will adopt in the following, joins theories on perception and bodily experience as advocated by Casey (1996) and Ingold (2000). Casey and Ingold both point out the direct sensory perception of the environment through the body, a body that in Ingold's terms is mingled with the environment (Ingold 2000, 2007), or, in Casey words "is as intelligent about the cultural specificities of a place as it is aesthesiologically sensitive to the perceptual particularities of that same place" (Casey 1996: 34).

Following the concept of local biology, people embody places through the consumption of local food and water, but also through their habits of eating. Both what one eats as well as when, how often, and how much affects one's biological body. As Nichter states, the relation of body, food, and environment, as well as season, shapes the ecological constitution of human beings. This constitution changes from place to place just as local climate and food, eating times, and so on, change. These changes are sensorially experienced in the body and commented upon culturally. Local biology and bodily experience are thereby influenced by an "analogical and metaphorical understanding of bodily processes" or "ethnophysiology" (Nichter 2008: 172). Exploring local biology means exploring how people experience and understand the feedback loop between their body, their mind, and the environment. Nichter suggests exploring in terms of local biology, among other things, the impact of different diets "on the bodies and lived sensorial experience of different populations across the life course and at times of illness and distress" (ibid.: 165). One example of the attention paid to local biology in relation to dietary regimes are the dietary practices in South Indian villages in Karnataka that are based on a staple diet of rice:

> The rice digestive cycle constitutes a state of physiological normality upon which the villager bases many notions of health. Daily rice consumption ... is responsible for a fairly routine food transit time, a hunger cycle so finely tuned that plantation agricultural laborers are able to tell time by their stomachs, and a set of body signs such as urine and fecal output, color, consistency and smell which serve as measures of normal health. (Nichter 1986: 188)

With a stable diet of rice, small deviations in eating patterns are felt as changes in bodily processes and become a matter of concern for the Karnataka villagers studied by Nichter.

The attuning of perception to ecological and bodily conditions shows that local biology is not just a metaphor, although it can be metaphorical. Local biology starts from the system of resonance between body, mind and environment. In this, its perspective of analysis differs from ethnosociological interpretations. As Francis Zimmermann points out in *The Jungle and the Aroma of Meats,* the ecological themes in ayurvedic texts that he analyzes deal with hidden properties of materials and savors of the soil, which do not stem from empirical observation but from a "revelation" proliferated in texts (Zimmermann 1987: 3). Thus, according to Zimmermann, the qualities of place in ayurvedic theory start from an idea and not from the observation of ecology. Marriott and Daniel, too, when talking about the matching of substances, talk about conceptions of body, person, and place. Albeit these ideas are embodied, they are sociological comments. Each substance carries a code that determines compatibility. Local biology, on the contrary, starts with practical knowledge and observation of ecological conditions of places as well as of one's body. In Nichter's terms, local biology focuses on ethnophysiology rather than ethnosociology. Both frameworks are not contradictory but rather take on different perspectives.

Interpreting phenomena in the framework of local biology draws attention to sensory perception and informed knowledge of local ecology. As Casey remarks, "To live locally, and to know is first of all to know the place one is in" (1996: 18). Local biology is linked to the physical body and experiences of and in the physical body: it refers not only to qualities considered inherent to different foods or water, but also to perceived changes in sensorial experiences of one's bodily processes.

Ethnographic Findings: The Concept of *Ādat*

When I went back to the field a second time, I had theories about the exchanges of substances between persons and places in mind. I concentrated on how people talk about place, belonging, and—so I was hoping—a matching of substances. I expected to find concepts of matching substances, similar to the ones Daniel describes for Tamil Nadu, among the Gaddi in North India. Seen from Heidelberg, ideas about substances of persons and places and their mutual compatibility seemed to make sense as an explanation of why water change affects people coming to new places. However, in conversations I had with people on the topic of water change, instead of notions of qualities or substances, the word *ādat* (habit), struck me as coming up repeatedly.

In its meaning of habit, *ādat* is used in expressions such as *ādat honā* (to have the habit, to be used to) and *ādat ban jānā* (to become accustomed to). The corollary of the notion of *ādat* is that if one is not used to something, one will have to get used to it, which implies a process of adjustment.

The idea of *ādat*, of being used to something, is closely linked to the explanation of falling sick through a change in place and water. The following explanations were given to me during a discussion I had with one informant on the meaning of water change:

> *Pānī badaltā hai* [the water changes] means that if you go to a different place the water there tastes different. There are different *vitamins* in the water. This does not apply to the filtered bottle water [which tastes the same everywhere].
>
> Your *digestion* has to adjust, especially when you travel [to that place] for the first time or if you travel too quickly. You can fall sick due to this. In any case, it will have an effect on your body. (From interview notes, translated by author)

To my question if he experiences water change, my informant, a man in his late fifties, who commuted regularly between his two homes in Bharmaur and Kangra, thus regularly changing environment and altitudes, replied,

> I am also affected. But with minor changes. But it does affect me, too. (From interview notes, translated by author)

To recapitulate this explanation: Water varies according to place in its composition. The differences in the water are perceivable in its taste. The bodily processes are disturbed by a change in water and the body needs to adjust to the unaccustomed water. This is notable in effects the consumption of water has on a person's digestive process when coming to a new place. The process of digestion is perceived to deviate from its normal state. The local water affects all travelers. However, adverse effects on one's health are less serious if one regularly travels to a place and more severe if one travels to a place either for the first time or travels very quickly. Generally, people who move from one place to another are vulnerable to water change.[1] Bottled water is explicitly exempted by my informant. It is perceived to taste the same everywhere and thus, I infer, lacks a connection to a concrete place. In local discourse, bottled water is often devalued as tasteless water and contrasted with "good" water from local springs.[2]

Another context in which people refer to a change in water that makes one sick until one has adjusted, is the case of women who change their place of residence after marriage. One example is the case of a woman, now in her late forties or early fifties, who grew up in Bharmaur subdistrict and was married to a man living in Kangra. She told me that the occasion of her marriage was the first time she had ever gone to Kangra. At first, she did not like Kangra at all, because she had left her *māykā* (natal home) behind, and, as she said, *apnā-apnā ilakā acchā lagtā hai* (one likes one's own place best). She reported having fallen ill for three successive years each April on the onset of the *garmī* (hot season). In April, the weather changes quite rapidly from cold to warm. She remembered having been sick with fever, headaches, and colds, and explained that this was due to the water. She said that it did not suit her. She was of the opinion that this would not have happened to her had she visited Kangra prior to her marriage. The fourth year, she said, she did not fall sick, since *ādat ban giyā* (she had adjusted to the new place). Contrary to the interview partner cited above, she strongly rejected experiencing difficulties going back to Bharmaur, her native region. She owns land in Bharmaur and travels there once a year to collect a share of the harvest from the tenants and to visit relatives, but reports not being affected by the change in water when going there.

Another case of ill-being that is considered to be caused by a change in environment after a shift of residence was related by a woman who married in the opposite direction, from Kangra to Bharmaur. In her case, she, now a grandmother, moved to Bharmaur only ten years ago when her husband was given a post there, which was several years after their marriage. She described herself as being from the plain and open Kangra region and reports to have been so terrified when she first saw the steep mountains of Bharmaur that she lay sick in bed with a fever for three days, not able to get up. Trying to get up she remembered being overcome by dizziness at the sight of the mountains, which rise like a wall across the valley from her house, so that she had to lie down again immediately. She related her illness to the sight of the steep mountains, not explicitly to the local water. However, *ādat* (habituation) is the clue to getting well again. She said she had become habituated to the environment and experiences no problems today, but she likes Kangra better because one likes one's own region.

In order to better understand the concept of *ādat* employed in the conversations cited above, I turn to three other contexts in which habit seems to be important, although not directly related to a change in water. Habit, like water change, is a common part of everyday discourse.

One feature of the seasonal migration that is practiced by the Gaddi is that one gets out of the heat in the plains in summer and the cold of the mountains in winter. One man from Kangra, about sixty years of age, had been telling me about the Gaddi's migration and their adaptation to the seasons. In his childhood, his family was involved in a small-scale seasonal migration not uncommon to the area around Dharamshala. They had two houses, one in a village at lower elevations and one close to McLeod Ganj on the slopes of the Dhauladhar. They lived four months of the year up in the hills and the rest of the year down in the valley. His family stopped moving and settled in the lower village when he was still in school. Since he mentioned how enjoyable and cool the upper villages are during the hot season, I inquired if he was not suffering from the heat in the lower villages. He declared not to be bothered by the heat in the valley, saying one would get used to the place where one lives. Since in his statement he did not elaborate on the meaning of the phrase "to get used to" in reference to the climatic conditions, it is not absolutely clear if his remark is linked to the concept of *ādat*. The next examples, however, strongly suggest that getting used to something is not a trivial phrase but carries meaning in terms of person-place or person-environment interactions.

My host families and several of their neighbors connected the illness experiences of my partner during his visit to the fact that he changed places too quickly—with and without referring to the water. Somewhat embarrassed about bothering my hosts with our illness episodes, I explained that he was usually very healthy back in Germany. This remark only confirmed their observation that it was the change in place that caused him trouble. I was reminded that I had also fallen sick at first. But as they said I had gotten used to the place: *tumhārī ādat ban gaī* (it has become your habit). Something which my partner who just arrived had not accomplished so far.

A further observation I made concerning habit or habituation was the expectation toward my adaptation to food in India, independent of illnesses. I was often puzzled by the naturalness with which people assumed that I would not like their Indian food, and their readiness to offer me to prepare my own dishes. Two questions that were frequently asked were if I would eat local food and if I was experiencing problems with the local food. Contrary to my hosts' expectations, I was eager to try out their food, being curious about its taste, which for me was new. What perplexed me even more was that by the time I was longing for the taste of German food again my hosts had decided that I had adapted absolutely well to the local dishes and did not need to go back to my German food. Although it still contrasts with my inner food cravings, I do understand my hosts better in the light of the concept of *ādat:* one will experience difficulties in eating new food, food that one is not accustomed to and that varies from one's usual diet. The more one gets used to the local food, however, the problems and thus the necessity to eat one's own food cease. What people comment on is a process of habituation and not a question of personal likings. Considerations about food and eating are not primarily statements of taste but relate to preoccupations with health and habituation to the conditions in a place.

To conclude, *ādat* is a concept about being habituated to or a process of habituation to the conditions of a certain environment or place. People take recourse to *ādat* as an explanation when, with a movement between places, a change in well-being occurs. Water as a vehicle through which this change in condition at a new place is experienced, and accordingly reference to water change, is only one instance, although a frequently mentioned one, of this perceived process of adjustment between body and environment.

Getting Attuned to Place

From my ethnographic findings, falling ill after a change in place is often explained as the result of a change in the local water. The change in the local water from one place to the other is experienced by persons through bodily processes, induced by the intake of the water into their body. Water change, in short, refers to observations of bodily processes in connection with changes in the environment. When traveling or moving to a new place, digestive problems as well as fever, cold, cough, and dizziness are often attributed to a change in the water and water change is even used as a comment on accidents. Explanations of the meaning of water change and its results on the body are not uniform. They vary from explanations that explicitly relate the taste and composition of water in different places to observations on the influence of travel on the digestive system, to little articulate matter-of-fact statements on water change that imply connections between unaccustomed places, adverse health effects, and the local water. Further investigation might show differences according to gender and age of the informants concerning the reference to water change as causing health problems. Since people's conditions and vulnerabilities are perceived to vary according to gender and to stages in life, such as childhood, old age but also pregnancy and lactation, or for persons already suffering from poor health conditions, susceptibility to water change is likely to be experienced and dealt with differently.

The phenomenon of water change is closely linked to the local concept of *ādat*. Reference to *ādat*, in short, expresses the idea of habituation, of being accustomed to something. Not being accustomed to a place is the explanation for a disruption of one's health. The concept of *ādat* makes water change as an explanation for illnesses comprehensible. What is considered to cause illness is what is contrary to one's habit, first and foremost abrupt changes in place. These changes occur as a consequence of changes in the local ecology. They are felt in the body and through bodily processes. Changes in digestion or body temperature are subsequently attributed to changes in place, often via the idiom of water. Local remedies for water change accordingly are the avoidance of abrupt changes in place, food, and water—for example, of proceeding too fast when traveling from one place to another. The advice I received to adapt my eating habits to the local water (eat one time a lot, not several times), too, points to observations on local biology: to the connection between bodily processes and ecology.

Thus when Gaddi talk about a change in water, they—contrary to my research hypothesis—do not refer to an inherent compatibility between person and place. One can get accustomed to new places with the bodily adaption to its ecology. The observation of ecological phenomena—namely, the influence of environment, food, water, and climate on bodily processes—is what people comment on when they relate illness to a change in water, and not ideas on ideational qualities of person and place. This is not to say that notions of person-place relations discussed in ethnosociological approaches are absent among the Gaddi. But in the context discussed here, it is rather the focus of the analytical concept of local biology—that is, attention to a sensory attuning to place and the feedback relation between the body and ecological conditions, that is commented upon, and that forms the basis for subsequent conceptualizations of these changes.

The focus on the perception of bodily experiences in the individual body is a new aspect in the framework of local biology in comparison to ethnosociological approaches. It shows that ideas of people-place relations are also informed by ecological and physiological observations. This matches Ingold's argument that humans are agents-in-an-environment with which they stand in a physical and sensory relation. Interchanges through the intake of water, as well as of food, and digestive processes that Nichter points to, are another example of these active involvements. And as the example of water change shows, people pay attention to these sensory, physical involvements of body and environment and endow them with cultural meanings.

Water as a Vehicle

Apart from its pronounced role in person-place interactions, water, especially its availability, is an important topic in regional mythology and religious practices: In several places in the region, women from the royal families are said to have sacrificed themselves in exchange for the flow of irrigation water in the canal system and are now revered as deities.[3] These goddesses and other deities presiding over the water flow in the irrigation channels are appropriated at the time of sowing rice on the irrigated terraces (see also Baker 2005). The Gaddi in Kangra who own irrigated land share in the system of irrigation management, including its rituals. Moreover, the appearance of springs is in several cases connected to boons granted by a *sādhu* (ascetic) or a deity. In other instances, the existence of springs—for example in places considered unlikely to harbor water sources such as ridge tops or rocky ground—is connected to its proximity to a deity's dwelling place. Water here is a life production force and as such is important for fertility, often related to females, whether goddesses or royal women, but also to *nāg* deities. Water can further be auspicious and has purifying as well as healing powers.

In short, water plays a prominent role in engagements with the environment among the Gaddi. It further receives attention in observations of ecological conditions. Many Gaddi people either through their experience as shepherds, through the experience of seasonal migration, or merely through social practices that lead them into the mountains have an intimate ecological knowledge of different places, especially of different altitudinal zones, corresponding climates, vegetational features, seasonal changes, and so forth. Perception of changes in water and notions of qualities of water form an important part in observations of local ecologies.

The characteristics of water are perceived to vary according to altitude. Generally it is said that the higher the altitude, the cooler the water. Shepherds report that the higher one moves into the mountains, the worse is the taste of boiled rice. Rice tastes worst on the high summer pastures in Lahul and best in the Kangra Valley. This was first mentioned to me as I sat in a shepherds' camp waiting for a meal of rice on the southern slopes of the Dhauladhar with two flock owners and one of their spouses. The two shepherds were preparing to cross the Indrahar Pass to Bharmaur from where they would move onwards, cross the Pir Panjal range, and take their flock to the summer pastures in Lahul. They, in short, complete the widest range of transhumance practiced by the Gaddi, in terms of latitude and altitude. They explained that the rice has little taste when cooked in the mountains because the water in the mountains is so cold that the rice does not cook properly, although, they added, the water in which the rice was cooked did of course boil. The observation is that the taste of cooked rice decreases as altitude increases. The shepherds related this to the decrease in the (unheated) water's temperature, which can be heated but is said to be so cold in itself that cooking with it has not the same effect as in water in lower altitudes.[4]

When I discussed this observation back in the village in Kangra, people there who practice a seasonal migration to Bharmaur immediately confirmed the shepherds' observation regarding the taste of boiled rice. They added that the difference in the water is also notable in cooking time. While rice, which is usually prepared in pressure cookers, needs "two whistles" (of the pressure cooker) to be done in Bharmaur, it needs only "one whistle" in Kangra. The longer cooking time in Bharmaur, just like the decrease in taste, was related to the coldness of the water. The water was said to be comparatively warmer in the lower-lying Kangra villages and thus the rice boiled quicker.

Moreover, concerning altitudes, the cool water in the mountains is said to increase one's hunger. Therefore going to temples or holy lakes in the Dhauladhar, going to Bharmaur, or visiting shepherds in their camp in the mountains, people commonly say that due to the cold water, they feel more hunger and eat more than usual.[5]

Gaddi people further elaborate on the quality of water—that is, on water that is good to drink and good for one's body—and they name places that have good water. This is not to say that traveling to these places one will not experience effects of water change. One general characteristic of *acchā pānī* (good water) is to be cool. Cool and good water is to be found at high altitudes—in other words, within higher elevations of the Dhauladhar and notably in Bharmaur. The perceived quality and coldness of water increase with altitude. While, in the context of the above-mentioned observation that with an increase in altitude and decrease in water temperature the taste of rice decreases, here coolness is valued positively. Spring water is also supposed to be better in high-altitude springs in Bharmaur than in springs in Kangra.

Regarding the intake of substances into the body, the role of water for health is stressed over the role of food. Through their consumption, both water and food pass the boundary of the physical body and affect bodily processes. Water as well as food such as rice or wheat grains, for example, through the soil in which they grow, can be seen as connected to place. However, it is water where the emphasis is made that it changes with place rather than the rice or wheat grains. One informant explained to me that rice and wheat vary from place to place because they grow in different water. Thus, water affects both humans and plants, and plants like humans are seen to relate to place through water.

Water is thus a marked feature of the environment, as indicated by its role in local biology, ecological perception, local mythology and religious practices. Water is used directly and metaphorically to express observations of body-ecology interactions; beyond being a vehicle through which person-place relations are expressed, however, its sources and qualities are emphasized in several ways when Gaddi people talk about the environment. Through their practices of seasonal migration, transhumant pastoralism, and their mutual involvements with their environment through social and religious practices, the Gaddi acquire an intimate knowledge of the local ecology. Their lifestyle in comparison to the majority of the Pahari population of Kangra thereby confronts them regularly with the different places in their local environment, including different altitudes, and makes them sensitive to the perceptions of changes occurring according to place and to the perception of connected phenomena such as water change.

Notes

1: See my comment below on possible differences between categories of persons in their susceptibility to water change. To elaborate this point, however, further research is necessary.
2. My informant treated bottled water as a uniform category. In Himachal Pradesh, depending on the production company, mineral water from springs as well as treated ground water is sold. I keep with the observation of my informant here. The comment was actually aimed at me since I often brought

a bottle or two of purchased water to the village with me and then switched to drinking the local spring water, which was encouraged by the local people. Several local people who watched me buy or consume bottled water voiced their doubts whether that water was good and had any taste.
3. The most prominent case is the story of the Queen Sunayana of Chamba, wife of Sahila Varman, revered as Sui Mātā and worshiped in the annual Chamba fair (see, for example, *Gazetteer of Chamba 1904* 1996). A similar story—with the exception that here it was the king's daughter-in-law, is told about the irrigation channel of Chari, a town west of Dharamshala.
4. Natural science, too, observes a change in the taste of rice according to altitude. In the network (to use Latour's term) of the natural sciences, the varying taste of rice in different altitudes is explained as a consequence of a change in air pressure that decreases the boiling point of water, the temperature of which in turn influences the release of the rice's flavors and thus its taste.
5. This connection that people make between hunger and altitude is also reported by Noble (1987: 30).

8

Cool Water, Short Green Grass, and Fir Trees

The Aesthetics of Environment

This last chapter is concerned with environmental aesthetics, foremost in the perception of places and landscapes. The focus on aesthetics takes up Casey's statement that places are sensed—that is, experienced through the body, which is both emplaced and an active agent in a place (Casey 1996: 34). This reinforces the argument that place-making also occurs through practical activities in—and therefore physical experience of—a place. As Ingold writes:

> A place owes its character to the experiences it affords to those who spend time there—to the sights, sounds and indeed smells that constitute its specific ambience. And these, in turn, depend on the kinds of activities in which its inhabitants engage. It is from this relational context of people's engagement with the world, in the business of dwelling, that each place draws its unique significance. (Ingold 2000: 192)

To understand ideas about environmental aesthetics—and thus to add this further dimension to the study of place-making—I propose to take seriously the idea that places are sensorily perceived and experienced through active engagements. However, beyond concrete activities of being in place, this sensing of places finds expression in ideas of aesthetics of environment and statements on good places. While relating to sensory perception, the term aesthetics also denotes a concept. In the following, I will thus be analyzing statements on aesthetics and their material expressions, having in mind that these are informed by practical experience and bodily perception, but I expect them to go beyond this direct engagement with the environment.

The Aesthetics of Environment

The term aesthetics has at least two meanings. On the one hand, it denotes a sense of beauty; on the other hand, it refers to forms of sensory perception. The term aesthetics is commonly used in the first definition and describes the perception of beauty, mostly concerning its visual perception. Aesthetics in this understanding is shaped by a European understanding of and discourse on beauty. Gell in his writing on art has therefore cautioned against the search for the aesthetic in other cultures: "In fact, . . . I am far from convinced that every 'culture' has a component of its ideational system which is comparable to our own 'aesthetics'" (Gell 1998: 3).

My research in Himachal Pradesh revealed that the people there do have an explicit sense of aesthetics, especially when talking about landscapes. Aesthetics as used here thereby implies a positive evaluation. The way people talk about landscapes and places reveals that aesthetics in its meaning of visual perception, albeit present, falls short of grasping what people perceive to be the attributes of a good place. When talking about environment and place, aesthetics here, as I will show below, has to be defined as sensory perception, above and beyond the sense of vision. Several authors have pointed to perception through the senses in engagements with environment and landscape. Bloch (1995) has described the stress put on visuality in evaluation of landscapes by the Zafimaniry of Madagascar who treasure clear views over the landscape. That environments and landscapes need not primarily be perceived visually has been put forward by Gell for the Umeda (1995), Feld for the Kaluli (1996), and Weiner for the Foi (1991). These authors have shown that in Papua New Guinea rainforest societies the sense of hearing is crucial in people's perceptions and representations of their surroundings.

The people I met and conversed with during my fieldwork frequently and explicitly commented on aesthetics of places according to their ecological features. Environmental aesthetics is a topic that is frequently mentioned when people talk about places. People also readily comment on aesthetic features when asked which places they like. They further inquire about aesthetic judgments of places by others. There are certain attributes of environments that lead to descriptions of these environments as *acchā*. The word *acchā* covers a range of meanings and can be translated as good, nice, fine, pleasant, or healthy. In respect to aesthetics of place, these shades of meaning all figure in judging a place as being *acchā*. In the following, I translate *acchā* as good.

Places that are described as being good places usually convey a striking conformity concerning their characteristics. Variations according to personal likings, of course, do occur, but they are in my experience rather rare regarding the core attributes. Good places are usually situated in the mountains. The environment is said to be good because it is *ṭhaṇḍā* (cool).[1] It has cool air and cool water. Several people responded to my question of how they had liked their stay at a certain place, usually at higher altitudes, by saying it had been *acchā* and the water had been *bilkul ṭhaṇḍā* (absolutely cold). Again, it is water that figures prominently in expressing involvements of humans with their environment (see chapter 7). A good environment is further said to be *śantī* (peaceful). Peaceful here means at a distance from roads, loud traffic, many passers-by, crowded neighborhoods, and the like. In spite of being located in the mountains, good places are quite plain, and they are *khulā* (open). They enable an open view, which might very well be a view onto the mountains. What is more, people comment that a place is *acchā* because it is green, and particularly because it has *chotā-chotā, hārā-hārā ghās* (very short, very green grass, the doubling being intensive).[2]

Aesthetic judgments of places are not absolute but vary according to the season. This time component of place evaluation is especially explicit in the elder generation's appraisal of seasonal migration as a life style. Many old people consider it a good way of life to live the warm months up in Bharmaur and the cold months down in Kangra. Moreover, I learned that an absolute inquiry about which place is best is the wrong question, since which place is considered good depends on the season. Seasonality matters—concerning aesthetic ideas and preferences, but also concerning activities. There are right times to be in a place as expressed by the statement "in winter there is no one in the mountains" cited in the introduction. The timing of activities was already mentioned in chapter 6 in connection with the respective seasons to visit temples on the southern side and on the northern side of the Dhauladhar. This time-place matrix is further reflected in what people consider to be the best time of the year. When I asked people about their favorite month or season, most respondents in Kangra answered either the season *hair* (mid-September–mid-December), which is after the monsoon rains but still warm, or the season *hīyūnd* (mid-December–mid-March, Hindi: *sardī*). Kātī (mid-October–mid-November) was the favorite month for most respondents in Kangra. It is cool but not too cold yet, not raining, and the weather is clear. The worst season in

Kangra is said to be *barsālā* (monsoon). In Bharmaur *barsālā* is considered to be the best season because during the monsoon—which rains off on the southern slopes of the Dhauladhar and does not hit Bharmaur—Bharmaur's vegetation is green, it is warm but still cool compared to Kangra, and fruits and vegetables ripen. Not only is *barsālā* the time to go on pilgrimage or visits to Bharmaur for people from Kangra, but also it is the best time to come and visit their area, according to the Bharmaur villagers I met. They repeatedly informed me that I had chosen the wrong season when I came to Bharmaur in November for my first month of fieldwork.

In spite of the seasonal evaluation of places, the descriptions cool, peaceful, green, and open are in a general sense—that is, independent of concrete places and times—positive descriptions of places in terms of notions of aesthetics. Cool as an attribute of a pleasant place confirms the necessity to define the aesthetic with reference to sensory perception beyond the sense of vision. The descriptions of good places show that feeling as a way of perceiving is as important in evaluations of places as seeing (green, open). Coolness as a positive quality of a place illustrates that places are felt, and conversely ideas about what is pleasant to feel feed into notions of good places.

Furthermore, following Halliburton (2003) in his writing on the aesthetics of healing, the description of something as cool or cooling "is an idiom for a pleasant effect based on lay South Asian concepts of health and aesthetics" (ibid.: 174). Here there might be a connection between classifications of food, emotions, and so on, as hot or cold, and cool as an attribute of a good place. Halliburton points to the fact that when people talk about something as causing heat or being cooling in relation to their body and to healing practices, they not only speak about abstract ideas, but also talk about processes that are perceived through the senses and judged as more or less pleasant. I suggest that in the South Asian context it is not surprising to come upon cool as an aesthetic quality. As Halliburton states, cooling "has the general, pragmatic meaning of a pleasant aesthetic effect and can be applied in many contexts" (ibid.: 175).

Good Places: The Mountains Revisited

The good place par excellence is Lahul, the region where the high alpine summer pastures are located. Lahul fits the above descriptions of a good place in almost every account that I was given of it, and is also generally explicitly said to be *acchā*. The majority of shepherds who move to Lahul consider Lahul to be the best place on their transhumance route in terms of aesthetic qualities. They qualify this by saying that the area is plain, and air and water are cool, which contrasts with the climate in the Kangra Valley at the same time of the year.[3] The grass is short and green, and nourishing for the sheep and goats. Lahul is peaceful, there are no mosquitoes, and for lack of forest trees there is no firewood, but also no bears or leopards. As one man put it, "Sheep and goats, and men live well there."

Although only those shepherds who have their summer grazing grounds in Lahul and move there with their flocks have actually been there, it is very common for other people, too, to describe the landscape of Lahul and its qualities—first and foremost that Lahul is plain and cool. In fact, going to Lahul is one of the few things Gaddi women do not do. While there is a gender-specific traditional division of labor among the Gaddi, with women occupied with domestic chores and the bulk of agricultural work, and men tending the flocks, activities and corresponding spatial zones are generally not strongly or exclusively gendered. Women also go into the mountains and help out in herding sheep. The only two things women cannot do are plowing and going to the pastures in Lahul. The prohibition for women to go to Lahul fits into Hindu ideas of purity and about high mountains as a pure space that might be polluted by women, among other things through menstruation. However, I found no one who gave me purity as a reason why women do not go to Lahul. That purity as an explanation is absent from Gaddi accounts on why women cannot go to Lahul fits with general attitudes toward women and purity. Among the Gaddi, there are no strong ideas on women as polluting. During menstruation, for example, women are not restricted in their cooking chores in most villages—unlike in many other parts of North India. There are further only a few temples that women may not enter at all because women are seen as generally impure. Moreover, in contrast to Lahul, women visit other high-altitude places in the mountains such as the Mani Mahesh Lake beneath Mount Kailash and other high-altitude lakes or alpine pastures in Bharmaur subdistrict. This is why the prohibition to go to Lahul sticks out as exceptional and cannot be generalized for high-altitude places. However, even if they cannot go there themselves, women and girls are able to give detailed descriptions of Lahul. It is remarkable that accounts of Lahul are more widely shared—at least verbally—than, for instance, descriptions of other parts of Himachal, Delhi, or Chandigarh, all places to which many people travel or migrate for work.[4]

Although Lahul is singled out as a good place par excellence, attributes of good places do not apply exclusively to Lahul. Concerning the qualities of place, there is, again, a contrast between the plains and the mountains. The mountains are explicitly contrasted with Punjab (i.e., the North Indian plain). Punjab is generally devalued vis-à-vis the mountains. In contrast to the notion of the mountains as an inside space, as the places where Gaddi people as well as Gaddi deities live, the Punjab appears as an non-Gaddi outside.

The way shepherds talk about Punjab when commenting on the places on their transhumance route is illustrative. The Punjab is generally the less liked part of the transhumance route. The landscape where the flocks stay in Punjab, referred to as *jañgal* (jungle), is the rather dry, bushy environment of the Shivalik foothills (here not to be translated as forest). Grazing areas in the *jañgal* are judged less appealing than grazing areas in the mountains, referred to as *pahāṛ* (mountain). One shepherd lamenting on the bad weather remarked that in the Punjab rain was worse than in the mountains: in the mountains there were always some rocks, caves, or sheds erected by people who bring their cattle to graze, whereas in Punjab there was nowhere to seek shelter. Many shepherds, moreover, consider herding flocks in the winter grazing grounds more difficult than in the mountains, because, as they say, the flocks need more supervision. Because the animals often have to be grazed in the proximity of the fields of local farmers, care has to be taken that they do not feed on the crops for which compensation will have to be paid. Furthermore, many herders complain that they have to protect their flocks from thieves. Therefore, more helpers—about twice as many people as on the alpine pastures—are needed during winter grazing. Axelby (2005) and Saberwal (1999) report a similar situation in the winter grazing grounds. More labor needed in Punjab also means fewer visits home for the shepherds than when they are in the mountains, albeit in Punjab coming and going is made easy by buses. The perception that herding in the Punjab is more problematic than in the mountains is paralleled by the notion of the Punjab as other people's area as compared to the mountains, which are more readily perceived as the own area.[5]

Apart from characterizations of the two broad categories—up and down, or Lahul and Punjab—people seldom comment on the mountains as a unit. Landscape is rather talked about in terms of concrete, named places. Casey's insistence that we live in a place world holds true here at an empirical level (Casey 1996). The landscape of the Dhauladhar, when evoked in everyday discourse on good places, consists of a network of place names including villages, temples, *dhār* (grazing tracts in the mountains), domains of deities, hillsides, and so forth.[6]

In the Dhauladhar range, there are several places that are said to be *acchā*. Around Dharamshala the temple of Gūne Mātā, described in chapter 6, is widely considered to be a good place for being up in the mountains, but *khulā* (open), *śantī* (peaceful), cool, often with a cool breeze blowing, and holy or powerful as the dwelling place of a deity. Two further places frequently characterized as good places are Triund and Laka. Triund is situated on the way to the Indrahar Pass; it is the flat top of the first mountain ridge that overlooks the Kangra Valley. Triund today is a destination for tourists, foreign as well as Indian, who enjoy the six-hour hike up to Triund and the rewarding view over the valley and onto the Indrahar Pass. Several tourists stay in tents or the government rest house at Triund overnight or camp close to Laka. Laka is situated another one to two hours hike from Triund at about 3,400 meters. Laka is the name of the plain ground about 1,000 meters beneath the Indrahar Pass. It is the resting and meeting point for shepherds and their flocks before they cross over the pass (see figure 8.1). At Laka, it is common for groups of shepherds to pool together to cross the pass. They set out one flock following the other with only small time intervals in between. Some flocks spend several weeks grazing in the area, others camp at Laka only one or two nights before they set out for the crossing. Apart from sheep and goats, people from lower-lying villages bring their cattle to Laka for grazing—where it is at times left to itself—during the warm season and monsoon (approximately between May and July). Laka and Triund are characterized by the vegetation of short green grass. Both are mentioned as good places for being foremost plain, peaceful, and cool by shepherds and other people, men or women from the villages, who have either visited the place itself or passed it on the way to Nāg Ḍal or Lamb Ḍal, two high-altitude lakes, behind the Indrahar Pass.

Figure 8.1 Gathering the flocks at Laka below the Indrahar Pass. Photo by A. Wagner (2007).

Bharmaur—Gaddern—is another region of which topographical descriptions are frequently given. As with Lahul, even those who have never been to Bharmaur are familiar with the descriptions of its landscape. When I accompanied a family from Kangra to their ancestral village in Bharmaur, the small daughters of the family, who were going to the area for the first time in their lives, shared their imaginations of Gaddern with me. These seven- to nine-year-olds told me about the *ūncī-ūncī pahāṛ* (high mountains) we were going to see on our trip. To demonstrate how steep the paths we would have to walk along were going to be, they held one hand in an almost vertical position and drew our zigzagging path on the back of the hand with their fingers. They were, moreover, excited about seeing the Ravi, the "big, beautiful" river, that would appear infinitely small down in the gorge below when viewed from the top of the hills. Although the mountains are impressively steep in Bharmaur, it turned out that the girls were disappointed by the real Ravi River. Interrupted by several dams, the Ravi, in addition to being near to its sources, appears quite small when one enters Bharmaur, and was judged to be tiny, "just like our seasonal river at home."

The descriptions of Gaddern, albeit carrying connotations of good places, differ from the description of Lahul. Contrary to Lahul, Gaddern does not carry unanimously positive attributes. As described in chapter 7, the sight of steep mountains might not be pleasant to everyone, especially not to women who have to shift their home from Kangra to Bharmaur after marriage. However, the cool water and air in Bharmaur in the summer, as well as other plain and open places in the mountains, in general, fulfill widespread ideals of aesthetic places. These attributes also appear in descriptions of good places to live. Concerning the environment of houses, several people commented that a nice home would be situated on mountain slopes above the valley, get cool air, be surrounded by green vegetation and flowers, be quiet, and have an open view.[7]

The discussion of environmental aesthetics adds arguments for the positive value attached to the mountains among the Gaddi in showing that places that play an important part in mythology, transhumance activities, identity constructions, as well as in religious terms as the previous chapters have shown, are also perceived as aesthetically pleasing. Meanings of places and their description as aesthetically pleasing reveal an interrelationship of social, religious, economic, ecological, and aesthetic dimensions. If, on the one hand, utilitarian aspects such as altitudes where sheep and goats find nourishing fodder are discernible in descriptions of good places, this applies, on the other hand, equally to ideas about the power of places, and connections between places and deities or the god Shiva. Social relations to place—that is, notions of inside and outside space—figure as much in locating good places in the mountains as do the practicalities of shepherding and climatic conditions.

Concepts of good places demonstrate that engagements with the environment not only have ideational components, but also are shaped by embodied experiences. Ideas on the aesthetics of environment, in spite of being expressed as abstract attributes, are informed by physical and sensory involvements—foremost seeing and feeling—of humans with their surroundings.

In the next section, I will show how notions of environmental aesthetics become visible in photographic practice. An understanding of local ideas of environment, landscapes, and aesthetics is thereby a prerequisite for being able to grasp the meaning of the photographs and intentions behind their choice as motifs.

Environmental Aesthetics in Photographic Motifs

> When I first started doing fieldwork in India in 1982 in Bhatsuda, a village in central India, I found myself taking what I perceived to be two different types of photographs: ones for myself and ones for villagers. (Pinney 1997: 8)

During my time in India, I had a similar experience to the one described by Pinney. In the first months in India, I was trying to take pictures that I wanted to take home in order to show what India looks like to me. My Indian acquaintances encouraged and asked me to take a second sort of pictures with different motifs, in different body postures, from different angles, and with a different zoom.[8] I believe I was initiated into the North Indian way of taking pictures in the course of my fieldwork, the success of which was proven to me by the demand for my photographic skills. While people also appreciated the shots I took for my own collection, which they sometimes termed natural, they insisted on having certain pictures taken of themselves, and I was meticulously instructed on how they wanted them to turn out.[9] What is more, friends insisted that I have myself photographed in the same way. My digital camera played an important part in instructing me on how to take pictures. The display made it possible to check the pictures on the spot and apply corrections right away to a second take, if I had not composed the picture the way people had intended it to be.

I was aware of the different ways of taking pictures and choosing motifs from the beginning of my fieldwork. My interest in photographs in connection to the topic of environment, however, emerged only later. One instance that triggered my attention was a photo session in front of a West Himalayan fir tree (Gaddi: *tos*). The motif of the fir tree struck me as odd.

In Germany, pictures with decorated Christmas trees are taken in the millions each year. Outside the context of Christmas, however, fir trees are rarely, if ever, chosen as a background for a picture.[10] Pondering on how a fir tree came to be a treasured motif, I realized that this and other images told a lot about environmental aesthetics. It is the notion of aesthetics of environment visible in photographic images that I trace in the following. The aesthetics of photographs themselves, convincingly analyzed by Pinney (1997), is beyond the scope of this work. I will start, with theoretical approaches with which I analyze photographic images as socially defined, then contextualize environmental motifs within Gaddi photography collections, and then put forward an interpretation of the meaning of short green grass and fir trees in photographic images and their connection to environmental aesthetics.

What Is in a Picture? Photography as Socially Defined Practice

As Bourdieu points out, only what is readable becomes visible in a picture. What is readable, is readable because it follows certain rules of reproduction of reality that define the social practice of photography. This according to Bourdieu includes norms regarding image composition, which if not followed interfere with the ability to judge the picture or even lead to its rejection (Bourdieu 1981a: 87). However, deciphering the meaning of a picture applies as much to its content as it does to its form. Kerstin Pinther, in her writing on photography in West Africa, comments on what has to be taken into account in order to understand the meaning of a picture. Messages of photographs, as Pinther highlights, are encoded in gestures, facial impressions, body posture, but also, for example, in dress (Pinther 1996). Decoding the message of a picture, thus, involves more than the picture itself. Understanding pictures implies understanding their social meanings.

We know from Bourdieu that photography is to be understood as a social practice that, notwithstanding the explicit intentions of its producers, is shaped by embodied rules that express likings, perception, and schemes of thought of a group (Bourdieu 1981b: 17). As Bourdieu notes, although in theory everything that is technically possible is "'photographable', it is still true that, from among the theoretically infinite number of photographs which are technically possible, each group chooses a finite and well-defined range of subjects, genres and compositions" (Bourdieu 1990: 6).

Bourdieu's findings from France regarding the social definitions of what is being photographed are backed up by Steven Sprague in his findings from Nigeria. In an article on Yoruba photography, Sprague states that although photographers claim that almost anything a client wants—except certain ritual objects—can be photographed, the analysis of photographs actually taken shows that in practice the motifs are much more restricted than claimed (Sprague 2002: 173). Sprague points out that Yoruba photography shares things with photography in other African and Western societies: "But cultural patterning exists, not only in subtle differences in these conventions but more importantly in the unique, culturally derived symbolic meanings and specific functions attributed to these seemingly similar forms" (ibid.: 174). Sprague suggests that the photographs he analyses "are 'coded in Yoruba' and can also give us much information about how the Yoruba see themselves" (ibid.: 184). I argue that this is equally true for North Indian, or, more specifically, Gaddi photography.

Gaddi Photography Collections

A few general remarks, concerning photographs in India and Himachal Pradesh and especially in Gaddi photo albums, are necessary to contextualize the pictures, which, as I contend, tell us about environmental aesthetics. Photo albums in India—in contrast to Germany—are not private family memories that only insiders get to see. Photo albums in Indian households are put on display and are shown to visitors (see also Pinney 1997). Accordingly, I draw my experience from Indian family photographs from the many albums and single pictures I was shown in the houses that I visited during my stays in India. Most elaborated is certainly the documentation of marriages, which could be said to form a genre in itself. Family collections also often contain photographs taken in photo studios and during trips to temples and other famous sites. Few families in my fieldwork area actually own a camera. Most pictures are acquired either through professional photographers or through a friend or relative who owns a camera, or today an accordingly equipped mobile phone, and who distributes the pictures to others.[11]

Body postures and facial expressions in these photographs are often highly formalized. The subjects photographed usually assume a formal posture and expression. A person is photographed in an upright position, preferably showing his or her full body and complete face without shadows, from a straight angle, with closed lips, and a serious facial expression. For details and further analysis I refer to Pinney (1997), since a discussion of this dimension of Indian photographic practices is beyond the scope of this work.

A type of image that I saw in almost every album collection was the image of people photographed in a certain dress: in the Gaddi dress of *nuāncarī* and *colā;* in clothes worn as costumes, such as pictures in Kashmiri dress taken, for example, at the Vaisno Mātā Temple in Jammu—men dressed as Sikhs with a turban, women wearing a sari; school children in their hockey (girls) or cricket (boys) team uniform.[12] Furthermore, there are certain popular accessories, such as sunglasses, that are worn for photographs. Pinney suggests that the formalized staging of pictures is among other things a form of exploration of roles that is brought into play in photography: "[T]he inventive posing that characterizes much of the imagery produced within studios is concerned with the transcendence and parody of social roles. The photographic studio becomes a place not for solemnization of the social but for the individual exploration of that which does not yet exist in the social world" (Pinney 1997: 178).

I hold this to be an important comment on the intercultural perception of photography. Ways of staging photographs and using seemingly modern accessories or backgrounds have too narrowly been interpreted as statements on modernity vis-à-vis tradition and ways of reaching for a world in pictures, a world that is out of reach in everyday life (e.g., Behrend 1996). Pinney convincingly shows that photographic practices in India do not merely copy images, but are creative and explorative in themselves.

For my fieldwork area, next to pictures of persons in a certain dress, pictures at temples (that again show a specific style), pictures of people with one or several goats and sheep, environment and landscape feature prominently in the pictures collected in family albums.[13] The pictures usually show one or several persons in a landscape and not a landscape without people. Individual or group pictures in front of mountain scenery is a common motif; I saw at least one such picture in almost every album collection. These pictures are most often taken in Bharmaur, but many families also own pictures taken on the Kangra side of the Dhauladhar, for example, at Triund or Gūne Mātā, in Jammu, or in the Pangi Valley. People leafing through albums are often stunned by images with high mountains and express their evaluation of the picture by exclaiming *vah-vah* (wow) or *kitnī acchī* (how nice) when coming across them. People also like having their picture taken with a background showing vegetation—wheat fields, bushes, flowers—and with snow. I came across such pictures with greenery or mountains in several Himachali households and was repeatedly asked to take similar images.

The photographs I am going to analyze in depth here are pictures with two very distinct motifs: persons sitting on lawn-like, short green grass, and persons in front of a West Himalayan fir tree. Both motifs appear less spectacular than people in front of mountain scenes and more specific than greenery as such. In most villages, particularly in those situated toward the lower elevations in Kangra, neither fir trees nor patches of the short green grass are to be found. So for a majority of people, both do not belong to the environment of everyday life. Short green grass and fir trees are connected to landscapes or to places that are visited on special occasions, and therefore the grass or fir as a photographic motif is distinct from green fields or flowers. At the same time, they are less readable for an unfamiliar audience. I hold that the choice of images of short green grass and fir trees tells us about notions of environmental aesthetics, which take up and reinforce arguments regarding engagements with the environment that were put forward in preceding chapters.

The pictures in my collection were taken during a trip to Bharmaur in August 2008. One of the families with whom I stayed in Kangra had invited me for a *jāgrā* to their ancestral village in Bharmaur. During the stay in this village, I joined a group of invitees who took the opportunity of being in the village to visit its different temples, including a goddess temple situated on the hill top above the village. Our group consisted of two men and one girl from the Bharmaur village who did not explicitly ask to be photographed. The rest of the group, all keen to be photographed with these motifs, were from Kangra. One woman was visiting the place for the first time. The others, three young women and the father of two of them, recognized the place as their ancestral village, although only the father had actually lived there as a child. One of the twenty-year-olds had come there for only the second time in her life. One of the other participants in this small excursion and I were carrying cameras. We first took pictures of everyone in front of the goddess temple and with the mountains in the background. On our way back down to the village, they asked me to photograph first the three men, and then, when the women who had descended a little slower caught up, the whole group on a stretch of short green grass (see figure 8.2). It is important to note that it was the expressed intention of those photographed to get a picture with the short green grass, and not primarily a picture of the group.

After having their picture taken sitting on the grass, the girls, who had commented on the *tos* (West Himalayan fir) already on the way up to the temple, asked for a photograph in front of a fir tree. The first try was not very successful. Given the slope of the mountain, it was not possible to fit a big tree in full size, or at least to show its needles and the group in the picture. Then the father of the girls discovered a small, somewhat crooked tree, which made it possible for us to sit on a branch of the tree and be photographed in front of its green branches (see figure 8.3). We all laughed heartily at the crooked tree, but still everyone was excited about the op-

Figure 8.2 "Short green grass." Photo by A. Wagner (2008).

portunity for the photograph it offered. I emphasize that the choice fell on the small crooked tree not because of its form, but because it was a *tos*. I have already referred to Pinney regarding how people are photographed in respect to body posture, clarity of facial expression, and camera angle. I suggest that these photographic conventions played a role in choosing the small tree in this case. Had a well-grown tree been available that made it possible to follow photographic convention and fit both tree and person in the picture, it would have probably been preferred.

After I had photographed the others one by one, my companions insisted that I have my picture taken with the tree as well.

Figure 8.3 The author with a *tos*. Photo by A. Wagner (2008).

Although I shared in the laughing about sitting on the crooked tree, I realized that—in contrast to the mountain scenery—I did not really share the wish to have my picture taken in front of the fir and only reluctantly agreed to it. As I pointed out above, from my German point of view an undecorated green fir tree makes a poor background for a picture. It carried no meaning for me. For Gaddi people, however, the image of oneself with a *tos* is generally treasured and was not merely chosen by chance on our short walk. This became obvious after we returned to the village. On hearing of the pictures we had taken, the other members of our group who had stayed in the village expressed their strong disappointment at not having been able to get a picture like that themselves. The photographs were also admired when printed and shown around back in Kangra by further family members and in-dropping neighbors, who once more stressed the *tos*, the short green grass, and the mountain scenery in the pictures.

On the Meaning of Short Green Grass and Fir Trees

Following Bourdieu and Sprague, short green grass and fir trees, independent of explicit intentions of individual actors, are motifs that are culturally patterned. If, according to Sprague, pictures and their subject matter are culturally coded, the task is to decode them, to understand what they stand for, and why they, out of all possibilities, are chosen. Although not everyone in Kangra might deliver a ready explanation of these motifs, it is important to keep in mind that these images form a part of the local photographic practice and are readable for a local audience. As Pinney remarked regarding the play on tradition and modernity in the studio photography in Central India, the meanings to be elucidated "are not obscure motifs to be conjured up through formal analysis by the anthropologist but are rather an absolutely fundamental feature of popular culture" (Pinney 1997: 181–182).

What do the fir tree and short green grass stand for? The vernacular name (in Gaddi) of the coniferous tree in the photographs is *tos*. *Tos* is identified as *Abies pindrow*, commonly known as West Himalayan fir or silver fir (*Gazetteer of the Kangra District 1897* 1899: 13; see also FAO n.d.; Tucker 1986; cf. van Gelderen and van Hoey Smith 1986). The "West Himalayan fir can become up to 60–70 m tall. In the western Himalayan [sic], it can be found at elevations between 2500 and 4000 m. It is best adapted to cool and moist conditions and is often found on northern aspects" (FAO n.d.). While deodar cedars are frequent in the higher elevations of the southern slopes of the Dhauladhar in Kangra, *tos* are more abundant in the district of Chamba than in Kangra. Tucker writes on the vegetational zones and distribution of tree species on the Dhauladhar:

> At the lower elevations, at around 1,500 m, a transition begins from chill pine forests to mixed stands of kharsu oak *(Q. semecarpifolia)* and several rhododendron species on the wetter slopes, and to the great Himalayan conifer forests. First come deodar *(Cedrus deodara)* and kail pine *(Pinus excelsa)*, the major timber trees of the region until recently. Above 3,000 m they gradually give way to Himalayan spruce *(Picea morinda)* and silver fir *(Abies webbiana or pindrow)*, which thrive as high as 4,000 m. At their upper limits, alpine pastures are flanked by stands of paper birch *(Betula utilis)* and pencil cedar *(C. tortulosa)*. (Tucker 1986: 18)

From its ecological distribution, one could conclude that in photographic practice the fir tree stands for a visit to the high mountains of Bharmaur. In one sense, this is certainly true. However, the practice of photography in India does not point to pictures being taken as a proof of physically having been to a place, as they do in the French photographic practices analyzed by Bourdieu (1981c: 48). As Pinney pointed out, "People who could very well afford to be photographed in Agra were still likely to be photographed in front of painted versions [of the Taj Mahal] in Nagda" (Pinney 1997: 175). What Pinney's remark points to is that the choice of the image is not primarily about authenticity. The question about a real or substituted background does not arise in the pictures discussed here, since people physically traveled to Bharmaur and climbed the hill where fir tree and short green grass grow. However, I argue that the intention behind taking a photograph sitting on short green grass or in front of a fir tree is about more than the obvious creation of a memory of a trip to Bharmaur. If Pinney is right about the general role of exploration in photography, rather than authenticity, for which backgrounds are another example, the meaning of the motifs *tos* and short green grass is to be found beyond the relation between photographed person and background.

If not primarily for the trip—for having been—to Bharmaur, what do *tos* and grass stand for? Fir trees and short green grass from an ecological point are characteristic of high-altitude stretches in the mountains. Not only coniferous trees, but also short green grass is strongly connected with high elevations. It is in particular the grass on the alpine meadows that is short and of a strong green color. This grass is called *niru* (Axelby 2005). The short green grass, thereby, is not only important to shepherds because of its nourishing value for the flocks, and not merely a feature of an ecological zone, but also is a general attribute of a good place.

A further indicator that short green grass and fir trees stand for high elevations is found in Gaddi songs. Physical elements of these mountainous landscapes are described in songs. Coniferous trees such as *tos* figure in these descriptions. In a song where the goddess Gaura asks her mother's brother to give her snow as dowry, Gaura looks outside several times to see if her wish comes true.[14] The fourth time she steps outside, there is finally snow. The song line expresses this by stating that the coniferous trees—*raī*, *kaleī*, and *tos*—are submerged in snow.[15]

पैले ता पैरे गौरा वारा जो आई अंवरभरूरा घणै तारै हो।	The first time when Gaura stepped outside, the sky was full of stars.
दूए पैरे गौरा वारा जो आई अंवरा ना बदली घाई हो।	The second time when Gaura stepped outside, there were clouds in the sky.
तीजै वो पैरे गौरा वारा जो आई रिमझिम बरखा लगुरी हो।	The third time when Gaura stepped outside, it was raining a little bit.
चौथे वो पैरे गौरा वारा जो आई दक्षिणारी झुल्लीठण्डी हवा हो	The fourth time when Gaura stepped outside, there was a cold wind blowing from the south.
रेई वो डूब वो कलेई वो डूबी तोस डूबे चुडी मोले हो	The *raī* trees were covered, the *kaleī*, too, were covered, and the *tos* trees were covered from top to stem [in snow].[16]
खिड़-र हिस्से मेरी गौरजा धीयां कीयां वो ईणा धुड़ुआ षियाणा हो।	My daughter was laughing loudly because how would Shiv-ji now manage to come [with his marriage party].

In a further song on Shiva's and Gaura's marriage, it is told how Gaura follows Shiva, who had left the marriage ceremony in anger, to Mount Kailash.[17] The song describes how Gaura, running along the riverbeds up into the mountains, passes coniferous trees on the mountain flanks. These songs are part of the *nuālā* repertoire and are widely known, including the passages describing landscapes, and so are the tree species mentioned in the songs. Moreover, Gaura in the song is running through the very real landscape of Bharmaur. It is the Bharmauri Kailash where Shiva lives and where she is following him. The coniferous trees mentioned in the song, thus, are intimately connected to a landscape to which Gaddi people feel intimately connected.

The lawn-like short green grass does not figure in the songs I collected, but it appears in the context of visual media. In VCDs featuring Gaddi *aincalī* (religious songs)—mostly compiled as *nuālā* songs—short green grass is chosen as the background for scenes depicting Gaddi dances. Men and women who dance in Gaddi dress are shown performing Gaddi dances on grass. These scenes are shot from an angle that shows only people and grass without a horizon in the background. People with whom I watched these VCDs enjoyed watching the dance and commented on the beauty of the pictures by pointing out the nice grass. Green grass is also a background motif employed in the Himachali folk music VCDs depicting Gaddi, as described in chapter 2. This might be another indicator as to why Gaddi people positively approved of the folk music imagery. It further shows that green grass as an attribute of the mountains—which are assigned to the Gaddi through the imagery of the VCDs—is employed and recognized by a wider audience and is not exclusive to the Gaddi. Concerning more specifically Gaddi connections to the environment, short green grass is also characteristic of Lahul, a good place par excellence, as well as other good places at higher elevations.

In sum, short green grass and fir trees are chosen as photographic motifs because they represent a specific landscape. The symbolic meaning of the images lies in associations with and attributes of the places, which are represented by fir trees and short green grass. The landscape that *tos* and short green grass stand for is positively marked in songs and other media and, as I have shown throughout this book, is meaningful in several ways: as an inside space, and, in a more narrow sense, as the Gaddi ancestral land, as the abode of Shiva and Gaddi deities, as pure and powerful places, as nourishment for sheep and goats, and, last but not least, as an environment that is pleasing to the senses (for at least half of the year).

To understand the meaning of these images, it is important to bear in mind that people engage with their environments not only ideationally, in terms of social relations, religious beliefs, or mythology, but that concepts of place are also informed by practical aspects of place-making—in other words through bodily experience and sensory perceptions. The attributes of good places are encoded in these photographic images. This is most obvious with regard to short green grass that is both photographic motif and attribute of a good place. But both fir trees and short green grass are plant species associated with high-altitude places.[18] These places are in turn considered pleasant to the senses for being green, peaceful, and above all cool. Thus, short green grass and fir trees do not represent just any landscape, but specifically aesthetically valued places. The understanding of ideas about the aesthetics of environment makes pictures taken in front of fir trees and short green grass readable, and enables the understanding of how short green grass or a fir tree becomes valued as an "object which is perceived as worthy of being photographed, which is captured, stored, communicated, shown and admired" (Bourdieu 1990: 6).

As a last remark, images of mountains, grass, and trees are not unique to Gaddi photographic practice, but are widely found in Indian imagery. Scenic mountain views and green meadows are commonly inserted into scenes of Bollywood movies. Posters depicting landscapes often decorate living room walls in middle-class homes in Himachal, Punjab, and cities like Chandigarh. Gaddi photographic imagery, living room posters, and Bollywood movies share certain environmental aesthetics that show a prevalence of mountains, greenery, and open spaces. From this follows that the cultural values encoded in Gaddi photography, at least partly, are embedded in a sense of aesthetics that is more generally prevalent in India. Thus, although foreign to a German anthropologist, references to environmental aesthetics in these pictures might, with Pinney, play on fundamental features of popular culture that are to some extent shared throughout North India.[19]

However, while environmental motifs in visual culture are not exclusively Gaddi, it would also be misleading to reduce Gaddi photographic motifs to quotations from Bollywood movies. The photographs analyzed above depict very specific motifs, which are intimately connected to landscapes that figure strongly in real or imagined topographies of meaningful environments and places within the Dhauladhar region. The places and landscapes represented by these images are moreover good places for their pleasing aesthetic qualities in embodied local experience. Thus, albeit participating in imagery of Indian popular culture, Gaddi photography displays distinctive markers of Gaddi identity and culturally distinct ways of engaging with place.

As a conclusion, it can be stated that Gaddi people do have an explicit sense of aesthetics regarding environment, which is clearly expressed in statements about good places. The analysis of photographic motifs underlines this sense of aesthetics, which is otherwise voiced in descriptions and judgments of places. The interpretation of photographic images shows that ideas about qualities of place become visible and materialize in photographic practice and in the corresponding cultural meaning of treasured images. Thus, the analysis of photographs has proven fruitful not only for the understanding of their motifs, but moreover to see how ideas of good places, besides being expressed in verbal comments, are inscribed in visual media. The examination of photographic images presented in this chapter, however, could be limited only in scope. There remains scope for analysis of photographic practices also regarding differences according to social background, age and gender, changes over time, and in respect to changing technologies—for example, the introduction of mobile phones with cameras, which started to spread rapidly among villagers during the time of my fieldwork. The investigation of photographic practices carries potential for extension in future research concerning the aesthetics of environment and beyond.

Notes

1. *Ṭhaṇḍā* can be translated into English as both cool or cold. If not otherwise indicated, such as in translations of statements used by my interview partners that indicate that *ṭhaṇḍā* is used in the sense of cold, I will in the following translate *ṭhaṇḍā* as cool, which captures better the range of meanings implied in descriptions of cool environments as aesthetically pleasing.
2. The appreciation of the mountains as cool and of their cool water as well as the positive judgment of an open or clear view parallel ideas of aesthetics present in other Himalayan regions (Lecomte-Tilouine 2009; Smadja 2009b).
3. The shepherds are well aware that in Lahul the temperature and weather can also become unpleasant and even harsh. There is a possibility of strong winds and snowfall even in the summer. This does not detract from the overall perception of Lahul as a pleasant place, however.
4. During my stays in India, there were many contexts in which people readily forwarded descriptions of places they had often heard about but never seen for themselves. It struck me that these accounts described features of places as if told by an eyewitness and did not include reference to the actual source of this knowledge whose descriptions they repeated, or to the fact that this was not first-hand knowledge. Thus, it is not surprising that daughters or sons, sisters or brothers of shepherds offer descriptions of the Lahuli environment.
5. I stay with the shepherds' own perceptions and accounts here. I have no data on the extent of financial loss due to compensation payments for damaged crops or stolen animals during the winter versus losses due to leopard attacks, falling rocks (a rather frequent occurrence), and other casualties in the mountains. Shepherding is a risky business throughout the year.
6. Note, while rivers and seasonal streams are commonly referred to by name, mountains are not, with the exception of Mount Kailash. It appears that it is usually not the mountain peak that is mentioned by name but the pass that leads over it.
7. This does not mean that people would necessarily choose to live at an aesthetically good place; in practice aesthetics is weighed against practical considerations such as proximity to roads.
8. Similar observations of discrepancies between one's own and the other's pictures have been reported from Africa (Behrend and Wendl 1996).
9. This is not to say that there is a natural way of taking photographs. Natural in this case rather refers to the person in the picture who is not posing in front of

the camera. My so-called natural pictures are highly formalized in their own way. The point is rather that German ways of image composition are subject to photographic conventions that are different from the ones I encountered in the field.

10. However, fir trees are not completely absent from German imagery. They appear, for example, in the films of the genre *Heimatfilm*. Their significance in this context would need further exploration, which is beyond the scope of this chapter.
11. A more general study on photography as a social practice would require a differentiated treatment that takes into account dimensions such as gender, age, income, and social background, and changes discernible over the years, which I largely ignore in the following characterization of photographic collections, since this is beyond the scope of this chapter. Furthermore, gender and age or income, for example, do not seem dominant factors in the choice of motifs I am concerned with here and their indication of environmental aesthetics (see below).
12. Himachali women usually wear *suit* (*salwar-kamiz*) on everyday and festive occasions, therefore, a sari becomes kind of a costume.
13. A further medium in which similar motifs are employed is, for example, the poster art (see chapter 2).
14. The story told in the song was summarized in chapter 3. The version that I collected is given in full in the appendix.
15. The song names three conifer species growing at about the same elevation in the Western Himalayas (see above). *Raiī* is the vernacular name for the Western Himalayan spruce (*Picea morida*, also *Picea khutrow*, *Abies smithiana*) and *kaleī* is most probably identified with the Himalayan white pine, also known as blue pine (*Pinus excelsa*) (cf. FAO n.d.; *Gazetteer of the Kangra District 1897* 1899: 13; Tucker 1986;).
16. *Raiī, kaleī, tos*: coniferous trees (*raiī*: Western Himalayan spruce, *kaleī*: Himalayan pine, *tos*: Western Himalayan fir).
17. For the corresponding story on Shiva's and Gaura's marriage, see chapter 3.
18. Certain tree species as markers of a specific environment and altitude have also been reported for the Magar of Nepal (Lecomte-Tilouine 2009: 165).
19. Although my interest in this chapter points me toward environmental aesthetics, expressions of aesthetics are, of course, not the only line of interpretation of environmental motifs, especially of what landscapes represent in South Asian popular culture or art (Pinney 1995).

Conclusion
Doing Place

In this book I approached the understanding of environment through an analysis of place-making. The aim was to redescribe human-environment relations among the Gaddi in terms of a symmetric anthropology and in doing so to highlight contemporary practices and activities through which environment is performed. The focus on place-making traces involvements of concepts, practices, narratives, and perceptions that make places meaningful in a given context. Places are not understood as abstract, objectively given categories. They are enacted by people who dwell in them, visit them, and connect to them in a meaningful way. Places, in short, are done.

The role of activities through which people do place was brought to the fore by applying Ingold's definition of environment as a process to place, which means that the environment (and its places) emerges through activities and in relation to the humans who inhabit it. The second insight I took from Ingold is the relational definition of environment that sees humans as agents-in-an-environment, and accordingly takes into account perception stemming from physical involvement. However, to move beyond practical engagements toward a more holistic understanding of human-environment relations, Ingold's approach had to be supplemented by taking into account the social and relational context of these activities. For it is not only direct engagement, but also mythology, photographic practices, and concepts of inside and outside spaces or of divine and spiritual entities through which environment is enacted.

Practices of doing place, thus, do not exist as such but are subject to involvements of different dimensions—of discourse and thinking as well as of technology and ecology, and one might further include politics. My understanding of the interplay and entanglements of different dimensions such as mythology, religious practices, social organization, economic activities, media practices, and ecological conditions drew on insights from Latour's study of networks. I did not concentrate on one particular network singling out one aspect of doing place, but rather applied the network approach to the writing of a holistic ethnography of human-environment relations.

With these aspects taken together, my activity-centered approach has proven fruitful in elucidating practices through which environment is enacted. By joining insights from environmental anthropology and new approaches in practice theory, the approach adds the aspect of sensory perception as well as a processual perspective on place to the study of social practice, thus giving a phenomenological twist to the classical approach to practice and embodiment.

The activity-centered approach, moreover, provides a perspective on environment that goes beyond the Western nature-culture dualism in that it makes environment a topic. I argued in chapter 1 that the Western notion of a nature-culture dualism found entry into the study of pastoralist societies and resulted in an identification of environment with the biophysical nature in the context of pastoralism. The task was here to reconsider the term environment for pastoralist societies in an ethnographic bottom-up approach in order to understand the meanings attributed to place and environment by people who dwell in them. Environment so defined can be approached through the study of place-making. Both, environment and place-making, aim at uncovering local perspectives and local meanings. By taking the study of environment beyond the nature-culture divide, this book has also taken the understanding of environment among the Gaddi beyond the study of pastoralism and transhumant practices.

The practices through which the local landscape comes into being divert attention to the landscape away from the physical features of the Himalayan mountains that a foreign observer might see toward the places in between the extreme points of the vertical movements that characterize Gaddi transhumance and seasonal migration. The consideration of place enables an understanding of how the mountains become meaningful and why they appear so prominently in visual representations. Chapters 2 and 3 have shown how the mountains figure in constructions of a collective Gaddi identity, in foreign as well as self-descriptions. The importance given to the mountains, for example in VCD images, reemerges in family photo collections. The significance of these images becomes comprehensible with knowledge of the local landscape. The local landscape in turn is a landscape produced through social practice. Here, landscape is best not thought of as an abstract space, but as Casey states, as a network of concrete places.

That ways of doing place are informed by their cultural context becomes apparent in the present work if compared to Basso's study of place-making among the Western Apache (1996). Basso highlighted verbal practice and references to the past as means of making place. Parallel to the role of references to the past for the Apache, place-making among the Gaddi is importantly accomplished through performances of social relations as well as through physical movements to places.

Chapter 4 and 6 have given examples of how the Dhauladhar, by and large, is enacted as a landscape through which people travel in visiting relatives, moving between Bharmaur and Kangra homes or going back to ancestral villages. Chapter 4 showed that performances of social relations are constitutive of relations to place. Resulting person-centric networks of places form a perceived inside space referred to as the own area. This inside is, however, not homogenous as a habitus that goes with different places shows. Women and their change in behavior between their natal and marital villages is only the most prominent example here. Furthermore, social relations are not only relations between humans, but also are relations between humans and deities. Relations to family deities, acted out in *jāgrā* and *jātar* rituals, too, are inside relations. Visiting deities is here similar to visiting kin. Similar to visits to relatives, journeys to deities' dwelling places, whether in the mountains or in villages, both in Kangra and in Bharmaur, carry the notion of habitual movements. Movements from and to places whether in religious practice or by children on vacation at their relatives' homes further establish practical and concrete connections and show that places are actively experienced and physically appropriated. Through these movements, intimate connections to places are established and place-networks come into being.

The topics covered in this book—from performances of social relations and the enactment of the mountains in religious activities to the concept of local biology and notions of aesthetics—are general aspects of how people make place. Approaching human-environment relations through place-making thus not only works for the Gaddi and the Himalayan region, but also points to a general importance of practices for an understanding of how humans engage with and enact their environment.

Nevertheless, this book has highlighted regional as well as more-local particularities in ways of doing place. The importance of social relations and kinship networks fits in well into the larger South Asian context, as the fact that I borrowed the concept of an inside space from a Pakistani ethnography shows. However, the concept of a perceived inside space receives a specific form and content through the characteristics of Gaddi kinship practices with symmetric alliances. Similarly, the prevalence of cool, green, open, and peaceful as attributes of good places more generally fits North Indian criteria, whereas aesthetics of environment at the same time show particular elements and connections such as the occurrence of fir trees as treasured photographic motifs. A third example is the phenomenon of water change analyzed in chapter 7. The complaint about water change well known throughout North India receives a distinctive connotation among Gaddi people who are specialists when it comes to becoming attuned to different places, whether as shepherds or through frequent movements between Kangra and Bharmaur. These themes situate the Gaddi within a larger regional context and thus deexoticize them. At the same time these themes point out specific characteristics that, in Sprague's words, code pictures and, I add, activities "in Gaddi."

Particular for this region of Himachal Pradesh is in addition the Gaddis' practice of a seasonal migration, the present state of which was discussed in chapter 4. The differences in relating to Bharmaur villages between seasonal migrants who connect to the village as their home and place of belonging, and families with one home in Kangra who see the Bharmaur village as their ancestral place and connect to it chiefly through their family deities, have thereby shown that ways of place-making are not uniform. Engagements with place and the activities with which they are accomplished differ between different groups of people, even if it is the same place that is meaningful.

The study of both, practical engagement and social practice, is made possible by ethnographic fieldwork based on participant observation that enabled me to follow people in their practices over a stretch of time. This was especially important since activities and movements around the Dhauladhar are strongly shaped by seasons. The role of activities that link people back to their ancestral villages in Bharmaur as well as visits to the high-altitude lakes, for instance, are only observable and become only a topic of conversation during the second half of the monsoon season.

My ethnographic fieldwork focused on the village and activities carried out from the village. It thus filled a gap in the literature in that I did not concentrate on shepherding practices, but brought in the perspective of women, children, the elderly, and nonshepherding men. The resulting descriptions of performances of social relations, journeys undertaken in the environment, and the attention paid to expressions of environmental aesthetics show that the mountains are of importance to the Gaddi beyond pastoralist practices and transhumant activities. In this, the approach does not only include the female perspective, but also it shows an ongoing connection to the mountains in a situation, where the seasonal migration over the passes on foot has long shifted to journeys by bus, and shepherds, at least around the Indrahar Pass, plan for their sons to continue in new professions. In my experience, practices such as *jāgrā*, *jātar*, or *nhauṇ* are also followed by labor migrants on their visits home that stay most of the time in the larger cities or are posted in the army. In this respect, the practices described in this book are quite widely shared.

However, the look at practice followed in this book enables a dynamic view on practices that acknowledges changing constellations. The ways of relating to Bharmaur villages by seasonal migrants and by families with one home in Kangra are only one example of differing practices in engaging with place. The local conception of environment in this understanding does not emerge as a specific kind of cosmology or pastoral worldview—and thus in an understanding that, as Ingold states, would imply the juxtaposition of a culturally framed and therefore also constrained indigenous knowledge with a more absolute knowledge available from an outside perspective (see chapter 1). While practices and related concepts might well be particular in and to a given place and time, they are not necessarily consistent or coherent. The concept of doing place here allows for a plurality of coexisting practices and therefore multiple enactments of reality. As Mol (2002) states, foregrounding practice means looking at things as they are done. If environment comes into being through activities, it is these activities that determine the conception of the environment and the latter will change with changes in them.

Appendix
Songs and Translations

1. A song from Gaura's wedding songs, version collected at Dharamshala in 2008. Translation by the author.

Gaddi	English translation
1. मामा वो मामा भानजी तेरीयां सामा मामा वो मामा भानजी जो दाज कै देला।	1. *Māmā o māmā* (MB), here is your niece (ZD). *Māmā o māmā*, what will you give your niece as dowry?
थाली वो देला वो कटोरी वो देला। सौगी वो देला ठठियारा हो।	I'll give her plates, give her pots. I'll give her a potter, too.
2. भैडा वो देला भानजीएं बकरी देला सौगी वो देला पहाल हो।	2. I'll give my niece sheep. I'll give goats. I'll give her a shepherd, too.
3. गाई वो देला भनजीएं भैंसी वो देला सौगी वो देला गुआला हो।	3. I'll give my niece a cow. I'll give a buffalo. I'll give her a cowhand, too.
मिरग खाए तेरी गाई वो भैंसी मरी चुकी जाए वो गुआला हो।	A tiger will eat your cow and the cowhand will kill the buffalo.
4. तूं वो ना सुणिदा मामा हिऊं वो पत्रिया मूं वो लेणा हिऊआं दा परौड़ हो।	4. Haven't you heard *māmā him rāj* (lord of snow)? I want only snow as a dowry.

Appendix • 179

5. पैले ता पैरे गौरा वारा जो आई अंवरभरूरा घणै तारै हो।	5. The first time when Gaura stepped outside, the sky was full of stars.
6. दूए पैरे गौरा वारा जो आई अंवरा ना बदली घाई हो।	6. The second time when Gaura stepped outside, there were clouds in the sky.
7. तीजै वो पैरे गौरा वारा जो आई रिमझिम बरखा लगुरी हो।	7. The third time when Gaura stepped outside, it was raining a little bit.
8. चौथे वो पैरे गौरा वारा जो आई दक्षिणारी झुल्लीठण्डी हवा हो	8. The fourth time when Gaura stepped outside, there was a cold wind blowing from the south.
रेई वो डूब वो कलेई वो डूबी तोस डूबे चुडी मोले हो	The *raiī* trees were covered, the *kaleī*, too, were covered, and the *tos* trees were covered from top to stem [in snow].
खिड़-र हिस्से मेरी गौरजा धीयां कीयां वो ईणा धुड़ूआ षियाणा हो।	My daughter was laughing loudly because how would Dhuṛūā (Shiva) now manage to come [with his marriage party]?

2. *Bhajan* to the goddess, devotional songs sung in Pahari, documented during a *jāgrā* from Kangra to Bharmaur in 2008. Translation by the author.

First song:

Pahari	English translation
मालिनी ने फूल सुट्यां मैया दे दरवारे आई के (2)	The gardener woman offered flowers coming to the mother's [goddess'] door. (2)
नैना देवी छम-छम रोए (2)	Naina Devi wept ceaselessly. (2)
माता ने पुत्र मंगया मैया दे दरवारे आई के (2)	A mother asked for a son coming to the mother's door. (2)
मालिनी ने फूल सुट्यां मैया दे दरवारे आई के (2)	The gardener woman offered flowers coming to the mother's door. (2)
नैना देवी छम-छम रोए (2)	Naina Devi wept ceaselessly. (2)

बहना ने भाई मंगया मैया दे दरवारे आई के (2)

मालिनी ने फूल सुटयां मैया दे दरवारे आई के (2)

नैना देवी छम-छम रोए (2)

बुआ ने भतीजा मंगया मैया दे दरवारे आई के (2)

Second song:
Pahari

मैया आज मुझे निंद नहीं आई है।
सुना है तेरे मंदिर में रस बड़ा है (2)

मैया के दरवार में अंधा खड़ा है (2)

अंधे को आँखे दे दो ना।
सुना है तेरे मंदिर में रस बड़ा है (2)

मैया आज मुझे निंद नहीं आई है।
सुना है तेरे मंदिर में रस बड़ा है (2)

मैया के दरवार में कोढ़ी खड़ा है (2)

कोढ़ी को कायाँ दे दो ना।
सुना है तेरे मंदिर में रस बड़ा है (2)

मैया आज मुझे निंद नहीं आई है।
सुना है तेरे मंदिर में रस बड़ा है (2)

A sister asked for a brother coming to the mother's door. (2)

The gardener woman offered flowers coming to the mother's door. (2)

Naina Devi wept ceaselessly. (2)

An aunt (FZ) asked for a nephew (BS) coming to the mother's door. (2)

English translation

Mother [goddess] today I could not sleep.
I have heard that in your temple, the power is plenty. (2)

At the mother's door stands a blind person. (2)

Do give eyes to the blind.
I have heard that in your temple the power is plenty. (2)

Mother, today I could not sleep.
I have heard that in your temple the power is plenty. (2)

At the mother's door stands a leper. (2)

Do give a (healthy) body to the leper.
I have heard that in your temple the power is plenty. (2)

Mother, today I could not sleep.
I have heard that in your temple the power is plenty. (2)

मैया के दरवार में लंगड़ा खड़ा है (2)

लंगड़े को टांगे दे दो ना।
सुना है तेरे मंदिर में रस बड़ा है (2)

At the mother's door stands a lame person. (2)

Do give legs to the lame person.
I have heard that in your temple the power is plenty. (2)

Glossary

acchā	good, nice
ādat	habit, habituation
ādat ban jānā	to become accustomed, to get habituated
ādat honā	to have the habit, to be used to
aincalī	(Gaddi) devotional songs
alag	different, separate
ammā	(grand)mother, term of address for old women
apnā	ones' own, reflexive pronoun
apnā ghar	ones' house
apnā-apnā ilakā	ones' area
āratī	act of worship involving the circling of a plate with an oil lamp in front of the image of a deity
bābā	ascetic renouncer, colloquial
bahin	sister
bahu	son's wife (SW)
bakrī	goat
bakrī leke jānā	to go with a goat (description for ritual)
bāl kaṭnā	to cut hair, ritual tonsuring
bali	sacrifice
ban khandī	forest dwelling
baṛā dhām	large festive meal given at the groom's home
barāt	the groom's party
Barsākh	a month, April–May (Gaddi)
barsālā	monsoon season (Gaddi)
barsāt	rain, monsoon season (Hindi)
bartan	ceremonial, reciprocal gift exchange of cloth and money

beṭī	daughter
bhābhī	brother's wife (BW)
Bhaḍom	a month, August–September (Gaddi)
bhagvān	god
bhāī	brother
bhāī/bahin bannā	to become a brother/sister, to accept someone as a brother/sister
bhajan	devotional song
bhamīrūḍūyān	a night-active bird
bheḍ	sheep
bhog	food offered to the gods
bhūā	father's sister (FZ)
bhojpatr	birch shavings
bhūmi	land
bhūt	ghost
bīṛī	leaf-wrapped cigarette
Birvār	Thursday
bītī huī bāt	past experience, bygones
boberū	leavened bread (Gaddi)
botwāl	the person performing the task of handing out *prasād* during the *nuālā*
cārbaukh	ceremony performed on the fourth anniversary of a death
celā	(Gaddi) oracle, literally student
charolā	gate (Gaddi)
chemahīne	literally six months; practice of living six months in one place and six months in another
chimaihanī	funeral ritual performed six months after a death (Gaddi)
colā	a long gown or cloak, Gaddi men's dress of white wool
chot, chūt	impure
chotā-chotā, hārā-hārā ghās	short green grass
cūlhā	hearth, fireplace
cūndāvand	per wife system of inheritance
cunje	beak (Gaddi)
dādī	father's mother (FM)

Glossary

dar	fear
darśan	sight, revelation, religious act of looking at the image of a deity/god
dev bhūmi	land of gods
devī	goddess, female deity
devī-devtā	deities
devtā	male deity
dhām	festive meal, deity's abode
dhār	mountain, mountain ridge or side
dharm bhāī/bahin	brother/sister by religion (fictive kinship)
dharmik	of religion
dholkī	small barrel-shaped drum
dhūp	incense
diū	daughter, married and unmarried (Gaddi)
diyā	oil lamp
drāt	flat multipurpose axe
dupaṭṭā	headscarf
dūsre log	other people
ḍal	holy lake
ḍerā	camp
ḍevar	husband's younger brother
ḍorā	a long, black woolen cord worn around the waist (Gaddi)
Gaddern, Gadderan	other name for Bharmaur
gaddī	seat
galat bāt	wrongdoing
gām̐v	village
gandā kām	dirty work
garmī	heat, hot season
ghaḍā	clay pitcher
ghaṇṭāl	see *thālī ghaḍā*
ghar	house, home
ghar ke ādmī	men of the house, patrilineal descent group
ghar ke log	people of the house, the patrilineal descent group
gharvālā	householder, the one of the house

ghūmnā	to travel
gode mem lenā	to adopt
hair	season after the monsoon, mid-September–mid-December (Gaddi)
halvā	sweet dish used as *prasād*
hamārā	our
Hāṛh	a month, June–July (Gaddi)
havan	fire offering/sacrifice
homā	see *havan*
hīyūnd	cold season (Gaddi)
ilakā	area, region
Itvār	Sunday
jāganā	to be awake, vigilant
jāgrā	night vigil, ritual performed for a deity (Gaddi)
jāgrātā	North Indian ritual, night vigil usually performed for the goddess
jai Shiv-jī	victory to Shiva
jajman	patron of a ritual
Jandhar	Gaddi for plains or winter grazing area
jañgal	wastelands, jungle
jātar	Gaddi ritual, in Bharmaur also a village festival
jātī	caste, type, concerning kinship also: clan
jhaṇḍā	flag
Jheṭ	a month, May–June (Gaddi)
jhot	pass
-ji	suffix denoting respect
jījā	sister's husband (ZH)
kālā	black
kaleī	pine tree, *Pinus excelsa*
kām	work
kaṛā	Gaddi for *halvā*
kathā, viśnu narayān kā kathā	literally story, sacred legend or narration, ritual for the god Vishnu (also performed for other gods)
Kātī	a month, October–November (Gaddi)
kharīf	summer/monsoon agricultural season
khās	special

khās riśtedār	close relatives
khelnā	to play
khuś	happy
kicharī	a dish of rice and pulses cooked together
kitnī acchī	how nice
kotwāl	person who has to stay awake during the *nuālā*, also police officer
kriyā	ceremony following a death, here a ceremony that lifts relatives of the deceased off death pollution
kul	descent line, family
kul devī/devtā	family deity
kul purohit	family priest
khulā	open
lāḍā	groom (Gaddi)
laṅgar	(free) community meal for devotees
lenā	to take
liṅg	phallus, lingam, symbol of Shiva
lok gīt	folk song
lotā	jug
luṅgerū	fern (tips) (Gaddi)
Māgh	a month, January–February (Gaddi)
mahal	neighborhood
mālā	garland
māmā	mother's brother (MB)
mān kī dāl	urad bean
Maṅgalvār	Tuesday
mātā	mother, also goddess
mātā dekhnā	to see the mother (goddess), act of worship
mausī	mother's sister (MZ)
māykā	natal home of a woman
mazā	fun
melā	festival
mitrā/sahelī bannā	to accept someone as a friend; see *bhāī/bahin bannā*
muṇḍan	Hindu life-cycle rite of the first tonsuring or haircut
mundāvand	per son system of inheritance
nāg (devtā)	serpent (deity)

nagārā	bowled drum
nāgin	female *nāg*
namaste	a greeting with joint hands in front of the chest
nanand	husband's sister (HZ)
nhauhaṇā	to bathe (Gaddi)
nhauṇ	bath (Gaddi), date and action of bathing in holy lakes around the Dhauladhar
nīce	down, below
nīce lenā	to take down, also to transfer a deity to Kangra
niru	a type of grass
nu	son's wife (SW) (Gaddi)
nuālā	Gaddi ritual for Shiva, also the garland used in the ritual
nuāncarī	dress worn by Gaddi women
pahāṛ	mountain
pānī	water
pānī badaltā hai	literally the water changes, also referring to a change in environment
pānī kī vajah se	because of the water
pattu	blanket from sheep wool (Gaddi)
paryāvaraṇ	environment
Phāgūṇ	a month, February–March (Gaddi)
prakṛti	nature
prasād	consecrated food offering
pūjā	religious worship
pūjārī	person who looks after a temple or performs *pūjā*
purānā	old
purānā gāṁv	old, ancestral village
pūrānī bāt	an old story or incident
pūrī	fried bread
purohit	Brahman priest
rabī	winter agricultural season
raiī	Western Himalayan spruce, *Picea morida*
rājā	king, ruler
rājmā	red kidney bean
rākhī	see *rakshā bandan*

rakshā bandan	North Indian holiday celebrating the brother–sister relationship
riśtedār	relatives, relation, kin
rīti-riwāz	custom
sakhā bhāī/bahin	real brother/sister
sālā	wife's brother (WB)
sālī	wife's sister (WZ)
salvār-kamīz	dress of loose trousers and long shirt worn by women
sangal	iron chain, symbol of deities
sardī	cold, cold season
sasurāl	marital home, in-laws' home
sāt phere	seven rounds around a sacrificial fire, part of Hindu marriage ceremonies
Sauṇ	a month, July–August (Gaddi)
sehrā	headdress/veil of the groom
sog	period of ritual pollution and mourning after a death
sthān	place
śakti	power
śantī	peaceful
śarik	local descent group, subcaste with common place of belonging
Śiv-jī	Lord Shiva
thālī ghaḍā	brass plate and clay pitcher, musical instrument
ṭīkā	an auspicious mark on the forehead
tīrthā	ford, crossing place, pilgrimage site
topī	cap
tos	West Himalayan fir, *Abies pindrow*
trimaihanī	funeral ritual performed three months after a death (Gaddi)
triśūl	trident
ṭhaṇḍā	cool, cold
ūn	wool
ūpar	up, above
vai	wedding (Gaddi)
yātrā	pilgrimage, journey

References

Adams, Vincanne. 1996. *Tigers of the snow and other virtual Sherpas*. Princeton, NJ: Princeton University Press.
Ahmed, Akbar S. 1983. Nomadism as ideological expression: The case of the Gomal nomads. *Contributions to Indian Sociology* (n.s.) 17 (1): 123–138.
Axelby, Richard. 2005. Pastures new. Pastoral development and the determination of grazing access in the Indian Himalayas. Ph.D. dissertation, School of Oriental and African Studies, University of London, London.
———. 2007. "It takes two hands to clap": How Gaddi shepherds in the Indian Himalayas negotiate access to grazing. *Journal of Agrarian Change* 7 (1): 35–75.
Babb, Lawrence. 1975. *Divine hierarchy: Popular Hinduism in Central India*. New York/London: Columbia University Press.
Baker, J. Mark. 2005. *The kuhls of Kangra. Community-managed irrigation in the Western Himalaya*. Seattle/London: University of Washington Press.
Balokhra, Jag Mohan. 1998. *The wonderland Himachal Pradesh*. New Delhi: H.G. Publications.
Barnard, Alan, and Anthony Good. 1984. *Research practices in the study of kinship*. London: Academic Press.
Barnard, Alan, and Jonathan Spencer (eds). 2002. *Encyclopedia of social and cultural anthropology*. London/New York: Routledge.
Barth, Fredrik. 1956. Ecologic relationships of ethnic groups in Swat, North Pakistan. *American Anthropologist* (n.s.) 58 (6): 1079–1089.
Basso, Keith. 1996. *Wisdom sits in places. Landscape and language among the Western Apache*. Albuquerque: University of New Mexico Press.
Basu, Badal Kumar. 2000. The Gaddis of Himachal Pradesh. An ethnographic profile. *Journal of the Anthropological Survey of India* 49 (1): 9–36.
Behrend, Heike. 1996. Bilder einer afrikanischen Moderne. Populäre Fotografie in Kenia. In *Snap me one! Studiofotografen in Afrika*, edited by T. Wendl and H. Behrend, 24–28. Munich/London/New York: Prestel.
Behrend, Heike, and Tobias Wendl. 1996. Afrika in den Bildern seiner Studiofotografen. In *Snap me one! Studiofotografen in Afrika*, edited by T. Wendl and H. Behrend, 8–16. Munich/London/New York: Prestel.
Berti, Daniela. 2001. *La parole des dieux. Rituels de possession en Himalaya indien*. Paris: CNRS Editions.

———. 2004. Gestes, paroles et combats. Pluralité rituelle et modalités d'action en Himalaya indien. *Annales de la Fondation Fyssen* 16:11–31.

———. 2009. Divine jurisdictions and forms of government in Himachal Pradesh. In *Territory, soil and society in South Asia*, edited by D. Berti and G. Tarabout, 311–339. New Delhi: Manohar.

Bhasin, Veena. 1988. *Himalayan ecology, transhumance and social organisation. Gaddis of Himachal Pradesh*. Delhi: Kamla-Raj Enterprises.

Blackburn, Stuart, and Joyce Burkhalter Flueckiger. 1989. Introduction. In *Oral epics in India*, edited by S. Blackburn, P. Claus, J.B. Flueckiger and S. Wadley, 1–11. Berkeley/Los Angeles/London: University of California Press.

Bloch, Maurice. 1995. People into places: Zafimaniry concepts of clarity. In *The anthropology of landscape. Perspectives in place and space*, edited by E. Hirsch and M. O'Hanlon, 63–77. Oxford: Clarendon Press.

Bourdieu, Pierre. 1977. *Outline of a theory of practice*. Cambridge: Cambridge University Press.

———. 1981a. Die gesellschaftliche Definition der Photographie. In *Eine illegitime Kunst. Die sozialen Gebrauchsweisen der Photographie*, edited by P. Bourdieu et al., 85–109. Frankfurt am Main: Europäische Verlagsgesellschaft.

———. 1981b. Einleitung. In *Eine illegitime Kunst. Die Sozialen Gebrauchsweisen der Photographie*, edited by P. Bourdieu et al., 11–21. Frankfurt am Main: Europäische Verlagsanstalt.

———. 1981c. Kult der Einheit und kultivierte Unterschiede. In *Eine illegitime Kunst. Die sozialen Gebrauchsweisen der Photographie*, edited by P. Bourdieu et al., 25–84. Frankfurt am Main: Europäische Verlagsgesellschaft.

———. 1990. Introduction. In *Photography: A middle-brow art*, edited by P. Bourdieu et al., 3–10. Cambridge, UK: Polity Press.

Campbell, Ben. 2010. Beyond cultural models of the environment: Linking subjectivities of dwelling and power. In *Culture and environment in the Himalaya*, edited by A. Guneratne, 186–203. London/New York: Routledge.

Casey, Edward. 1996. How to get from space to place in a fairly short stretch of time: Phenomenological prolegomena. In *Senses of place*, edited by S. Feld and K. Basso, 13–52. Santa Fe, NM: School of American Research Press.

———. 2001. Between geography and philosophy: What does it mean to be in the place-world. *Annals of the Association of American Geographers* 91 (4): 683–693.

Casimir, Michael, and Aparna Rao. 1985. Vertical control in the Western Himalaya: Some notes in the pastoral ecology of the nomadic Bakrwal of Jammu and Kashmir. *Mountain Research and Development* 5 (3): 221–232.

Chakravarty-Kaul, Minoti. 1998. Transhumance and customary pastoral rights in Himachal Pradesh: Claiming the high pastures for Gaddis. *Mountain Research and Development* 18 (1): 5–17.

Chhatre, Ashwini, and Vasant Saberwal. 2006. *Democratizing nature. Politics, conservation, and development in India*. Delhi: Oxford University Press.

Cronon, William. 1996. The trouble with wilderness or, getting back to the wrong nature. *Environmental History* 1 (1): 7–28.

Daniel, Valentine E. 1984. *Fluid signs: Being a person the Tamil way*. Berkeley/Los Angeles/London: University of California Press.

Department of Tourism and Civil Aviation. 2008. *Himachal tourism*, http://himach altourism.gov.in.
Descola, Philippe. 1994. *In the society of nature. A native ecology in Amazonia*. Cambridge: Cambridge University Press.
———. 2005. *Par delà nature et culture*. Paris: Gallimard.
Descola, Philippe, and Gísli Pálsson (eds). 1996. *Nature and society. Anthropological perspectives*. London: Routledge.
Diserens, Hélène. 1995–1996. Images et symboles des déesses de la haute vallée du Kulu. *Bulletin d'études indiennes* (13–14): 91–115.
Dhobal, Ballabh. n.d. *Hamāre pracīn tīrthasthān. Bhāgsūnāg aur unya devālay*. Dharamshala: privately printed.
Doniger O'Flaherty, Wendy. 1973. *Asceticism and eroticism in the mythology of Shiva*. London: Oxford University Press.
Eck, Diana. 1981. India's "tirthas": "Crossings" in sacred geography. *History of Religions* 20 (4): 323–344.
———. 1998a. *Darśan. Seeing the divine image in India*. New York: Columbia University Press.
———. 1998b. The imagined landscape: Patterns in the construction of Hindu sacred geography. *Contributions to Indian sociology* (n.s.) 32 (2): 165–188.
Elmore, Mark. 2006. Theologies of visibility and evidentary authority in eastern Himachal Pradesh. *Contemporary South Asia* 15 (1): 3–14.
Erndl, Kathleen M. 1993. *Victory to the mother. The Hindu Goddess of Northwest India in myth, ritual, and symbol*. New York/Oxford: Oxford University Press.
Escobar, Arturo. 1999. After nature. Steps to an antiessentialist political ecology. *Current Anthropology* 40 (1): 1–16.
Feld, Steven. 1996. Waterfalls of song: An acoustemology of place resounding in Bosavi, Papua New Guinea. In *Senses of place*, edited by S. Feld and K. Basso, 91–136. Santa Fe, NM: School of American Research Press.
Food and Agricultural Organization of the United Nations (FAO). 2001. *Pastoralism in the new millennium*. Food and Agricultural Organization, http://www.fao.org/DOCREP/005/Y2647E/y2647e00.htm#toc.
———. n.d. *Ecocrop. Abies Pindrow*, http://ecocrop.fao.org/ecocrop/srv/en/cropView?id=2558.
Fox, James. 1997. Place and landscape in comparative Austronesian perspective. In *The poetic power of place. Comparative perspectives on Austronesian ideas of locality*, edited by J. Fox, 1–21. Canberra: Australian National University.
Fuller, Christopher. 1992. *The camphor flame. Popular Hinduism and society in India*. Princeton: Princeton University Press.
Gazetteer of the Chamba State 1904. 1996. New Delhi: Indus Publishing Company.
Gazetteer of the Kangra District 1883–1884. 1884. Vol. 1, *Kangra Proper*. Calcutta: Punjab Government.
Gazetteer of the Kangra District 1897. 1899. Parts 2 to 4, *Kulu, Lahul and Spiti*. Lahore: Punjab Government "Civil and Military Gazettee" Press.
Gell, Alfred. 1995. The language of the forest: Landscape and phonological iconism in Umeda. In *The anthropology of landscape. Perspectives in place and space*, edited by E. Hirsch and M. O'Hanlon, 232–254. Oxford: Clarendon Press.

———. 1998. *Art and agency. An anthropological theory.* Oxford: Clarendon Press.
Gooch, Pernille. 1998. *At the tail of the buffalo. Van Gujjar pastoralists between the forest and the world arena.* Lund: Lund Monographs in Social Anthropology.
———. 2004. Van Gujjar: The persistent forest pastoralists. *Nomadic Peoples* (n.s.) 8 (2): 125–135.
Gosh, Amitav. 2008. Wildnisfiktionen. *Lettre international* (83): 62–69.
Government of Himachal Pradesh. n.d. *Himachal Pradesh. The official website. Religious Tourism,* http://himachal.nic.in/tour/relig.htm.
Grierson, G. A. (ed.). 1986. *Indo-Aryan family, central group: specimens of Pahāṛī languages and Gujuri.* Reprint ed. vol. 2. Delhi: Motilal Banarsidass.
Guneratne, Arjun. 2010. Introduction. In *Culture and environment in the Himalaya,* edited by A. Guneratne, 1–16. London/New York: Routledge.
Gutschow, Niels, Axel Michaels, Charles Ramble, and Ernst Steinkellner (eds). 2003. *Sacred landscape of the Himalaya,* Vienna: Austrian Academy of Sciences Press.
Halliburton, Murphy. 2003. The importance of a pleasant process of treatment: Lessons on healing from South India. *Culture, Medicine and Psychiatry* 27: 161–186.
Handa, O.C. 2004. *Naga cults and traditions in the Western Himalaya.* New Delhi: Indus Publishing Company.
———. 2005. *Gaddi land in Chamba. Its history, art and culture.* New Delhi: Indus Publishing Company.
Harder, Hans, and Gautam Liu. 2008. Transliterationskonventionen für die Devanagari-Schrift (Hindi). Heidelberg: Südasien-Institut der Universität Heidelberg.
Himachal Pradesh State Electricity Board. 2006. *H.P. State Electricity Board,* http://www.hpseb.com/index.htm.
Hirsch, Eric. 1995. Landscape: Between space and place. In *The anthropology of landscape. Perspectives on place and space,* edited by E. Hirsch and M. O'Hanlon, 1–30. Oxford: Claredon Press.
Hoon, Vineeta. 1996. *Living on the move. Bhotiyas of the Kumaon Himalaya.* New Delhi/Thousand Oaks/London: Sage Publications.
Hornborg, Alf. 2009. In defense of the nature/culture distinction: Why anthropology can neither dispense with, nor be reduced to, semiotics. *Cognitive semiotics* (4): 92–115.
Ingold, Tim. 2000. *The perception of the environment. Essays in livelihood, dwelling and skill.* London: Routledge.
———. 2004. Culture on the ground: The world perceived through the feet. *Journal of Material Culture* 9 (3): 315–340.
———. 2006. Up, across and along. *Koht ja Paik / Place and Location. Studies in Environmental Aesthetics and Semiotics* 5: 21–36.
———. 2007. Earth, sky, wind, and weather. *Journal of the Royal Anthropological Institute* (n.s.): 19–38.
Ingold, Tim, and Jo Lee Vergunst. 2008. Introduction. In *Ways of walking. Ethnography and practice on foot,* edited by T. Ingold and J.L. Vergunst, 1–19. Farnham: Ashgate.

Kapila, Kriti. 2003. Governing morals: State, marriage and household amongst the Gaddis of North India. Ph.D. dissertation, Department of Anthropology. London School of Economics, University of London, London.

———. 2008. The measure of a tribe: The cultural politics of constitutional reclassification in North India. *Journal of the Royal Anthropological Institute* (n.s.) 14: 117–134.

Kaushal, Molly. 1998. Sacred response to environment. The Gaddi and his mountain. In *The cultural dimension of ecology*, edited by B. Saraswati, 65–71. New Delhi: Indira Gandhi National Centre for the Arts.

———. 2001a. Cultural concepts of space and time. In *The nature of man and culture. Alternative paradigms in anthropology*, edited by B. Saraswati, 75–83. New Delhi: Indira Gandhi National Centre for the Arts.

———. 2001b. Divining the landscape: The Gaddi and his land. In *The human landscape*, edited by S. Geeti and A. Banerjee, 31–40. New Delhi: Orient Longman.

———. 2004. From mythic to political identities: Folk festivals and cultural subtexts. In *Folklore, public sphere and civil society*, edited by M.D. Muthukumaraswamy and M. Kaushal, 186–196. New Delhi/Chennai: Indira Gandhi National Centre for the Arts and National Folklore Support Centre.

Khapatiyā, Umarsingh. 1981. *Himācalī lok-sāhitya*. (One copy in the Public Library, Dharamshala, H.P., India.)

Kreutzmann, Hermann. 2004. Pastoral practices and their transformation in the north-western Karakoram. *Nomadic Peoples* (n.s.) 8 (2): 54–88.

Lamb, Sarah. 2000. *White saris and sweet mangoes: Aging, gender, and body in North India*. Berkeley: University of California Press, http://ark.cdlib.org/ark:/13030/ft458006c0/.

Latour, Bruno. 1993. *We have never been modern*. New York/London/Toronto: Harvester Wheatsheaf.

———. 2004. *Politics of nature. How to bring the sciences into democracy*. Cambridge: Harvard University Press.

———. 2005. *Reassembling the social. An introduction to actor-network theory*. Oxford: Oxford University Press.

———. 2009. Perspectivism: "Type" or "bomb"? *Anthropology Today* 25 (2): 1–2.

Lecomte-Tilouine, Marie. 2009. The Nepalese landscape: Exegis and appropriation of the country. In *Reading Himalayan landscapes over time. Environmental perception, knowledge and practice in Nepal and Ladakh*, edited by J. Smadja, 161–197. Pondicherry: Institut Français de Pondichéry.

Liechty, Mark. 2003. *Suitably modern. Making middle-class culture in a new consumer society*. Princeton, NJ: Princeton University Press.

Lock, Margaret, and Patricia Kaufert. 2001. Menopause, local biologies, and cultures of aging. *American Journal of Human Biology* 13: 494–504.

Luchesi, Brigitte. 2002. Haḍimbā Devī—hinduistische Volksgöttin mit überregionaler Bedeutung. In *Hairesis. Festschrift für Karl Hoheisel zum 65. Geburtstag*, edited by M. Hutter, W. Klein and U. Vollmer, 327–340. Münster: Aschendorf Verlag.

———. 2006. Fighting enemies and protecting territory: deities as local rulers in Kullu, Himachal Pradesh. *European Bulletin of Himalayan Research* 29–30: 62–81.

Lutgendorf, Philip. 2005. Sex in the snow: The Himalayas as erotic topos in popular Hindi cinema. *Himalaya* 15 (1–2): 29–37.

Lye, Tuck-Po. 2008. Before a step too far: Walking with Batek hunter-gatherers in the forests of Pahang, Malaysia. In *Ways of walking. Ethnograpghy and practice on foot*, edited by T. Ingold and J.L. Vergunst, 21–34. Farnham: Ashgate.

Malamoud, Charles. 1996. *Cooking the world. Ritual and thought in ancient India*. Delhi/Bombay/Calcutta: Oxford University Press.

Manuel, Peter. 1993. *Cassette culture. Popular music and technology in North India*. Chicago: University of Chicago Press.

Marriott, McKim. 1976. Hindu transactions: Diversity without dualism. In *Transactions and meaning. Directions in the anthropology of exchange and symbolic behavior*, edited by B. Kapferer, 109–142. Philadelphia: Institute for the Study of Human Issues.

Mauss, Marcel. 1973 (1935). Techniques of the body. *Economy and Society* 2 (1): 70–88.

Mehta, Lyla, and Anand Punja. 2007. Water and well-being. Explaining the gap in understandings of water. In *Waterscapes. The cultural politics of a natural resource*, edited by A. Baviskar, 188–210. Ranikhet: Permanent Black.

Michaels, Axel. 1998. *Der Hinduismus. Geschichte und Gegenwart*. Munich: C.H. Beck.

Michaels, Axel, Cornelia Vogelsanger, and Annette Wilke (eds). 1996a. *Wild goddesses in India and Nepal*. Bern/Berlin/Frankfurt am Main: Peter Lang.

———. 1996b. Introduction. In *Wild goddesses in India and Nepal*, edited by A. Michaels, C. Vogelsanger and A. Wilke, 15–34. Bern/Berlin/Frankfurt a.M.: Peter Land.

Ministry of Tribal Affairs. n.d. *Ministry of Tribal Affairs*, http://tribal.nic.in/index2.asp?sublinkid=542&langid=1.

Mitra, Swati (ed.). 2007. *The temples of Himachal*, New Delhi: Good Earth.

Mol, Annemarie. 2002. *The body multiple. Ontology in medical practice*. Durham/London: Duke University Press.

Moreno, Manuel, and McKim Marriott. 1989. Humoral transactions in two Tamil cults: Mirikan and Mariyamman. *Contributions to Indian Sociology* (n.s.) 23 (1): 149–167.

Mumtaz, Zubia, and Sarah Salway. 2005. "I never go anywhere": Extricating the links between women's mobility and uptake of reproductive health services in Pakistan. *Social Science and Medicine* 60: 1751–1765.

Narayan, Kirin. 1986. Birds on a branch: Girlfriends and wedding songs in Kangra. *Ethos* 14 (1): 47–75.

———. 1997. Singing from separation: Women's voices in and about Kangra folksongs. *Oral Tradition* 12 (1): 23–53.

Newell, William. 1960. Goshen: A Gaddi village in the Himalayas. In *India's villages*, edited by M.N. Srinivas, 56–67. Bombay/Calcutta/New Delhi: Asia Publishing House.

Nichter, Mark. 1986. Modes of food classification and diet-health contingency: A South Indian case study. In *Food, society, and culture. Aspects in South Asian food systems*, edited by R. S. Karve, 185–221. Durham, NC: Carolina Academic Press.

———. 2008. Coming to our senses: Appreciating the sensorial in medical anthropology. *Transcultural Psychiatry* 45 (2): 163–197.
Noble, Christina. 1987. *Over the high passes. A year in the Himalayas with the migratory Gaddi shepherds.* London: Collins.
Osella, Caroline, and Filippo Osella. 2007. Muslim style in South India. *Fashion Theory* 11 (2–3): 1–20.
Paniyari, Surinder. 2006. *Dhoban.* VCD, Pathankot: Nagma Music.
Paniyari, Surinder, and G.D. Maity. 2004. *Bhedliyān carāndī reshmā. Himāchalī lok gīt.* VCD, Kangra: Jayanti Mata Cassette (JMC).
Parkes, Peter. 1987. Livestock symbolism and pastoral ideology among the Kafirs of the Hindu Kush. *Man* (n.s.) 22: 637–660.
Parry, Jonathan P. 1979. *Caste and kinship in Kangra.* New Delhi: Vikas Publishing House.
Phillimore, Peter. 1982. Marriage and social organisation among the pastoralists of the Dhaula Dhar (Western Himalaya). Ph.D. dissertation, University of Durham, Durham, UK.
Pickering, Andrew. 1995. *The mangle of practice. Time, agency, and science.* Chicago/London: University of Chicago Press.
Pinney, Christopher. 1995. Moral topophilia: The significance of landscape in Indian oleographs. In *The anthropology of landscape,* edited by E. Hirsch and M. O'Hanlon, 78–113. Oxford: Clarendon Press.
———. 1997. *Camera Indica. The social life of Indian photographs.* London: Reaktion Books.
Pinther, Kerstin. 1996. "Wenn die Ehe eine Erdnuß wäre . . . ." Über Textilien und Fotografie in Afrika. In *Snap me one! Studiofotografen in Afrika,* edited by T. Wendl and H. Behrend, 36–41. Munich/London/New York: Prestel.
Polit, Karin. 2006. Keep my share of rice in the cupboard. Ethnographic reflections on practices of gender and agency among Dalit women in the Central Himalayas. Ph.D. dissertation, Heidelberg: University of Heidelberg, http://www.ub.uni-heidelberg.de/archiv/10671.
Raheja, Gloria, and Ann Gold. 1994. *Listen to the heron's words. Reimagining gender and kinship in North India.* Berkeley/Los Angeles/London: University of California Press.
Ramanujan, A.K. 1989. Is there an Indian way of thinking? An informal essay. *Contributions to Indian Sociology* (n.s.) 23 (1): 41–58.
Rana, Karnail. 2008. *Gaddan.* VCD, Mumbai: Big Home Video.
Raṇapatiyā, Amarsingh. 2001. *Gaddī. Bharmaur kī janjātīya loksanskriti evam kalāem.* Shimla: Himachal Kala Sanskriti Bhasha Akadami.
Rao, Aparna. 2000. Blood, milk, and mountains: Marriage practice and concepts of predictability among the Bakkarwal of Jammu and Kashmir. In *Culture, creation and procreation. Concepts of kinship in South Asian practice,* edited by A. Rao and M. Böck, 101–134. New York: Berghahn Books.
Rao, Aparna, and Michael J. Casimir. 2003. Nomadism in South Asia: Introduction. In *Nomadism in South Asia,* edited by A. Rao and M. J. Casimir, 1–38. Oxford: Oxford University Press.

Registrar General and Census Commissioner of India. 2007. Census of India, http://www.censusindia.gov.in.
Rival, Laura. 2002. *Trekking through history. The Huaorani of Amazonian Ecuador.* New York: Columbia University Press.
Robbins, Paul. 2001. Tracking invasive land covers in India, or why our landscapes have never been modern. *Annals of the Association of American Geographers* 91 (4): 637–659.
Rodman, Margaret. 1992. Empowering place: Multilocality and multivocality. *American Anthropologist* (n.s.) 94 (3): 640–656.
Rose, H.A. 1980 (1919). *A glossary of the tribes and castes of the Punjab and North-West Frontier Province.* Delhi: Amar Prakashan.
Saberwal, Vasant. 1999. *Pastoral politics. Shepherds, bureaucrats, and conservation in the Western Himalaya.* Delhi: Oxford University Press
Salzman, Philip C. 1971a. Introduction. *Anthropological Quarterly* 44 (3): 104–108.
———. 1971b. Movement and resource extraction among pastoral nomads: The case of the Shah Nawazi Baluch. *Anthropological Quarterly* 44 (3): 185–197.
———. 2002a. Nomadism. In *Encyclopedia of social and cultural anthropology,* edited by A. Barnard and J. Spencer. London/New York: Routledge.
———. 2002b. Transhumance. In *Encyclopedia of social and cultural anthropology,* edited by A. Barnard and J. Spencer. London/New York: Routledge.
Sarkar, Rajendra. 1996a. Gaddi Brahman. In *People of India. Himachal Pradesh,* edited by B.R. Sharma, and A.R. Sankhyan. Delhi: Anthropological Survey of India/Manohar.
———. 1996b. Gaddi Rajput. In *People of India. Himachal Pradesh,* edited by B.R. Sharma, and A.R. Sankhyan. Delhi: Anthropological Survey of India/Manohar.
———. 1996c. Rihara. In *People of India. Himachal Pradesh,* edited by B.R. Sharma, and A.R. Sankhyan. Delhi: Anthropological Survey of India/Manohar.
———. 1996d. Sipi. In *People of India. Himachal Pradesh,* edited by B.R. Sharma, and A.R. Sankhyan. Delhi: Anthropological Survey of India/Manohar.
Sax, William S. 1991. *Mountain goddess. Gender and politics in a Himalayan pilgrimage.* New York/Oxford: Oxford University Press.
———. 1996. Draupadī and Kuntī in the Pāṇḍavlīlā. In *Wild goddesses in India and Nepal,* edited by A. Michaels, C. Vogelsanger and A. Wilke, 355–382. Bern/Berlin/Frankfurt am Main: Peter Lang.
———. 2002. *Dancing the self. Personhood and performance in the Pāṇḍav Līlā of Garhwal.* Oxford: Oxford University Press.
———. 2009. *God of justice. Ritual healing and social justice in the Central Himalayas.* Oxford: Oxford University Press.
Sharma, Jai Karan. 2004. *Nuālā. Himāchalī Shiv vivāh.* VCD, Gaggal, H.P.: Jai Maa Music Co.
Sharma, Kishore. n.d. *Jai Bannī Mātā. Yātrā Sahit.* VCD, Jassure, H.P.: KM Audio.
Sharma, Kamal Prashad. 2001. *Manimahesh Chamba Kailash.* New Delhi: Indus Publishing Company.
———. 2004. *Folk dances of Chamba.* New Delhi: Indus Publishing Company.

Sharma, Kamal Prashad, and Surinder Mohan Sethi. 1992. *Biunsuli. Folk musical instruments of Chamba.* Jalandhar: Neelam Publishers.
———. 1997. *Costumes and ornaments of Chamba.* New Delhi: Indus Publishing Company.
Sharma, Khushi Ram. 1974. *Kangre di sanskriti kanain lok-jivan* (The culture of Kangra and life of its people). Una: Rajkeey Mahaavidhalay.
Singh, Chetan. 1998. *Natural premises. Ecology and peasant life in the Western Himalaya 1800–1950.* Delhi/Chennai/Mumbai: Oxford University Press.
Singh, Kuldeep. 2004–2005. Famous religious places of Chamba and Kangra. M.Phil. thesis, Himachal University, Shimla.
Sircar, D.C. 1973. *The sakta pithas.* Delhi: Motilal Banarsidass.
Smadja, Joëlle. 2009a. Introduction. In *Reading Himalayan landscapes over time. Environmental perception, knowledge and practice in Nepal and Ladakh,* edited by J. Smadja, 1–28. Pondicherry: Institut Français de Pondichéry.
———. 2009b. A reading of the Salme Tamangs' territory and landscape. In *Reading Himalayan landscapes over time. Environmental perception, knowledge and practice in Nepal and Ladakh,* edited by J. Smadja, 199–239. Pondicherry: Institut Français de Pondichéry.
Sprague, Stephen. 2002. Yoruba photography: How the Yoruba see themselves. In *The anthropology of media. A reader,* edited by K. Askew and R.R. Wilk, 172–186. Oxford: Blackwell.
Stellrecht, Irmtraud. 1992. Umweltwahrnehmung und vertikale Klassifikation im Hunza-Tal (Karakorum). *Geographische Rundschau* 44 (7–8): 426–434.
Sutherland, Peter. 1998. Traveling gods and government by deity: An ethnohistory of power, representation and agency in West Himalayan polity. Ph.D. dissertation, Institute of Social and Cultural Anthropology, Oxford University, Oxford.
Tapper, Richard. 2005. Correspondence. *Journal of the Royal Anthropological Institute* (n.s.) 11:841–842.
———. 2008. Who are the Kuchi? Nomad self-identities in Afghanistan. *Journal of the Royal Anthropological Institute* (n.s.) 14:97–166.
Thakur, Rakesh. n.d. *Satarangī merā colā kālā merā ḍorā.* VCD, Gharoh, H.P.: Shailen Music Company (SMC).
Tucker, Richard P. 1986. The evolution of transhumant grazing in the Punjab Himalaya. *Mountain Research and Development* 6 (1): 17–28.
van Gelderen, D.M., and J.R.P. van Hoey Smith. 1986. *Das große Buch der Koniferen.* Berlin/Hamburg: Paul Parey.
Verma, V. 1996. *Gaddis of Dhauladhar. A transhumant tribe of the Himalayas.* New Delhi: Indus Publishing Company.
Vikās. 2008. "Ḍal jhīl men baḍā nhauṇ āj". Newspaper, *Panjāb Kesrī:* Palampur, India, September 2008.
Vogel, J. Ph. 1972. *Indian serpent-lore or the nagas in Hindu legend and art.* Delhi/Varanasi: Indological Book House.
Voss, Martin, and Birgit Peuker (eds). 2006. *Verschwindet die Natur? Die Akteur-Netzwerk-Theorie in der umweltsoziologischen Diskussion.* Bielefeld: Transcript.

Weiner, James. 1991. *The empty place. Poetry, space, and being among the Foi of Papua New Guinea*. Bloomington/Indianapolis: Indiana University Press.

Widlok, Thomas. 2008. The dilemmas of walking: A comparative view. In *Ways of walking. Ethnography and practice on foot*, edited by T. Ingold and J.L. Vergunst, 51–66. Farnham: Ashgate.

Zimmermann, Francis. 1987. *The jungle and the aroma of meats. An ecological theme in Hindu medicine*. Berkeley/Los Angeles/London: University of California Press.

Index

Adams, Vincanne, 6
ādat, 143–48
aesthetics, 152–54, 159–60
affinal relations, 81–82, 85–87
agropastoralism. *See* pastoralism
Ahmed, Akbar S., 22
altitude, 112, 114, 129–32
ancestral villages, 65, 70–71, 77–79, 90
Axelby, Richard, 8, 24nn5–6, 40; on Gaddi settlement in Kangra, 66; on pastoral cycle, 4, 157; on sacrifice, 117; on seasonal migration, 71

Babb, Lawrence, 107
Baker, J. Mark, 8, 140
Bannī Mātā, 112, 115–20
Barth, Fredrik, 21
Basso, Keith, 5, 175
belonging, 73–77
Berti, Daniela, 63n21, 125, 133n1
Bhagsu Nag, 126–29, 135n23
Bharmaur: deities of, 104; and environmental aesthetics, 159; physical features of, 2; religious practices in, 101; and Shiva, 40, 60; temples of, 61, 134n7
Bhasin, Veena, 8, 20–21, 67–68
Blackburn, Stuart, 59
Bloch, Maurice, 153
Bourdieu, Pierre, 16, 85, 94, 161, 166, 170

Campbell, Ben, 18
Casey, Edward, 4–5, 9n1, 141, 143, 152, 157
Casimir, Michael, 20
caste, 7, 9nn2–3
celā, 49, 52, 56–57, 63n21, 111, 118–19
Chakravarty-Kaul, Minoty, 21, 32, 90
Chamba, 2, 32, 65–66, 63n18, 151n3
chemahīne, 41, 61n1, 65, 75
Chhatre, Ashwini, 26–27
children and place, 68, 83–85, 90
clan, 7, 9n3, 70–71
couples and place, 86–87

ḍal. See high altitude lakes
Daniel, Valentine E., 139–40, 142–143
darśan, 58, 64n33, 97, 102–4, 110, 129
death, 35, 46, 75–76, 91nn3–4
deities: and accessibility, 105; and affliction, 109; benevolent and fierce, 106–7; deity-*bhagvān* distinction, 105; forest dwelling, 106–7, 113, 117; Gaddi, 101–8; Gaddi versus Pahari, 111–112; and pastoralism, 116–17; of place, 106; and transfer to Kangra, 77–78; travelling, 121. *See also* family deities; *nāg* deities
descent, 67
Descola, Philippe, 10–12, 17, 100, 132
Dharamshala, 2, 66, 101, 113–15, 122. *See also* seasonal migration

dharm bhāī/bahin. See fictive kinship
Dhauladhar, 2, 46, 61, 122–23, 157–58. See also mountains
Doniger O'Flaherty, Wendy, 39
dress, 28, 34–36, 37n8, 38n9

Eck, Diana, 103–4, 124, 134n5
environment: and body, 141–42, 147–48; and degradation, 19; definition of, 15, 18; processual understanding of, 15–16, 95, 98, 100, 132, 173–74
Erndl, Kathleen M., 42, 102–103, 106–107, 120–21

family deities, 77–78, 109, 114,117–18, 120–21
FAO, 19–20, 22
Feld, Steven, 5, 153
fictive kinship, 87–89, 92n13
first haircut, 88, 92n12
Flueckiger, Joyce Burkhalter, 59
Fuller, Christopher, 62n7, 105–6

Gaddern, 40, 90, 159. See also Bharmaur
Gaddi: festivals, 61n4; language, 7; meaning of, 6–7; migration stories, 6, 91n1; and Pahari, 8, 59–60, 102–4
Gaura, 40, 43, 45–46, 62n11, 168
Gell, Alfred, 153
goddess temples, 102–3
Gooch, Pernille, 24n7, 73
good places, 114–15, 154–58
Gosh, Amitav, 130–31, 135n25
Gune Mātā, 97, 112–15, 157
Guneratne, Arjun, 2, 18, 24n3

habitus, 85–87, 93–94, 96
Halliburton, Murphy, 155
Handa, O.C., 32, 61, 125–27, 135n23
high altitude lakes, 122–24, 135n19
Himachal Pradesh, 3, 25–27, 112, 120
Hindi cinema, 30, 33, 170
Hirsch, Eric, 2–3, 9n1
Hoon, Vineeta, 73

identity, 25–26, 30–37, 39–41, 59–60
Ingold, Tim, 10, 14–16, 18, 173; on sensory perception, 141, 148, 152; on walking, 94–95, 98
inheritance, 67–68, 91n2
inside space, 80–83, 87, 89–90, 104, 120

jāgrā: and ancestral villages, 78–79; description of, 108–12, 118–19; and family deities, 109; and mobility, 108, 112, 120
jāgrātā, 59–60, 121
jātar. See *jāgrā*
joking relationships, 55–56, 82, 92n8
jungle, 29–30, 96, 157

Kailash, Mount, 6, 40, 46, 61n2, 122,124
Kangra, 2, 7–8, 60, 66, 102, 133n1. See also seasonality; water
Kapila, Kriti, 8, 28
Kaufert, Patricia, 141
Kaushal, Molly, 22, 41, 133n1, 135n20
Kelang, 42, 61n1, 125, 135n21
Khapatiyā, Umarsingh, 125, 135n22
kinship: groups, 49, 51–52, 75, 77–78, 82, 92n9; and place, 79, 89, 120
kriyā rituals. See death

Lahul, 1, 116–17, 149, 155–56
Laka, 157–58
landscape, 2–4, 9n1, 153, 157; local, 46, 79–80, 90–91, 100–1, 168–69, 174
Latour, Bruno, 4, 10, 12–14, 17–18, 24, 132
Lecomte-Tilouine, Marie, 171n2, 172n18
Liechty, Mark, 36
local biology, 141–43, 147–48
Lock, Margaret, 141
Luchesi, Brigitte, 134n14
Lutgendorf, Philip, 30, 33
Lye, Tuck-Po, 93, 98

Malamoud, Charles, 106
Mani Mahesh Yatra, 40, 122

Manuel, Peter, 25–26
Marriott, McKim, 139, 142
mātā dekhnā. *See darśan*
Mauss, Marcel, 93–94
McLeod Ganj, 66, 71–72
Mehta, Lyla, 138
men and place, 86–87
Michaels, Axel, 39, 107
Mol, Annemarie, 5, 18, 107, 177
mountains, 36–37, 102, 104, 156–57, 174
Mumtaz, Zubia, 80

Nāg Ḍal, 122–24, 128, 130, 158
nāg deities, 43, 106, 110, 121–22, 124–26
Narayan, Kirin, 8
nature-culture dualism: and adaptational approach, 21; and anthropology, 11, 14–15; critique of, 10–15, 174; and Gaddi, 32–33; and pastoralism studies, 23
networks: Latour, 14, 17–18, 24n1, 151n4, 174; place-, 65, 87–91, 98, 132, 157, 175
Newell, William, 8, 9n3
nhauṇ, 40, 121–22, 128–29
niche, 21, 32
Nichter, Mark, 141–143
Noble, Christina, 40, 62n12, 135n20, 151n5
nomadism, 19–22
nuālā, 46–60, 108, 112, 168

oracle. *See celā*
Osella, Caroline, 30
Osella, Filippo, 30

Pahari, 7–8, 37n1, 96, 98. *See also* Gaddi
Parry, Jonathan, 8, 81–82, 92n9
Parvati. *See* Gaura
pastoralism, 1–2, 19–23, 32, 174. *See also* transhumance
person and place, 139–43
Phillimore, Peter, 8, 9n4, 81, 63n22, 92n9, 133n1

photography, 34–35, 161–67, 170
Pinney, Christopher, 29, 160, 162–63, 166–67, 172n19
Pinther, Kerstin, 161
Polit, Karin, 79–81, 86, 140–41
priest (Brahman), 42, 45, 48–51, 57–58, 105, 134n9
Punja, Anand, 138
Punjab, 89, 102, 156–57

Raheja, Gloria, 85, 87
Ramanujan, A.K., 139
Raṇapatiyā, Amarsingh, 125, 131
Rao, Aparna, 20, 24n7
residence, 67, 70, 77, 86. *See also* seasonal migration
Robbins, Paul, 17

Saberwal, Vasant, 8: and discourse on pastoralism, 21, 24n3; on fictive kinship, 89; on Himachali identity, 26; on pastoral cycle, 4, 157
sacrifice: description of offering, 51–52, 54; and fierceness of deity, 107; *jāgrā* and *jātar*, 110–11; opposition to, 62n8; and shepherds, 62n9, 117; and Shiva, 42–43
śakti pīṭhā, 102–103, 134n5
Salway, Sarah, 80
Salzman, Philip, 20–21
Sarkar, Rajendra, 9n2
Sax, William S.: on deities, 62n7, 62n11, 107; on kinship, 81; on landscape, 100–1; on person and place, 140–41; on place, 4, 75–76; on ritual performance, 59; on sacrifice, 42
Scheduled Tribe, 27–28, 37n4
seasonal migration, 2, 41, 65–73, 176–77; and agriculture, 70, 72; in Dharamshala, 66–73; heterogeneity of, 70–71; as life-style, 23, 72–73, 145, 154; and marriage, 71; persistence of, 70, 72–73; and Shiva, 41; within Kangra, 71–72; young generation, 69

seasonality, 1, 96, 115–16, 132–33, 154–55
sensorial anthropology, 5, 141, 174, 176
sensory experience, 16, 18, 141, 143, 152–53
Sethi, Surinder Mohan, 37n7, 50, 62n5, 63n17, 63nn19–20
seven sisters. *See* goddess temples
Sharma, Kamal Prashad, 32, 37n7, 62n5; on *nuālā*; 50, 63n17, 63n19–20, 135n20
Sharma, Kushi Ram, 32
Shiva, 39, 103, 135n23; and deity-*bhagvān* distinction, 105; and Gaddi, 6, 39–46, 59–60, 168–69; and Gaddi deities, 104–5; and *nāg* deities, 126; and *nhauṇ*, 121–22; and sacrifice, 42–43; and sheep, 43. *See also nuālā*
sibling relations, 81, 87–88
Singh, Chetan, 27
Smadja, Joëlle, 24n3, 125, 171n2
songs, 37n1, 46, 54–55, 58, 111–12, 168
Sprague, Stephen, 161–162, 166
Sutherland, Peter, 125, 133n1
symmetric anthropology, 4, 14

Tapper, Richard, 19, 22, 31
tīrthā, 124
transhumance, 2–3, 19–20, 23, 27, 41, 155–56. *See also* pastoralism
Trilochan (story of), 123–24
Triund, 97, 157–58
Tucker, Richard P., 2, 167

VCD, 25–26, 28–30, 33–34, 169
Vergunst, Jo Lee, 94–95, 98
Verma, V., 32
Vogel, J. Ph., 106, 124–25
Vogelsanger, Cornelia, 107

walking, 1, 93–98, 132
water, 138, 144, 148–50, 154
water change, 137–39, 143–48
wedding, 36, 43–48, 51–52, 58, 62n13, 63n14
Weiner, James, 153
Widlok, Thomas, 93, 98
Wilke, Annette, 107
women and place, 74–75, 85–86, 144–45, 156

Zimmermann, Francis, 106, 142